WHY PEOPLE SUCK

Abe Surde

Sugar Coin Press

Why People Suck. ©2016 by J.Y. Lee. All rights reserved. This book or any portion thereof may not be reproduced or used in any manner whatsoever without express written permission from the author and copyright holder. Library of Congress.

This is a work of fiction and is for entertainment purposes only. Any resemblance to actual persons, living or dead is highly probable (can't get away from bad behavior, it's everywhere), but is also purely coincidental. Recommendations are not to be taken seriously. Do not throw eggs at dangerous people. In fact, avoid them altogether. Then go have yourself a hot chocolate with a shot of whipped cream.

Contact: sugarcoinpress@gmail.com
photos by: damedeeso@123rf.com, Arina Zaiachin@123rf.com

All his life he tried to be a good person. Many times, however, he failed. For after all, he was only human. He wasn't a dog.

—Charles M. Schulz

Table of Contents

Introduction *5*
The Adrenaline Junkie *9*
The Adulterer *12*
The Ageist *15*
The Angry Person *18*
The Antisocial *21*
The Apathetic *24*
The Arguer *27*
The Asshole *30*
The Backstabber *33*
The Bitter *36*
The Blabbermouth *39*
The Blackmailer *39*
The Braggart *45*
The Brat *48*
The Bully *51*
The Cannibal *55*
The Co-Dependent *58*
The Competitive *62*
The Conformist *65*
The Control Freak *68*
The Coward *71*
The Creep *74*
The Critic *77*
The Cusser *80*
The Denier *83*
The Destroyer *86*

The Diva / Divo	88
The Downer	91
The Drama Queen	94
The Drunk	97
The Entitled	100
The Exhibitionist	103
The Fanatic	105
The Fickle	108
The Flaker	111
The Fool	114
The Freeloader	117
The Gold Digger	120
The Grudge Holder	123
The Hater	126
The Hedonist	130
The Hellish Houseguest	133
The Hoarder	136
The Hypersensitive	139
The Hypochondriac	142
The Imposter	145
The Inconsiderate	148
The Indecisive	151
The Inflexible	154
The Ingrate	157
The Insecure	160
The Insensitive	163
The Irresponsible	166
The Jealous / Envious	169
The Judge	172
The Killer	176

The Killjoy 180
The Know-It-All 180
The Liar 186
The Litigious 189
The Loudmouth 192
The Manipulator 195
The Miser 198
The Moody 201
The Nag 204
The Name Dropper 207
The Napoleon 210
The Narcissist 213
The Passive Aggressive 216
The Pollyanna 220
The Power Tripper 223
The Prankster 227
The Prude 230
The Psychic Vampire 233
The Psychopath 236
The Sadist 239
The Sarcastic 242
The Scene Stealer 245
The Seducer/Seductress 248
The Self-Absorbed 251
The Self-Disparager 254
The Skeptic 257
The Slanderer 260
The Sleaze / The Slut 263
The Slob 266

The Snob	269
The Snooper	272
The Stalker	275
The Stoner	280
The Superstitious	282
The Sycophant	285
The Talker	288
The Tempter	291
The Thief	294
The Troublemaker	297
The Type A	300
The User	303
The Victim	306
The Weirdo	310
The Worrier	313
About the Author	317

Introduction

I have had the great fortune of knowing extremely difficult people. I have also been told I am a big pain in the neck. I consider this very instructive for it has forced me to look within and ask, "Why am I such a jerk? Why are you such a prick?" Why do we say awful things to each other like, "You'd look great if it weren't for your face" and "Are you sure your mother wasn't a donkey, because you're such an ass?"

These questions and more plagued me for twenty years until I had an epiphany one day, caused by a most unusual event.

One warm Tuesday in July last year, I absentmindedly strolled the length of my lush, untamed garden when I came face to face with a chupacabra hiding in an overgrown patch of blackberry bushes. You can imagine how shocked and nervous I became. My first thought was *how did this monstrous thing get in my yard* and *what was it doing in my part of the continent?* Luckily, there were no goats in my yard and my Whippet, Snippet, was in the house chasing his tail.

This chupacabra had eyes the color of charcoal and a surprisingly penetrating gaze. We stared at each other for a few minutes, caught in some type of unspoken animalistic mind meld. Then he stepped forward into the sunlight revealing his true size—he was over four feet tall with extremely long fangs!

I could see its expression clearly and it wasn't a happy "rub my chin" face. It dawned on me he might be hungry, and I might be lunch. I ran away as fast as I could. As fate would have it, I tripped on the edge of a lawn chair and was knocked out cold.

I awoke in a hospital room with the worst headache of my life but also with the sharpest clarity I had ever had. I had been unconscious for almost 24 hours. When I fell, I hit the front of my skull on a small statue of Athena situated near some wild roses in my backyard.

In Greek mythology, Athena is known as the goddess of wisdom, and I believe she bestowed upon me a gift of insight that day. I suddenly understood what eluded me before—what truly caused people to behave like stinkers.

This divine illumination is not surprising given my history and interests. I have the great fortune to be the grandnephew of the sister of one of the cousins who was the niece of the aunt by marriage to the brother of Anna R, a patient of Dr. Carl Jung from 1932 to 1934. My connection to Dr. Jung could not be any closer.

Anna saw him for an eating disorder—an addiction to sausage salad that was causing great turmoil for her parents. Based on Anna's journal of her sessions with Dr. Jung, my family was able to gain some understanding into Jung's process.

For the last eight decades, Anna's journal has been treated as if it was the bible of psychoanalysis in our extended household. I pored over her carefully scribbled journal with great attention.

In addition, I have also read the work of Maslow, Freud, Sacks, Fromm, Castenada, Erikson, and many grim looking men who wore glasses. In short, I was primed for Athena's intervention.

The blow on the head has helped me comprehend the true origins of many undesirable personality traits. Having this intuitive understanding has helped narrow my search for answers and discover strong connections between seemingly unrelated events.

Through research and channeled information from the universal consciousness, I am able to see with great clarity the reasons for many difficult behaviors seen in daily life. I share those with you today in hopes that you may better understand how to deal with certain shitty behaviors when confronting them in your relationships. I also offer some basic recommendations that may help make a difficult situation more bearable.

Many of the conclusions presented here are not aligned with the traditional views or treatments in the psychoanalytic field. For that reason, some readers may balk at my ideas, will say that I'm a headless twit with the brain of a jackal, that my theories stink like a wet donkey covered in its own piss, but I ask you to have an open mind.

A note of warning to sensitive readers—there is "R" language, references to drugs, sex, and only minimally to rock and roll within these pages.

The bad behaviors are arranged in alphabetical order with short descriptions for each one, followed by discussions on the probable causes, catalysts, or origins of the behavior. These theories are born out of field and academic research combined with knowledge channeled from a higher source. At the end of each described behavior, simple recommendations are offered for those seeking solutions.

When eating peanuts, you can never stop at one. Similarly, when someone is a jerkface, they will probably act lousy frequently and in several different ways. For example, an angry person could also be an arguer. A psychic vampire might also be a thief. In such situations, you may be dealing with a very troubled person who has a highly unusual past. They will require a great deal of your patience and understanding.

Some of this material may offend or even anger those who recognize their own behavior in this compilation. Nobody enjoys feeling bad about themselves, except for the self-disparagers. To admit we have behaved in a shitty way can make us feel guilty and ashamed. We would rather forget the past and pretend like it didn't exist.

I must admit, I thoroughly offended myself several times when I read the pages I wrote aloud. I went as far as my bathroom mirror to give myself a serious talking to and a few times, berated that face staring back at me with some choice four letter words. I tried to kick myself in the nuts too—a pretty hard thing to do. The truth hurts.

If only we could turn back time and undo that mistake of manipulating a buddy's girlfriend into sleeping with us or stealing that Porsche during a moment of envy or borrowing the neighbor's dog for a week without permission, we would have an easier time in life.

It helps to remember that many of these bad behaviors are not really our fault. We are triggered in ways we do not realize. Many factors are involved with shaping who we are and the behaviors we exhibit. To truly change, we must first recognize we have a problem. We must have a picture painted for us (not literally, but that may be helpful for the artistically inclined) so that we may see clearly how we are hurting ourselves and pissing others off.

Once we understand why we do what we do, it is time to take charge, to reclaim the past and to do something about it. The moment we realize we didn't have a choice—that we were shaped by things out of our control—we suddenly gain a choice. We can wallow in excuses or we can whip it. "We can whip it good!" (Devo, "Whip It", 1980). Sometimes, you can whip it yourself, and other times, you will need a friend or possibly a professional with strong wrists to help you through the really tough, heavy stuff.

This collection is by no means exhaustive or complete. Some truly horrible behaviors have been excluded as I continue to seek answers and mull over recommendations and as new behaviors arise from our technologically advancing world. This is an ongoing project that will possibly be revised as more insights make themselves known.

As for what happened to the very large scary friend on my property that instigated my fall into enlightenment? It mysteriously disappeared. I was left unbitten, my blood untouched. The appearance of such a rare creature in such an unusual place and the resulting psychic breakthrough from my serious fall lead me to believe that what I encountered wasn't a real animal, but actually a spirit guide sent to lead me on a path to help others in the world.

In honor of Mr. Chupacabra, I humbly offer this collection of divinely channeled and researched explanations into the causes of various bad behaviors and the possible ways of handling them.

Abe Surde

The Adrenaline Junkie

aka: the danger junkie, the daredevil, the risk-taker, the thrill-seeker

Skydiving off the Empire State Building is the best idea Rocky has had all month. He isn't particularly smart and he should never be in a relationship. Of any kind. Unless it's with blow-up doll. Because he's an adrenaline junkie and no one needs the stress of being involved with him. On the other hand, he is a rich fart. Maybe having a relationship with him is the smartest thing anyone can do, as long as there is a good life insurance policy involved and he's shared his ATM password.

Adrenaline junkies are folks who love danger so much they will regularly do crazy things that make people with common sense go, "WTF?"

Spurred on by the thrills, chills, and goosebumps they get from adrenaline, dopamine, cortisol, and endorphins coursing through their blood, these danger junkies would rather die in a blaze of glory than live a safe existence behind a white picket fence eating Pop Tarts.

Humans are hardwired to react in situations of danger when survival requires quick reflexes and fast thinking for those times when a rascally coyote strays your way, keeping you from reaching your burning ribs on the grill.

Our heart rate speeds up, we go on high alert, and adrenaline courses through our bodies, motivating us with a sense of urgency to get those ribs off the grill as soon as possible.

If the coyote growls and shows his fangs, the flight or fight response kicks in and we might do one of the following: wrestle with the coyote until we win, run from it like a scared 2nd grader, shoo it away with a lawn mower, or scream insults at it until it sprints away with hurt feelings. What we do all depends on how much those ribs mean to us.

For most people, this fight or flight response is a natural reflex reserved for times of real danger but for some, reliving dangerous situations is the name of the game.

Those who enjoy the exhilaration of danger need to put themselves in heart pumping scenarios where their head might be torn off. They can't get that same high wiping down a keyboard or clipping their toenails. Nope, they'd rather play hopscotch in a pen of poisonous vipers. Adrenaline rushes can be very addictive and feels much better than a spinal tap.

You may wonder why adrenaline junkies have been included in this collection; their behavior is hardly rotten, say, compared to a psychopath (see *The Psychopath*). Adrenaline junkies do make their loved ones fret, but that's not so horrible. But the adrenaline junkie can be a real jerk when they rope, harass, inspire or trick weaker-minded folk into following their dangerous pursuits, leading others into serious injury or early death.

There are all sorts of activities that can get the heart racing, including cliff diving, tsunami surfing, and tornado chasing—all activities guaranteed to put the adrenaline junkie under a pile of dirt at some point.

If you enjoy the security of a safe environment, you don't want to be near these daredevils, because they might fool you into coming along for the ride.

CAUSE:

It is said a child develops food preferences based on their mom's diet during pregnancy; if mommy scarfs down ghost pepper chocolates, their child will develop a taste for it too. By extension, whatever a mother does during her baby's gestation also influences the unborn child's behavior. For adrenaline junkies, you can trace their addiction back to mommy dearest.

"How?" you might ask. Most pregnant women avoid thrilling activities, preferring sedate and safe environments where they can wallow in misery, but not all women. Those with an adventurous spirit will continue to do the things they enjoy. Don't mention roller coasters and skydiving around them.

If the mom is addicted to adrenaline, the fetus will have this addiction too. When these babies finally make their exit out of mom's safe flesh cave, they will search for ways to relive their in utero environment. Like mama, like child. This is how the love of adventure passes from one generation to another.

If the child's father is equally enamored of life-threatening games, then the child will have a woefully short but exciting life. If the father is the couch potato type, the padre's chillin' influence will mitigate the child's desire for excitement.

If the child is female, the girl will have a better chance of survival than males; girls have better judgment than boys, usually stopping at asinine, suicidal acts.

The female child of an adrenaline-addicted mother will continue the cycle of begetting new generations of thrill-seeking kids, unless she becomes addicted to downers, plays Portishead tunes, or becomes physically debilitated during pregnancy, all of which contribute to a sedentary lifestyle.

RECOMMENDATIONS:

To stifle thrill-seeking tendencies in children, warm milk with some Nyquil PM can do the trick.

To slow down an adult-sized adrenaline junkie takes effort; the desire for terrifying adventure is always in the back of their mind. A tranquilizing dart and a lecture on statistics would help. So would graphic videos of surgeries performed on accident victims. If that doesn't quell the call of adventure, a good life insurance policy should make up for your worries.

Also, ensure that the thrill-seeking friend, spouse, or family member has decent medical coverage and keep track of where their nice toys are so you can inherit them once the adrenaline junkie is gone. Watch for special deals from your local funeral homes.

The Adulterer

aka: the cheater, the two-timer

James feels a sore throat coming on after eating a giant five-cheese pizza. He decides he needs to head home and nip it in the bud before his vacation next week. He opens the front door and hears all kinds of screams from his wife inside the bedroom. Alarmed, he rushes in to find her having a ball, literally, dangling in front of her delighted face from an unknown man in a sexy leopard suit. She's naked in a complex yoga position. Shocked by her husband's sudden appearance, she quickly pushes leopard man off, mortified at being caught.

The adulterer is a married person who is having a good ole' time while naked with someone else, without a thumbs up or a written permission slip from their significant other.

Adultery is a very common problem in relationships. At least a quarter of marriages end with a husband or wife "doin' it" with someone who doesn't share their underwear drawer. This has the effect of making the duped spouse very upset, enough to cry for a few weeks, down a pint of whiskey, and yank all the hair off the cheating partner's body. This behavior is much frowned upon in cultures that treat monogamous marriage as sacred.

In older times and even now in certain tribes, religions, and cults where polygamy is practiced, adultery is not considered a bad behavior.

It is usually the male who gets the prerogative of boning lots of women—not the other way around. Unfortunately, this is not acceptable to most women in the western world and should not be practiced as women expect to be treated as equals and can be quite terrifying with a flat iron.

Anyone scorned by an adulterer can do lots of damage. For men, the worst damage involves a very sharp object and a very vulnerable appendage.

When a person is caught two-timing, the results are never the best case scenario, which would be if the partner said, "Wow, this looks fun. Let's have a three-way!" Instead, you'll get a vase thrown at your head.

If you wish to go funning around with someone you shouldn't, it might be wise to file for a divorce first and not do the nasty in the same house that your partner has a key to.

CAUSE:

FOMO, a newly minted expression to describe the old phenomenon known as "fear of missing out," has been around as long as people could host parties in their homes. It was never given an official name before 2014 but has always existed. The cause of adultery is due to a person's deep seated fear of missing out on more sex before they lose interest in doin' it or start decomposing.

Bananas, pickles, muffins, and frosting are all quite tasty, but having the same flavored muffin and frosting over and over again, or dealing with overripe bananas and eating flaccid pickles on a daily basis can get boring real fast. After a while, no one wants them anymore and all that food begins to get moldy.

Then along comes a person with a big old basket filled with exciting new flavors and nice firm bananas. This makes a person with a case of FOMO very hungry for those goodies. They are going to try hard to get invited for a sumptuous dinner where they can sample new flavors.

The partner not invited to the meal, once they find out there was a great dinner party without them, is going to be very upset and may do everything in their power to ruin any future meals. Think pails of puke.

If you haven't figured the obvious, we're talking about sex. When someone who is afraid of missing out on all the booty they can get in their lifetime—while their apparatus still works—tends to go after it as if their ass is on fire when there are suddenly new peeps who want a piece of them, and they can still attract something that doesn't remind them of Gollum.

RECOMMENDATIONS:

Sex is a three letter word.

If you are hurt by a cheating partner and have a broken heart, don't do anything that can earn you a felony count. Dump the loser, heal your wounds, and go enjoy your life with or without pickles, bananas, muffins, or frosting. Better yet, try something entirely new. Pumpkin pie? Apple strudel? Go for it.

If you want to cheat and have a strong case of FOMO in the pants, then for fuck's sake, break it off with your partner instead of sneaking around like a thief.

You should not be in anything committed. If you have kids, your kids are better off without your lame ass being only half present anyways.

Reclaim your coveted single status and screw to your heart's content, at least until you get an STD. Then you'll have to stop for a bit but once cured, can screw and screw again. Don't be draggin' others into the mud with your issues.

The Ageist
aka: the biased

Eighteen-year-old Darrell chances upon an elderly couple groping each other like two hormone-infested teenagers as he walks through the park. He tries not to stare, but man, those two are going at it. It's kind of gross, but he's enthralled nonetheless. He didn't know senior citizens still had such desires at their mature age. Things are getting pretty heavy—they've gone horizontal on that park bench. He shakes his head. He thinks their behavior is highly inappropriate for their years. His attitude reveals his ageist ideas.

An ageist is a person who has preconceived ideas or holds negative or judgmental views towards another individual or group based strictly on the other's age. For example, they are the first to tell great grampy he shouldn't be swinging with other couples. It can strike anyone at any stage of life, making ageism commonplace.

As a bad behavior, ageism tends to be less irksome than having a cut finger dipped in acid, but it can be problematic in areas such as employment.

In the current digital age, ageism seems to be rampant among younger adults. To stay relevant, people must tweet, friend, Link in, Facebook, and click all sorts of crap that fry their eyeballs and mess up their thumbs.

Many older adults have yet to be consumed by the digital bug, preferring activities, namely in-person get togethers and telephone conversations. They also enjoy picking flowers and watching live theater with friends.

As a result, younger people tend to view elders as inept, slow, easy to prank, and dispensable in today's work environment, while more mature adults find younger ones to be impatient, socially stupid, illiterate, and incapable of having a five-minute conversation without fondling their phones.

This conflict in perception is one of the main reasons older adults get passed over for employment by young employers. That and somewhere in the back of a young employer's mind, they secretly harbor a wish to hook up with that cute employee they hired; very few want to hook up with anyone who could stand in as their grandparent, unless that employer was sexually open minded, or they were once lovers in a previous life, or the older person is a rich mofo.

With everyone wired and plugged in, instant gratification from a finger tap or an eye movement is expected. The slower paced world of older adults becomes exponentially more alien to young people who have learned to feed their ADD tendencies with each new gadget, which helps foster ageist ideas.

At one time, aging was connected with wisdom and experience; having elders around meant having sound advice within arm's reach. Now it means easy identity theft.

CAUSE:

Because ageism seems to strike everyone, no matter the race, gender, creed, and age, the cause of ageism must be rooted in a widely shared resource—water. In turn, this causes limb disturbances affecting a person's activities, which in turn, affects how others perceive them.

Solar flares emitting high levels of radiation have affected the world's water supply, causing cells in our bodies to become more electrified. Higher charged cells stimulate limb restlessness, especially in the hands and arms, resulting in Fidgety Finger Syndrome (FSS).

This syndrome makes fingers tingle with nervousness and anxiety, needing something to relieve their restlessness, and that relief comes from hitting hard surfaces.

There have always been solar flares, but we have had more protection from the sun due to a stronger stratospheric ozone layer (the precious gas up in the sky that protects us from radioactive solar flares).

In the last 30 years, we've made a hyper leap forward in energy use through computers, devices, video, and appliances, all of which contribute to the depletion of ozone layer. We are more exposed to the sun's radiation than ever and as a result, FSS has gotten more severe and extreme.

The degree of FSS between age groups is the core reason for ageism. Young people have a more severe case of FSS while older people suffer much less from it.

Young people drink more water, being thirstier from eating salty crap, while older folks drink less water, being more apt to pee in their pants.

Plus, they usually eat less salt, having indulged in their fair share of junk food until they become prone to dying a crummy death if they continue.

FSS makes a person want to slam their fingers down on hard surfaces. That's why so many people under 35 have their heads bent down with their fingers busily texting and playing video games. That's also why they prefer to have relationships through email and messaging—it provides their fingers great relief.

When people drink less water, they are less driven by fidgety fingers. They can do other things, not to mention have verbal conversations and play poker with friends.

Those with a severe case of FSS have the consequence of becoming super wired and speedy with those fingers engaged in a variety of different online games and tools. Those who don't have FSS don't have a strong online presence and don't give a shit about League of Legends.

Ageism is expected to remain with us in the foreseeable future and may expand as a rotten behavior. As more devices are created, more nuclear and coal energy is needed to power them. As a result, we will have more greenhouse gasses, which will further deplete the radiation-blocking ozone. It's a vicious cycle that increases with every new electronic gadget.

In twenty years, young people will be pounding keyboards with their foreheads as Fidgety Fingers Syndrome grows more fervent in their bodies, spreading to other areas.

RECOMMENDATIONS:

Don't drink water with irradiated particles. If you can, filter it. If you have no filter, you can pour water through a layer of clean sand. Hey, it's better than nothing. If you must drink that toxic brew, sing "Bridge Over Troubled Water" by Simon and Garfunkel loudly and play Hot Tuna's "Water Song."

As Dr. Masaru Emoto discovered and made popular with his published articles, water has consciousness, able to change its properties based on words and thoughts directed at it. Your cheerful words will help negate some of the bad charge irradiated water has on your fingers.

Do not cuss and swear in the presence of your H_2O while dealing with any device glitches. Your frustration will surely upset the water's consciousness, making it more toxic to your body.

The Angry Person
aka: the hothead, the irate, the meany, the pissed off, the psycho

Bruno craves chili cheese fries. It's the only thing that sounds good to him. Not pizza. Not a burger. Not even a steak sandwich served by a naked Megan Fox. He sits down at a diner, his mouth waters with anticipation. The waitress comes over. He gives his order and tells the waitress to pile on the cheddar, but she regretfully tells him, "Sorry, we're out of chili tonight." It takes a moment for Bruno to understand the full implications of her words, but when he does, he goes ballistic. For the next five minutes, he screams at the poor waitress while waving a butter knife in the air. Bruno has an anger issue and when he doesn't get what he wants, his head explodes.

An angry person is an easily disturbed individual who overreacts in a hostile manner to every situation imaginable, from having a minor hangnail to dealing with a sinkhole in their front yard.

These people can be very unpredictable as you won't necessarily know what will set them off. It is nearly impossible to carry on a conversation with an angry person, because they will not really hear what you say. When you say "good morning" to such a person, what they hear is, "I wanna stab you in the neck mothafucka!" Words of kindness, compassion, or compromise are not in their vocabulary.

Angry people are ticking time bombs; if you happen to say the wrong thing at the wrong time, expect a loud rant with references to your IQ, your weight, your body odor, and your mother's sexual habits. The only way to calm an angry person is to put them into a straightjacket.

CAUSE:

Due to the amount of gesticulating an angry person does while shouting at you, the cause of this bad behavior is Death Metal Syndrome (DMS).

Metal is a form of music with subgenres, one of which is death metal. Death metal consists of loud guitars, unrecognizable melodies, and lyrics shouted at incomprehensible levels by dudes with, ideally, long black hair.

Hotheads tend to enjoy angry music or perhaps it's the other way around. It's hard to know which came first. No matter. Some of the angriest people on Earth are teenagers and a good many of them love death metal.

Death metal contains emotional, gory, angry, simplistic words that include at least one or more of the following: die, kill, fuck, corpse, torture, death, blood, bleed, rot, evil, cry, scream, claw, slaughter, grave, attack, murder, demon, shoot, hammer, burn, knife, and so on.

Listening to a stream of pissed-off directives and macabre stories accompanied by ear-splitting discordant riffs affects the mind. This violent mantra hypnotizes young adults, while the obligatory head banging— integral to enjoying metal music—causes brain damage.

For those in the dark, head banging is the act of swinging the head up and down vigorously as if to shake lice off the scalp. This motion, done with fervor, knocks the brain against the skull, causing trauma as well as imprinting song lyrics blasted into the ears of a death metal head.

Similar to a piece of vinyl imprinted with grooves, the injured brain likewise imprints the lyrical directives screamed at them through the music, making the listener feel aggressive and pissed off all the time for no apparent reason. A daily ritual of death metal can transform the nicest PTA mom into Lizzie Borden.

In previous decades before death metal became so popular, angry people were created through rock and punk genres, both of which were more melodic with tamer lyrics, and were distributed through radio, records, tapes, and compact discs (cds). You couldn't just download one song but had to commit some moolah to an entire cd or album and had to make a trip to a record store in order to get it.

This extra step slowed down the distribution of music in general, preventing rock and punk music from reaching a wider audience. Also, head banging was not a ritual part of rock and punk, although body slamming in mosh pits did require listeners to physically bump up against each other.

Exposure to rock and punk was limited to radio play, live concerts, Walkmans, and home stereo systems during the '70s through the '90s, just as death metal began to emerge in the mid '80s.

And 50 or more years ago, anger was less prevalent in the general public than it is today, as music pre-'70s focused more on dancing, love, getting dumped, and tripping instead of killing and goring.

And before the advent of telecommunications, in the very old days, a songstress or orator would belt out their angry words to an attentive crowd when desiring an audience, but this was usually a one-off performance. Any angry residue from an orator's speech could easily be dispelled by a lavish meal of roasted pig.

RECOMMENDATIONS:

Unless you are a psychopath, a troublemaker, another angry person, a killer, or just plain clueless, you are not going to win an argument with a pissed off person. No words should ever be spoken and eye contact must be avoided completely. Get away immediately, for the intent of angry person is to spread his or her hostility. It's an unconscious thing.

If an encounter is unavoidable and you have had to exchange barbs and blows with an angry asshole, try not to let their anger infect you.

Heal yourself by getting to the nearest dog park where you can find the smile of a happy Labrador with a slimy chewed up ball in its jaw. Gaze into the mesmerizing blue and brown eyes of an Alaskan Malamute that can say "I ruv you" in dogspeak. Take in the joy of a happy domestic pet enthralled in a game of fetch with its owner. It will stop the poisonous anger venom from spreading to your heart.

If you are an angry person and don't wish to be, start listening to elevator music and smoke lots of weed. You will slowly feel the calm close in on you.

The Antisocial

*aka: the loner, the lone wolf,
the reclusive, the solitary, the unfriendly,
the unsocial, the withdrawn*

variation: the misanthrope

You're having a housewarming party and decide to invite Jenny, the oddball co-worker in your department who shoots daggers from her eyes whenever you smile at her. She never says "please" or "thank you," but that's not such a big deal. The worst thing about her is that she talks to no one and eats a plain potato without fixings—not even a dab of sour cream—for lunch every day at her desk. Your attempts to start a conversation with her are met with silence. You can't believe anyone can resist your winning personality and start to wonder if you aren't half as charming as you think you are. It's not you. You are dealing with an antisocial person.

If you've been confronted with an anti-social person, you know it immediately from their *I wanna kill you* look. A person who is anti-social does not want to talk to you. They act as if you've told them to go blow their brains out when you invite them to join you for a burger.

This bad behavior is not to be confused with apathy, which can also garner the silent treatment. Apathy is due to indifference, lack of motivation, and the comfort of an ass on a couch as a result of hydrogen sulfide exposure (see *The Apathetic*), while anti-social behavior is based on seeming antipathy towards the world.

However, don't be misled. Not all anti-social behavior is rooted in animosity; some of it may be anxiety. That is easy enough to figure out once you engage in a little tête-à-tête with the person.

Ask that hostile face, "How are you today?" Note the eyebrows. Are they furrowed in a V-shape, indicating how much they despise you or more of a half M-shape, as if you might bite them any second?

If the corner of the antisocial's eyebrows slope downward at the outer edges, then anxiety plagues that soul and you can draw them out with compliments like "Damn! Your hair looks so good I thought it was wig." But be warned, if the brow is in a V-shape, then your attempts at friendly banter will be shot down.

CAUSE:

If someone seems frosty and treats you like you're carrying the plague, there's good reason for their crappy demeanor. That ice-cold person hasn't been human for long due to their previous life as a display mannequin. Their newfound birth into mortal flesh occurred through a series of screw ups from bumbling magicians engaged in reckless horseplay.

Throughout the nation, magic schools exist to educate aspiring magicians who yearn to work in the entertainment industry. At these schools, magicians learn real spells from master wizards able to perform amazing feats. They practice their tricks in front of a fake audience composed of mannequins, because real people don't have all damn day to hang out in magic schools.

As we all know, there is always a troublemaker in every classroom. Magic schools are no different. Naughty, overly curious students messin' with charms and incantations stolen from their teacher's private journals can cause unforeseen consequences, one of which is animating objects to life.

Fearful of reprimand and possible expulsion, magic students then push the newly live mannequins out into the world, without any proper orientation, to rid themselves of the incriminating evidence.

Over the years, countless mannequins have been thrust into this new life in such a manner—a rather shocking start for any immobile plastic figure.

Adjustment is not easy. In their previous world, mannequins stood around on cold cement floors, sometimes hung out in warehouses, sat in supply rooms, or if lucky, dressed in the latest designer wear while displayed in swank department store windows.

The only social interaction a mannequin ever had was when it was placed alongside another mannequin as stiff as they were. No conversation ever came from working together.

Occasionally, the mannequin would get felt up by some hornball handler who couldn't resist touching their smooth surface. Being groped didn't affect the mannequin much; it couldn't feel and didn't have consciousness.

But one day, that changed. The mannequin found itself able to speak, to feel hunger, to caress textures, to become bruised, and to move around—thanks to a bunch of lame magicians bringing life to mannequins throughout the nation.

As a result of this quick and unusual birth, the mannequin hasn't received any preparation on how to use their new human shell. One day, they were suddenly alive and that was it.

As breathing entities, they haven't figured out the stuff we humans have had a lifetime to work on. For this reason, when people want to engage with anti-socials, it makes them uncomfortable. Hence, the unfriendly cold demeanor.

Mannequins were made to have whistle-worthy bodies and nice faces. In becoming human, they retained their "easy on the eyes" appearance but don't have the personality to match. Still, people are drawn to them because they are shallow jerks taken in by a pretty face, no matter if the antisocial has the charm of a plastic mat.

Don't blame the antisocial for being true to their nature. Blame those stupid magic students for fooling around with things they shouldn't.

RECOMMENDATIONS:

In dealing with an anti-social person, you must remember, they are not used to being with real people, only pretend people in the form of fiber and plastic. Asking a mannequin-turned-human to chit chat and mingle with people is similar to forcing a cow to eat with a fork—it's unnatural.

The only way to engage the newbie human is to approach them on their terms; do activities that would help them feel at ease. Strike a pose before their eyes and freeze your position as long as you possibly can.

When they see you behaving like a mannequin, they will warm up to you. It may take a while, but you'll know you've made good headway when they strike a pose back at you. Together, standing solidly without words is the best way to relate to the antisocial. It will offer the anti-social a chance to be their natural selves.

Eventually, you'll be able to introduce words, but start slow. Initially, go for simple topics that might generate a response. After an hour or standing still, for example, you could ask, "You hungry?" or "Cramp much?"

After a few months of this routine, your verbal exchange will grow, allowing you to share longer sentences with one another.

The Apathetic

aka: the disinterested, the dispassionate, the emotionless, the indifferent, the lazy, the slacker, the unmotivated

The physical exertion of moving a jelly donut to your mouth is strenuous. When you see someone injured by a hit and run driver, you yawn and continue walking. A picture of a battered baby seal inspires a desire to nap on a furry pillowcase. All these and more make you so very bored, because you are an apathetic.

An apathetic is one who shows no motivation, no concern, no desire, no movement, no passion, and no interest for something as epic as the next Star Wars pic; a person who seems to be lacking a pulse.

Is that so bad you ask? After all, apathy is the highest form of chillin'. We all have the right to be a gelatinous blob on a sunny beach once in a while. As with all the bad behaviors, it is the extreme that is a concern.

Apathy becomes a serious problem when it takes over a person's life. That means the "down unders" go unwashed, phone bills become napkins, toilets don't get flushed. A baby porcupine couldn't inspire this slacker to get up and take a gander. (Google it. They are fucking adorable.)

Sleeping away one's life, unless you suffer from narcolepsy, is not an admirable or healthy choice.

If you have a roommate, parent, child, or significant other that is an apathetic person, you know how hard it is to get them off their asses.

This bad behavior is by no means the worst offender of the lot, but it can be said that apathy inspires contempt and contempt is as pretty as a herpes scab.

CAUSE:

Psychologists say apathy is connected to mental issues, such as boredom, anxiety, depression, and other emotional problems. I say the real culprit is hydrogen sulfide.

Hydrogen sulfide is a highly dangerous, rotten smelling gas present in flatulence and poop from all humans and animals. With that, a small amount of methane is also present in this offensive output.

These two gasses don't dissipate after release, no matter what public health experts say. Instead, they compete with oxygen in the air, reducing the amount available to us humans. This is not good. In high amounts, methane can asphyxiate a human body.

Oxygen is a necessary component for human cell survival, but with hydrogen sulfide and methane in the air, less oxygen reaches those cells, thus, destroying them. When a person breathes this noxious air for extended periods of time, nerve endings in the body die off and that really messes a person up.

Occasional exposure is smelly but tolerable. However, repeated exposure over months and years can have bad effects. With dulled or dead nerve endings, sensitivity is compromised. This is why apathetic people are so unmoved and unmotivated; they can't feel anything.

Junk food junkies and hedonists eat a high amount of nasty foods and do so in weird combinations guaranteed to produce plenty of these toxic gasses and a pretty foul gut.

Those living with junk food junkies are at high risk from second-nose exposure and could develop apathy as well. Also, junk food addicts tempt others to eat poorly, creating the domino effect of double gassing. Who wants a pile of lettuce when ranch-style chips are two feet away?

And worse, if the junk food eater lives in a wooden house, they are getting daily doses of methane off-gassed by termites eating their house up; termites produce methane as a by-product of their digestive system. That nasty gas is everywhere!

RECOMMENDATIONS:

If you or a loved one suffers from apathy, open your windows and air out your smelly home. Make sure your bathrooms have air vents, a fan, or a window.

Next, throw out all junk food in the house and get yourself and your friend on a liquid diet of veggie juice for a few days. Try being a breatharian for 24 hours.

Meanwhile, to stimulate emotion and feelings, watch five hours of nature shows featuring pandas, meerkats, and baby lions.

Keep a megaphone nearby and scream "hallelujah" whenever the apathetic person seems unmotivated to take action.

If you are the person with apathy but wish to be more engaged with the world, volunteer at an animal rescue shelter, but make sure you wear a gas mask when you go.

The Arguer

aka: the combative, the contentious, the contrarian, the debater, the disagreeable, the disputer, the quarreler

Did you say Macs were better than PCs? You are an idiot with no brains to speak of. Everyone, except for the paid brainwashed drones at Apple, knows PCs are the best. I have data to prove you wrong on every level! So crawl back to your hole and make out with your overpriced MacBook, because I'm always right and agreeing with you would feel as natural as wearing a chimp on my head.

An arguer is a person who must contradict you on everything you say, because a little voice inside them drives them to disagree with you on very important things like cornflakes, space debris, and note pads.

Arguing is the same as breathing for these disagreeable souls. Even if an arguer secretly agrees with you, they will never fess up. The need to rebut you is compulsive, the way a bull is compelled to gore a matador—it doesn't feel very good on the receiving end.

If you question their motives, they'll put up defenses that may or may not make sense, like "My great grandfather was a soldier at the Battle of Gettysburg so I know which hemorrhoid cream works best."

You won't have a chance to reflect on their answers, because their tactic is to throw supposed facts, evidence, and quotes from experts in rapid-fire succession, in a loud voice, to overwhelm your wimpy objections.

You're never quite sure if some of these facts are real or made up, but no matter. The arguer's sole purpose is to convince you of their supreme knowledge and your supreme stupidity. If you engage in any of their baited subjects, you'll be sorry.

Arguers lose friends, lovers, and jobs on a regular basis, because arguers will not stop until the other person gives in, admits defeat, confesses their ignorance, or busts a blood vessel.

Some arguers quarrel calmly while other arguers show visible physical changes, specifically a hot red face, pursed lips, and flared nostrils.

In some instances, arguers may actually want to correct a falsehood or a bit of misinformation, in which case, the ignoramus who spouts garbage deserves the full brunt of the most obnoxious contrarian in the world. But, for the average person who wants to participate in an exchange of ideas without a shower of saliva spray from another's mouth, stay clear of these contentious people.

CAUSE:

Arguments are inevitable when a little voice inside—a gargoyle head lodged in an arguer's throat—eggs the person on until victory is assured.

Most people know of gargoyles as grotesque faces carved in stone and placed outside on building facades to protect the structure from evil forces. What people don't know, however, is that gargoyles are also real living beings, hideous in appearance, which causes them to hide from public view.

In the Middle Ages, people caught glimpses of these poor homely creatures—that's how we know of them today.

Surprisingly, gargoyles are emotionally fragile when it comes to their feelings, yet highly abrasive in their verbal exchanges. They become weepy when someone runs away from them screaming.

In an overpopulated world, there are few places a gargoyle can hide. As a brilliant adaptive measure, they have discovered new places to hide in plain sight—the human throat. How can they do this? They have the unique ability to disembody themselves at will, with the head and torso surviving as separate entities.

When a gargoyle spots a homo sapien with a large neck, they see an opportunity to protect themselves by making a home inside that cavernous tunnel. Once embedded, they nest for a long residency. Being small monsters, they have no trouble fitting comfortably in the throat with room to spare for masticated food to pass through. They are much smaller than we think, being almost the size of Tinkerbell.

The gargoyle head detaches from the rest of their body to go make a new home in the human's throat while the rest of the body finds a nice place in a nearby garden to bury itself for a long hibernation while they are separated.

In the middle of the night when the human is asleep, the head bounces its way into a gaping mouth where it will slip through and attach itself to the walls of the throat. Initially, it may feel uncomfortable for the host, but eventually they'll forget about it if the gargoyle head doesn't fidget too much.

The person harboring a gargoyle may not be aware of their new inhabitant, but the human host's behavior changes—for the worse.

Being abrasive, gargoyles are great at dishing out verbal abuse but can't handle it when they get the same. This carries over to the host. The unsuspecting gargoyle carrier becomes combative, desiring to argue points on every topic, whether that be peanut butter or politicians. That's because the gargoyle head takes control, preventing the host from the peaceful conclusion of a discussion.

Once controversy is introduced, the human carrier's ego sometimes gets involved and the stage is set for a contentious verbal battle.

RECOMMENDATIONS:

Bitter, salty, sour, and moist foods are what gargoyles enjoy most. They hate scones and biscotti for they are sweet, dry foods.

If you wish to keep an arguer at a distance, try to get something dry and sweet into the arguer's mouth while taking away any available liquids. This will help the gargoyle choke back their words.

Avoid beer at all costs and no bar snacks of any kind. You do not wish to feed the nasty little head, for it only gets nastier with fuel.

If others view you as an arguer or you find that friends, coworkers, and family suddenly avoid you like the plague, you've got a little gargoyle stowaway inside you.

The gargoyle is usually lower in the throat and can't be easily seen with a mirror, but an ear, nose, and throat specialist should be able to examine whether there is an ugly, disembodied face lodged near your Adam's apple. If so, the only way you will get it out is by starving it to death (starving yourself in the process) or feeding it with only sugary treats.

The Asshole

aka: the bastard, the cocksucker, the cunt, the dick, the dickhead, the fucker, the jerk, the jerkwad, the piece o' shit, the prick, the son of a bitch

variation: the bitch

A sweet redhead sidles up to you with big tits all in your face. You make meaningless banter, but it's clear what you both want. Things go swimmingly; she invites you back to her place, which is only a block away. You say yes and your heart does a high five inside. Problem is, you're here with your girlfriend who is stuck waiting in a long line for the bathroom. You must decide quickly. What to do, what to do. And you decide to make a quick getaway dumping your girlfriend at the bar, by herself, without any words or a way to get home. But you hesitate. Her dog was killed by a drunk driver yesterday. And she was fired from her job last week. And she found a lump in her breast this morning. But you decide to go anyways because you're an asshole, and assholes are stinkers. No way around it.

An asshole is an individual who does things—sometimes delights in doing things—that are thoughtless, dickish, inconsiderate, soulless, selfish, and just plain shitty to others, making these bozos one of the top ten bad baddies to avoid.

Unfortunately, there's no shortage of examples when it comes to asshole behavior. The dude who sideswipes you on the 405 and then hollers at you is a prick. The nasty neighbor who poisons your cat is a most certainly an asshole. The stranger who slips a roofie in another's drink is definitely a prick plus a complete loser in bed. So many people act like assholes that you're forced to be a dick once in a while not to get stepped on.

Asshole behavior is not specific to men, although they do seem to make up a good majority. Plenty of women act like assholes too, but they are usually referred to as bitches.

Similar to the arguer, the asshole loses friends on a regular basis, but always manages to find some poor fool to sleep with—someone that tolerates being treated as trash. Any asshole or bitch who says your face would be greatly improved with a nose job should probably go on your "get lost" list.

CAUSE:

After evaluating more than five dozen studies conducted on the origin of asshole behavior and with Athena's guidance, it can be surmised that this unpalatable behavior was possibly formed during the toddler stage when an infant crawled on the ground on all fours and inadvertently obstructed their intestinal tract, which is why this bad behavior references the excretory system.

In the wanderings of a small child, an asshole-in-the-making found his or her mother's tampons in the bathroom cabinet and believing it to be a tasty food item, shoved the cylindrical object into their mouth.

If the child didn't choke and managed to get the tampon down the esophagus, the tampon would have gone down without a parent's knowledge.

Once in the stomach, acids burned away the outer plastic or paper casing of the tampon, releasing the cotton structure inside the applicator. Once the cotton met liquid, it expanded, with much of it lodged inside a pocket of the small intestine where it has festered and fermented, unable to free itself from the wee one's body.

For decades, the little one must live with this embedded cotton structure lodged inside them where it can help trap pieces of chunky food items until the whole thing becomes a hardened little ball inside.

An obstruction of that size can affect mental processes through pain and discomfort, which in turn, creates a bitter temperament that gets diffused through aggressive demands, shitty behavior, and denigration of others.

In short, assholes have to act like douche bags in order to feel better, primarily because there is something similar to a douche bag—a tampon—stuck in their gut.

RECOMMENDATIONS:

Laxative relief in the form of castor oil (organic) should help expel the irritating tampon. This process should be followed by an enema of chamomile extract in a quart of warm water and a dab of rose oil on the neck.

For more extreme cases where hydro-cleansing fails to do the trick, a beat down in a dirty alleyway will fix the asshole right up.

The Backstabber

aka: the betrayer, the fink, the snitch, the tattletale

You and your childhood friend invent the most incredible device known to humankind, a machine that converts ordinary urine into expensive craft beer. It was an idea you got one day while sitting on the crapper thinking about nothing much when your thoughts led you down a path of weird ideas called the "what ifs." What if cows could fly? What if lobsters ate human babies? What if urine could be converted to beer? It was enough to get you in the garage tinkering, and after years of yucky taste tests, you and your friend finally perfected the urine beer machine. But before you have a chance to get your great invention to the patent office and save local municipalities loads of money on wastewater treatment, your friend goes and sells your precious plans to a major beer manufacturer for a billion bucks without your consent or knowledge. That friend is called a backstabber.

A backstabber is a friend, lover, co-worker, boss, partner, or relative who breaks an unspoken code of trust between the two of you by the horrible sin of betrayal that makes you feel so down in the dumps that you believe demons have taken over the human race. You probably didn't see it coming.

Not all betrayals are equal. Some are no big deal while others are real heart stoppers. Any of them done once—no matter how small—should serve as a warning that you will be stabbed in the back more frequently in the upcoming future.

For example, a fairly common hurtful betrayal is the friend putdown. Some friend of yours blurts out an embarrassing story involving you, some poor guy's wienerschnitzel, some really soggy bread, and an angry box turtle, details of which you would never want spoken aloud to strangers or acquaintances. Everyone is amused, laughs heartily *at you*, not with you, and your so-called friend is suddenly the most popular person at the party—all at your expense.

If your friend can turn on you for a few cheap laughs, you can bet that friend will sell your little sister for the right price.

In rare cases, you may come across a backstabber of the literal kind; the crazy-eyed nut job, switchblade in hand, who goes on a stabbing rampage at lunchtime. This type of backstabber is probably the worst kind, the kind you should never go to happy hour with.

CAUSE:

Backstabbing has always been around, just like many of the other bad behaviors noted here. However, in the last decade and a half, there seems to be more backstabbing behavior than ever, concurrent with the rise of reality television.

In the days before reality television, soap operas and dramas in the '70s, '80s, and '90s elevated backstabbing behavior on primetime as entertainment for our pitiful enjoyment. Viewers spent their evenings watching a whole lotta bad backstabbing behavior on such shows as *Dynasty*, *90210*, and *Dallas*.

Having common sense, most people knew these shows were for entertainment and not to be taken seriously, but for a small minority of viewers out there, these shows were more than that. They became instructional courses on how to succeed in life with plotlines taken as literal models to follow. Luckily, only a small percentage of viewers fit into this category.

But reality television changed everything. *Survivor* was the new kid on the block in 2000 and it was so different from anything seen on network television before.

Suddenly, real people, not actors, could be seen inside a little box in millions of homes throughout the nation, and they didn't have to look like Ford models.

These people on reality television weren't acting either. They were real people put into highly stressful situations and encouraged to backstab, snitch, fink, and do really crappy things to win. Those who did were way more successful than those who didn't.

As a result, reality television has become the training ground for viewers to behave badly, because people love to imitate winners.

Reality television has exploded into every country on nearly every subject imaginable—wife swapping, celebrity wife swapping, child swapping, cooking, singing, dancing, fear, fashion, and more than the average brain can imagine.

And don't count on it stopping anytime soon. It seems like everyone knows at least one person who has been on a reality show, and the networks are getting desperate for more ideas. In the future, expect to see: *America's Got Pimples, Race with a Hernia, Biggest Wart on the Block*, or *The Cancer Countdown*.

As more and more reality shows are created, backstabbing will grow exponentially as people get rewarded with more screen time by successfully betraying others on the show. And more people will watch these new shows, ensuring a constant crop of newly minted backstabbers who will practice this horrendous behavior.

RECOMMENDATIONS:

If you are a backstabber and wish to stop, take a vacation from reality television shows and for Pete's sake, stay far away from *Game of Thrones*.

Offer profuse apologies to your victims and offer reparations that count. Think along the lines of a Segway or a lifetime supply of cheese balls.

If you have been backstabbed by someone trusted, there are things you can do to comfort your broken heart. One of them requires handling a big metal key, over a shiny paint job, in the dead of night. Throw in some cat puke while you're at it.

Revenge is a dish best served with Tigger's hairballs. Just kidding! Bad joke. Better to take the high road and let it be. Yes. Turn the other cheek and all that biblical stuff.

The Bitter

aka: the acerbic, the grouch, the grump, the sourpuss
variation: the cynical

*You woke up this morning staring into the eyes of the most beautiful and smart woman you've met in your entire life, and your head feels a little dizzy, and the air smells fresh, and you can barely walk 'cuz your mind is still intoxicated by the outrageous sex you had the night before, and you want to kiss everyone you see, including the meter maid writing you a ticket for parking in a street cleaning zone. You enthusiastically say, "Good morning" to all the other employees you work with in that crap job of yours, which today, feels like the best job on Earth. Then you run into your miserable boss, Mr. Bitter, who takes one look at your obviously besotted expression and says "love stinks, the sooner you get this into your head, the faster you'll recover when she dumps you, and she **will** dump you."*

A bitter person is one who views life from a very negative perspective, has a generally unpleasant personality, and quite possibly sports a haircut befitting a poodle.

Bitter people contain such negative energy that mere mention of a bitter person's name can ruin a perfectly good orgy. Bitter people do not trust others. They have grey auras, love sour cream, and have the ability to coagulate milk by looking at it. They are definitely not the life of a party.

Like many of the other unpleasant personality types listed here, bitter people don't get on well with others and if they manage to somehow make a new friend, won't keep them for long.

Being around such an acrid person can make your ice cream taste as yummy as puke, so unless you enjoy having your dreams smashed into little tiny pieces, minimize exposure to these grumps.

You'll know you've encountered a bitter person when the world as you know it suddenly smells as fresh as a wrestler's armpit on a hot summer's day.

CAUSE:

Blame it on lemons. Lemons are sour, so sour that imagining a tablespoon of fresh squeezed lemon juice entering your mouth makes the mouth scrunch up involuntarily. Sucking on a high number of lemons can cause a person to unconsciously train their facial muscles to freeze into a permanently puckered expression. People who love the sour taste of lemon juice are at risk of becoming bitter people.

Psychologists have found a correlation between facial expression and mood. They say facial expressions can affect mood and vice versa. For example, forcing yourself to smile throughout the entire day even when you want to gut the noisy guy at the next table, can transform your mood into a better one.

Likewise, sucking down a tart little lemon throughout the day makes your face contort into an unpleasant, sometimes hideous expression, enough to turn you into an acerbic, biting, negative human being.

Psychologists call this "facial feedback hypothesis." You are what your face expresses. If you scrunch it from sucking lemons constantly, then you can become an acidic person from all that tartness.

And that's not all. The acid from lemon juice eats away surface enamel on teeth, which in turn, makes chewing feel similar to chomping on a pickaxe.

RECOMMENDATIONS:

When a bitter person enters your life, it takes great effort to combat their bad juju. A talisman, something like a Hello Kitty charm, might work for a temporary fix.

To permanently cure a bitter person requires much more effort: an IV drip of sugar water (with vitamins) that has been exposed to laughing children, and it must be administered by an enthusiastic clown.

It's not the cheapest cure and not a particularly easy one to procure but so beneficial to the bitter person that it is worth the effort.

Eliminate all citrus and vinegary foods. Avoid tart things in general.

An alternative method that may work, but not necessarily as well as the IV drip, is to gather family and neighbors for a group hugging session that lasts at least five hours with occasional food and bathroom breaks. This will possibly cause the bitter person to have an emotional breakdown, destroying the bitter barrier around their bosom, allowing the inner Care Bear to come out.

The Blabbermouth

aka: the big mouth, the spoiler

variation: the gossiper

Two days ago, your obstetrician told you some shocking news—that baby inside your stomach is not fully human. It's part armadillo and it definitely lives! It's a miracle and a nightmare at the same time. You don't know how it happened, but you do vaguely remember one day last month when you couldn't account for five hours of missing time. One minute you were chowing down some tasty lasagna and the next thing you know, you were staring up at the overhead lights from your bed; the time in between somehow disappeared. You tell your sister about the whole armadillo thing, begging her not to say anything to your folks as you try to figure out what to do next—you don't want to shock your mom into a stroke. But a day later, your mom calls you up on the phone anyways, in hysterics, rambling something about a sin she committed with a boy in her class when she was 16 and now you're all cursed. Not what you needed to hear when a shelled mammal wriggles inside you. Tell your little sister, "Thanks for being a blabbermouth!"

A blabbermouth refers to a person who can't keep their lips sealed during a time when it most needs to be sealed. It doesn't matter if they didn't mean any harm—that would be the backstabber (see *The Backstabber*)—harm is done anyway, because the blabbermouth's lips flapped open with juicy details that should have remained unspoken until some beer could be chugged down.

That means the blockbuster you wanted to see, the mystery novel you wanted to read, the surprise party you wanted to give, the engagement you wanted to keep under wraps—all ruined by the blabbermouth who cannot keep their lid shut.

You tell them, "Don't spoil it for me," and they always promise not to, but it means nothing, because they will burst unless that secret tidbit flies out of their mouth and out come the spoilers you didn't want to know, until you were camped out in a dark room with buttered popcorn. Not a big deal for movies, but a phenomenal nightmare if someone spills all to your fiancée about that brothel you secretly own.

Children are natural blabbermouths. Restraint isn't in their skill set yet—that comes with age—so don't tell anything to a kid you don't want publicized. Best to say nothing at all to those immature little chipmunks if you want to keep those skeletons buried deep.

CAUSE:

Big mouths become that way due to a condition called foot in mouth disease. The sickness, as the name implies, strikes the victim down with the propensity to say things at random without discretion. The disease arises from sucking on a grimy big toe for an extended period of time.

Early on, many children find comfort sucking their thumbs, which replaces a mother's nipple. When mama ain't around, the big thumb comforts the same way a mom's breasts do. But for some children, however, a big toe is preferred to the thumb, and it is with these children that foot in mouth disease has its foothold.

Hands, which are exposed to air, sunlight, water, and soap, tend to be cleaner than a foot at any given time. Feet are usually on the ground—sometimes they are actually barefoot—on dirt where billions of microbes live.

Feet are also shrouded in socks and shoes, giving rise to sweat and fungus over long periods of time. If the socks are made of wool, you can bet there's at least a tablespoon of sweat perspired by a foot over an entire day. Placing the toe in the mouth allows these germy items to get swallowed.

Why children prefer the toe to the thumb is probably the flavor. The taste of sweat mixed with grime and wool is a strong savory attraction, but it is hard to know for sure. Perhaps it is simple enjoyment of a toe's size and sensation. Unfortunately for those who prefer the toe, they end up sucking a whole lot of disgusting stuff, enough to do some serious damage. As the kid is growing up, they develop a blabbermouth condition, a condition that will plague them for the rest of their lives.

Some of the most unsanitary feet belong to kids who walk barefoot on city streets and public beaches where all sorts of filthy detritus accumulate. Nasty microorganisms live there and can cause serious permanent damage; hearing can become impaired and the throat can become infected with all sorts of gross looking critters that creep upward into the brain, impairing the areas that control judgment, good sense, and ability to shut up when needed.

The person with foot in mouth disease can ruin many potentially good mysteries, surprises, and secrets.

RECOMMENDATIONS:

Toe diversion is necessary to prevent young children from becoming future blabbermouths.

When a child is seen going for their toe, you must stop them. Grab their foot and pull it away from their anticipating lips.

Sometimes, you can't prevent toe sucking unless the child is strapped to you 24 hours a day—a pretty difficult task if you have to take a dump.

If you know a child with toe sucking problems, it's better to scrub that child's feet every hour and tie small bells to their ankles so you can hear them when they raise their feet.

If you are dealing with adult blabbermouths, divulge nothing and retrain them from this bad behavior by sealing their lips together with glue, clothespin, or tape as they start to gossip details you know you shouldn't be hearing. Make sure you insert a straw into their mouth first so they can breathe. The intent is to keep their indiscreet mouth sealed, not suffocate them.

The Blackmailer

aka: the extortionist

Everyday you pick up your mail at 6 pm like clockwork. You sift through the usual—bills, ads, more bills. A crudely addressed envelope catches your eye. It looks to be written by a ten year old. You open the mysterious envelope to see a poorly scribbled message on a piece of paper. "I saw what you did with the babysitter in the bakyard I gonna tell your wife unles you give me 1000 snickers bars. Meet at jungle jim in swan park tomorow nite and you better have what i want." If you have ever received such a note in your life, then you have been blackmailed by a rotten little punk with cavities in their future.

A blackmailer is a person who has you by the balls, metaphorically speaking but sometimes literally, in which to extract some type of demand—usually large sums of money or other tangible goods and services from you.

If you don't comply, something shitty happens involving loss of some kind—your reputation, money, genitals, a pet horse.

Maybe you've become famous, and some jerk from your past threatens you with a "tell all" about that time in sixth grade when you were caught doing something nasty with a goat during a farm field trip. Or perhaps a certain co-worker saw your hands touching something they shouldn't, perhaps some gonads or mammaries belonging to someone with a higher rank. Whatever it is, you know your unflattering secret is going to go public soon if you don't pay in a big way, and that can make you extremely fearful.

Being blackmailed causes most people to break out into a big sweat, lose sleep, and a whole mess of other afflictions. Once blackmailed, a person is never quite the same.

CAUSE:

The act of blackmail may seem a crime of pure evil. In outcome, that would be true. But to view the blackmailer as an irrepressible malevolent force driven by a purely crooked mind is to focus on the result and not the impetus for the crime, kind of like stepping on dog shit and blaming the dog rather than the owner. Blackmailers could be thwarted if more people understood the motivation for their sick and disgusting behavior. These menacing fiends are driven by their noses, addicted to the smell of fear, a real tangible though subtle smell that leads a blackmailer into a euphoric state.

For these individuals, the smell of fear triggers a physiological and emotional response similar to ecstasy. Fear gives off a scent only a special nose—belonging to a dog or a blackmailer—can sniff out. For these unusual folks, smelling someone's terror is as enjoyable as smelling baked brownies for most people.

Scents—gardenias, soaps, colognes/perfumes, and rain—make blackmailers hurl. Instead, their unusual nasal olfactory receptors are enthralled by the scents most people would find super offensive: rotting eggs, cow manure, dirty hair, and as mentioned, fear.

Having this unusual sensory response makes it difficult for normal employment. In most work situations, employees unknowingly contribute scents and fragrances to an environment through their daily habits.

Tilly might bring a loaf of sweet smelling pumpkin bread one morning to share with her co-workers. Jack might come in slathered in cheap aftershave he got on sale at Walgreens. Laquisha might have a vase of stargazer lilies from the dude she's doing this month.

Also, most work sites use some type of janitorial service for common areas, which leaves a place smelling sterile or of Lemon Pledge. This is dreadful for a fear-lovin' soul, kind of like living in an elephant cage for the rest of us.

With the exception of a zoo, a pet store, a junkyard or some other odorously unpleasant environment, blackmailers have a hard time dealing with the fragrances at most places of employment. For lack of money, they have learned to monetize their unusual ability and get pleasure out of it, which is how blackmailers come to exist.

RECOMMENDATIONS:

To prevent from being the target of a blackmailer, first, don't do stupid deeds that you can get busted for.

If you have no self-control and must do dumbass things, then carry around some air fresheners, scented oils, or maybe a small bottle of bleach in a spray pump. This way, if you should be confronted by someone who has accidentally spotted your immoral act and decides to blackmail you, you have some basic tools of protection.

Mist the air with the clean smell of perfume or bleach between you and the blackmailer, forming a fragrant barrier between the two of you. What this will do is mask any fear (smell) emitted from your body and instead, replace it with a repulsive odor.

The blackmailer will learn to associate you with unpleasant fragrances, replacing the enjoyment of scaring you with the loathsome odor of perfume or cleanliness. This will deter them from dealing with you any further.

Beware of backlash if the person has allergies to perfume or if the bleach should land on any exposed skin, causing a burning sensation and rash. Things might worsen if you piss off the blackmailer by giving them a skin condition.

If all fails, you might see about hiring a former Navy SEAL to help you take care of it. Explain your situation and he'll know exactly what to do.

The Braggart

aka: the boaster, the conceited, the egotist, the hotshot, the pompous, the self-important, the showoff

"If you were as smart as me, you'd still have your job," says your buddy Joe. "I'm great at what I do. Last week, I scored a million in sales, because I bust ass harder than everyone I know and I fucking rock." Joe's supposed pep talk ends up making you feel like shit when he goes on to list all his accomplishments and tells you in great detail how he was honored with an Employee of the Year Award. You find yourself wishing he would get smacked in the head by an errant baseball so he would shut up already.

A braggart is an individual who spends the majority of a conversation telling you how fuckin' amazing they are; how ginormous their wanker is; how rich they are; and how everyone thinks they are a god among mortals, because the braggart feels these details will enrich your existence in some way, and they must remind you whenever they see you in case you mistake them for a giraffe.

Occasional bragging is no big deal. Excessive gloating is. That's because the boasting buffoon, by virtue of their nonstop self-glorification, is not really interested in any of your accomplishments or comforting you when you're down. They are more interested in letting you know how woefully inadequate you are by comparison.

Hubris, we know is a big fat no no in the world of Greek tragedies where the prideful protagonist gets bitch slapped by the gods in the end.

Braggarts don't seem to know this literary rule and don't understand that the rest of us are waiting eagerly for their big divine kick in the butt to knock them back down. If it turns out Zeus can't do the job, maybe a local felon adept at nicking cars can. We can only hope.

CAUSE:

The inflated ego of an egotist would almost be entertaining if it didn't make you feel want to stuff an entire grapefruit in their mouth. These hyped up individuals were tolerable once upon a time—that is—before they got their lips wrapped around a helium tank.

Helium, a hit at parties with big and little kids alike, can have some serious side effects if abused, used, or swallowed too many times. Due to the unbalanced ratio of oxygen to helium in some tanks, inhalation for long periods of time can kill neurological cells.

Helium occurs naturally in our world in small amounts and is found with natural gas deposits. It is listed as a safe element, but the truth is, it is neither safe nor fun when brain damage is the end result. Helium, used long term, is not amusing when it causes showoff, braggy, and egotistical behavior.

The helium-injured person can also have visual and auditory hallucinations; they can mistake other people's bored expressions as great enthusiasm. When people say, "Do you ever stop talking about yourself?" The braggart hears, "Please tell me *more* about yourself!" The ability to read faces, to understand social cues gets screwed up as well. Eye rolling, for example, is mistaken as adoration.

Access to helium is dangerously easy. Every city seems to have helium tanks available to rent for children's parties.

Children, of all people, should not be inhaling the stuff. It may be fun to sound like a munchkin for ten seconds, but it is no laughing matter when the brain gets deprived over and over again of adequate oxygen.

Yes, tanks do come with oxygenated helium, otherwise, we'd have cute little corpses at birthday parties, but not all helium tanks are created equal. Some have less oxygen than others due to disgruntled employees who hate their company and want to see them get sued.

Make no mistake—helium is public enemy number 536, regardless of what party rental companies say. The stuff should not be inhaled long-term or you can end up with an egotistical brain damaged child/friend/student/GF/BF/spouse that won't shut the hell up when they should.

RECOMMENDATIONS:

To deter helium use, ban the Wizard of Oz movie from children's eyes and certainly don't have it playing in the background during the holidays. If that is impossible to do, dub over the munchkin scenes with Tom Wait's voice or add trance music to cover up the appealing, overly cute munchkin lines. Helium sucking should be discouraged at all costs.

If you are forced to get a helium tank for a birthday party, release the helium out of the tank before the party and fill it with broccoli puree. That way, children will get healthy antioxidants instead of dangerous gasses, and you technically fulfilled your obligation of procuring the tank. You also do the world the favor of not producing future braggarts.

The Brat

aka: the impudent, the little shit, the rascal, the spoiled, the stinker

It's a beautiful sunny day. You head over to the nearest lake with your Kindle. As you get there you see an adorable little tyke, about five years old, polishing off a cherry popsicle, half of it down the front of his shirt. You claim a good sized plot of grass and settle in for an afternoon of Stephen King. Suddenly, an ear-splitting scream erupts from your right side. Panicked, you look up expecting to see blood spurting from that kid's eye. Instead, you see a little foot stomping up and down, a face twisted into a tight coil and a whole lotta words flowing from that tiny little mouth. "YOU NEVER GIVE ME ANYTHING I WANT! YOU'RE SO MEAN. YOU'RE THE WORST MOTHER I'VE EVER HAD. I HAAAAAATE YOU!" The boy catches your amused look which only makes him scream louder, in your direction, at you. You have been the lucky witness to a brat having a full on tantrum.

A brat refers to a child but can also refer to an adult behaving like a child, when that individual has a tantrum, a hysterical fit, or makes a scene when not getting exactly what they want, making others want to give that person a little extra something called knocked out teeth.

When a child acts out, we excuse their behavior while resisting the urge to break their neck, because children are supposed to act like little shits. It's expected.

When an adult stomps their feet and gets whiny, it's harder to bear, because they make an ass of themselves, which makes you want to hide from the world that you are actually involved with this man-child or infantile wench. If you're lucky enough to witness this bad behavior early in a relationship, count your blessings, because you can still opt out before it's too late.

Brats are not easy to rehabilitate, because their behavior is deeply embedded into their psyche. It takes great effort, persistence, and plenty of tranqs to change these difficult types.

CAUSE:

Brat behavior has become an epidemic in the last 30 years, much worse now than it has ever been in history. If you believe weak parenting skills are to blame, you are partially correct. But it is not because parents have become overly sensitive fools subscribing to the new age creed of keeping their children's spirit intact by using only positive reinforcement; it is really because these children's parents had their muscles damaged by the KGB, the Russian security agency.

In the mid '60s, the Soviet Union began a campaign to weaken U.S. citizens by sending spies to record making (vinyl discs that play music) manufacturing plants.

These spies, once in the record duplicating plants, were tasked with dumping toxic chemicals into vats of black poly vinyl chloride—the raw material for vinyl records. These toxic, damaging vapors got released into the homes of music lovers once that diamond needle hit the vinyl disc.

All sorts of unmentionable chemicals were dumped into those vats, many of which are outright banned now, because they cause cancers. (People who worked in these plants suffered greatly from inhaling poisonous fumes, causing many to have industrial accidents and fall into the vats.)

For the average Joe listening to records at home, the gasses that got released from the record player led to muscle cell breakdown and ultimately, destruction. The KGB's intent was to weaken the U.S. economy by knocking down the workforce, thus disabling financial growth.

The covert operation worked well. The toxic vapors turned teenage music lovers into sluggish beings with muscle damage as they continued playing rock and roll records in their bedrooms, shaking their asses to the music for a decade or more, until they stopped being able to.

Once these teens reached parenting age, their bodies were so weakened that they were physically unable to discipline their children, lacking the strength to chase them down for a time out or a spanking.

These children, unable to get much reaction from their damaged parents, had to speak louder, be more theatrical, and throw tantrums to get their parents actively moving. The kids also seemed to be able to do whatever they want without any consequences. Get caught stealing a Mars bar from the local corner store? No problem, dad won't do anything, because he couldn't run after his kid if his life depended on it.

Once these brats started having their own children, they let their children go wild, following the model of parenting they were brought up with. Even though these grown up brats weren't as exposed to vinyl records as their parents were (due to the emergence of analog tapes) and had the physical ability to chase down their little snots for punishment when they acted out, they didn't because they hadn't experience a thing called discipline and didn't know how to deliver it.

Luckily, not all teenagers from the '60s loved music enough to play it daily in their bedrooms. Some who were obsessed with studying or had strict parents or were too poor to buy records were spared from exposure and retained all their muscle strength. Their children and grandchildren, being born or raised at present, will compensate for their out of control peers.

The KGB knew they could inflict damage on Americans by polluting music, but did not expect the secondary bonus of creating bratty children, which has helped them succeed in their covert mission of having a less effective workforce.

RECOMMENDATIONS:

Avoid playing vintage vinyl records. Records made after 1991 are relatively safe, although the Soviet Union now uses other means to inflict damage on American listeners. What we can only hope to do now is modify the behavior of brats by using training methods including those used on cats and dogs.

A squirt gun filled with ice cold water is an effective tool when shot in the brat's face; it can stop a child or an adult mid-tantrum, surprising the recipient temporarily, until they regain their senses and throw a bigger fit. That's when another blast of ice water must be utilized as quickly as possible, double the time, double the squirts. However, you don't want to shoot so much that you drown the child or adult, but you do want to stop them from their irritating fits.

When they finally shut up and dry their face, that's when you have a treat of some sort to reward their momentary silence; try a juicy strawberry, a compliment, a warm hug.

Warning: if the brat is a sly little devil with quick hands, that squirt gun could be taken from your clutches and used on you. Be prepared for your own soaking and have another squirt gun as a backup, bigger than the first one used in order to defend yourself appropriately.

The Bully

aka: the coercer, the goader, the harasser, the intimidator, the meany, the oppressor, the tormentor

Once upon a time, a mean boy got in your face. His big fat mouth hovered over your head with his chin jutted out. He always knocked you down when you weren't looking, tripped you, and threatened you as if you were some gnat he could step on. You weren't the most popular boy, but you weren't the most unpopular either. One day, your stupid mom gave you the most hideous haircut you ever got, because she had a thing for '80s New Wave, and you were stuck with a 'do that made you look like a band member from the Flock of Seagulls. You could have killed her for doing that. Everyone in your P.E. class laughed at you, and it was all started by that bonehead jerk, the bully of your 6th grade class.

A bully is a person who harasses, taunts, or beats up one or many individuals for identifiable differences, whether those differences are overt, subtle, or exaggerated in the obnoxious bully's mind, making these baddies a good target for a dodge ball.

Elementary and high schools are hotbeds for bullying behavior where half-witted goons and goonettes pick on someone a little different (a boy with a limp, a girl with bad teeth). The bully harasses their poor victim until the bullied kid is so stressed out that they end up bringing an AK-47 to math class.

Bullying makes their victims feel crappy. This bad behavior is one of the few that has worsened over time, once social media became the go to form of interaction.

In pre-web days, bullying primarily consisted of physical beatings, verbal assaults, intimidation, local humiliation, and group taunts. Eventually, with time, those horrible experiences faded until they became an unpleasant glitch in the photo album of the mind.

Now with social media, bullying has all the former and the added joy of global humiliation that is forever etched in the online world, one that follows the poor victim through life, or at least, until a massive natural disaster blows all storage servers into the ether.

CAUSE:

Bullies seem to be a curse among decent folk. These ogres inspire fear, loathing, and emotional pain for people who can feel sympathy and compassion. If bullies seem subhuman to you, you would not be far from the truth—bullies aren't people, they are actually reptiles.

If you've heard the phrase "wolf in sheep's clothing," you may be able to understand this concept more clearly.

You might know that chameleons are reptiles best known for their camouflage abilities; they can change the color of their skin to blend in with their environment, offering them security from would be predators.

What you might not know is that a number of these highly intelligent lizards have evolved beyond merely changing colors to actually changing shape.

Having lived as pets among humans for so long, they have learned, over centuries, to change into human form. In doing so, they have learned to walk upright and use their hind legs bipedally as humans do. Their front legs have become their hands and their long tails now retract into their body, acting as a spine for their upright position. The chameleon's great evolution is one of nature's miracles, though not well publicized in the mainstream press.

Japanese herpetologist Gray Komodo has spent more than twenty years documenting this unusual phenomenon and has proven without a doubt the link between bullying behavior and human-posing chameleons among us.

He first discovered this unlikely connection by noticing similarities between bullies and lizards, mostly in physical and behavioral aspects: the similarity in the shape of the tongue, in the texture of the skin, in their repulsion to human touch, and their love of eating bugs.

These noted similarities inspired Komodo to track down a number of notorious bullies, swipe their blood by putting nails and spikes on surfaces where bullies would likely injure themselves, and taking these blood-stained objects for testing. It was in the lab that Komodo found human bullies to have some reptilian chromosomes, enough to suggest the evolution of reptiles into human form.

Much of Komodo's theories help explain why bullies behave the way they do. Lizards aren't fond of humans. Their speech and actions, in human shape, reflects this. They are mean and aggressive due to their reptilian brain. They have basic survival instincts and threaten others when they feel bothered. They don't reason, cannot be objective, lack compassion, don't have critical faculties and other higher functions. In short, they behave the way any lizard would, threatening, posturing, flaring their gills, and acting nasty, because they are mean little shits.

But how did they learn to speak you might ask? Lizards generally don't have vocal chords. Komodo asked the same question.

After years of field observation, he found that bullies were somewhat incoherent and illogical, focused on threatening words, just as he imagined lizards to behave if they could talk.

Because humans are constantly trying to handle lizards without the lizard's consent, the lizard's aversion to touch and need to communicate that aversion in a manner that humans could comprehend, probably instigated the spontaneous creation of vocal chords. After all, necessity is the mother of invention.

Komodo's theory also answers the question of why bullies don't listen very well—a lizard's hearing is much worse than a human's.

Komodo's lifelong work contributed greatly to the understanding of bullying behavior. Unfortunately, his work has not received the attention it should due to Komodo's unpleasant demeanor, biting personality, and ethically questionable methods of data gathering.

RECOMMENDATIONS:

When a bully plagues the playground, the neighborhood, or workplace, they can be a source of fear. You must be careful around a bully for they are unpredictable, having only a primitive brain. Forget logical conversation, they aren't capable.

What you can do is to distract them from threatening you or others by appealing to their true amphibious nature—toss a big, fat, juicy bug towards their mouth. You want their basic instinct to take over so they will stop bothering you. By feeding them, you subdue their aversion to humans, making you seem an ally rather than a predator.

Make sure you have a pocketful of insects. Feeding one isn't enough and may actually generate aggression towards you if you stimulate their appetite without satiating it. Big bugs are better; they are much easier to grasp in an emergency so keep a stash around.

You might prefer the bugs to be dead, but that may not be as appetizing to a bully/lizard. A fresh crawly is much more appealing.

Feeding the bully a handful of insects might entice the bully into shape shifting back to its original form where it would be easier to manage and contain.

Certainly do not try to fight back when they are in human form unless you can really knock them down for good.

The Cannibal

aka: the flesh eater, the man eater

Mortika has a hankering for a particular kind of meat not available in most supermarkets. In fact, it's not available in any supermarket, but it is available everywhere she looks. She feels the urge for a humanburger and if she wants it, she's going to have to do something bad to get it. For Mortika, human flesh is no different than beef, but to others, she's a scary cannibal.

A cannibal is a person who eats human flesh of any kind, namely muscles, organs, brains, skin, and will do so without using any spices or sauces.

When lost in the wilderness, trapped on an island, or stuck in the desert without any food sources available, people can resort to cannibalism.

In some tribal societies, cannibalism is practiced as part of the cultural dining experience—captured enemies and prisoners become the main entrees.

In modern society, it is deeply frowned upon, is very rare, is against the law, and is considered highly distasteful.

CAUSE:

The reason some people desire to eat human flesh in modern, civilized society is because they are zombies—the dead brought back to life by sorcerers—and infected with Toxoplasma gondii.

When most people die, they usually stay dead, but sorcerers can revive a corpse to enslave for selfish purposes—for doing chores, such as mowing the back lawn, fetching beer from the store, wiping mold off windowsills, dumping trash into a neighbor's garbage bin, and so on.

Being unethical people, sorcerers aren't great about mealtimes or feeding their slaves but when they do, a couple of raw cow organs can be enough to keep the zombie satisfied.

However, if the sorcerer has cats in their living quarters, a corpse becomes exposed to Toxoplasma gondii, a parasite found on felines and rodents. This changes the behavior of a zombie, making them very aggressive.

Unlike live people, corpses do not have a good immune system and become easily overwhelmed by this little parasite, especially when one of their chores is to scoop out the litter box.

When a zombie is hungry and their poverty-ridden master doesn't feed them enough, they will do something about it. But as zombies, they can't visit the local Safeway for raw chicken, pork, beef, or lamb. (Seafood, being relatively bloodless, doesn't really cut it.) They don't have the same varied options available to plant eaters. Actually, meat eaters have relatively few choices for flesh. The most convenient meat becomes human flesh.

Human flesh can fulfill a zombie's daily nutritional needs to keep them working throughout the entire day. On an average human, there's lots of flesh to gnaw on, providing many days of meals. It also satisfies more than a couple of raw pig hearts. Additionally, humans that have just eaten a spicy meal taste better than pig parts anyways.

When the cannibal wants a meal, watch out!

RECOMMENDATIONS:

If someone with glassy eyes, a distant vapid stare, and pale bluish skin approaches you some dark evening on an empty street, cross to the other side immediately. Do not attempt to start any conversation. Do not try to pass by them quickly. They will lunge for your butt—the meatiest part of your body—and bite a chunk off of you. If you have big tits, that makes you doubly vulnerable. Once you're in their grip, escape is difficult but not impossible.

If you are in the clutches of a cannibal zombie, you must fight your way out by any means necessary. You must aim for their face with everything you got. Sometimes, this means fingers in gross places. Don't be squeamish. Zombies certainly aren't and they won't think twice about eating your nostrils.

If you cannot escape, try to hold your breath. Your living essence whets their appetite, but if you can hold your breath for a long time and play dead, they might leave you. Zombies don't enjoy eating dead people—they taste terrible.

If you've dodged a zombie, try to keep your eyes open for the sorcerer, who may be nearby and might throw a stun spell in your direction to make it easy for their servant to come nab you for a few bites, which saves them the trouble and liability of illegally procuring free human flesh. It also saves them money on their grocery bills.

The Co-Dependent

aka: the glued at the hip,
the interdependent, the overly attached

Manuel and June invite you over to their house for a lobster dinner Friday night, and they're gonna have your favorite chocolate flourless cake for dessert. It's tempting as hell considering there's only a bottle of Ex-Lax in your fridge, which you keep cold, because it tastes better that way and kind of passes for food. Problem is, you're not sure you have the stomach for an evening with the dysfunctional pair; Miguel and June speak as if they were one person, finishing each other's sentences. They won't ever disagree with each other even though Manuel was a former anarchist, until he met June and became a hardcore Republican. Even worse, they need to be within constant sight of each other. It disgusts you to no end. Manuel was the buddy who used to put on raves and pop-up parties. Somehow, he has morphed into a Siamese twin with his girlfriend, and you lost a good pal in the process.

Co-dependents involve at least two people in a relationship—not necessarily romantic—where there is a dearth of independence and plenty of mental enslavement, usually in one of the following scenarios: a) one barking the orders and the other following them; b) one or both always agreeing with the other even when the other is wrong; c) one or both dropping their previous friends so that nobody can take their time away from each other; or d) one or both refusing to end the relationship when they would each be better off with a parakeet. There are other forms of co-dependency, but these seem the most common.

If you try to make plans with a co-dependent, you will find only frustration as you witness the inability of that co-dependent to make a decision without consulting the other, as in, "is it okay for me to go take a piss now?"

Co-dependency can happen between a romantic couple, a parent and child, siblings, and between friends. When co-dependency happens between family members, it gets a little weird. "Mom, can you help me shave the hair off my butt before the party?" "Sure honey, but let me go buy your 40 birthday candles first."

If you know a co-dependent couple, it would be good to keep a barf bag handy if you have to visit them. If you accidentally hurt one of the pair's feelings, the other one will come after you with sharp tongs. You will also get booted out the door and banned from ever visiting again, and that's a good thing.

CAUSE:

When two people are unable to act independently from one another, you can assume their co-dependent behavior is a carryover from a previous incarnation as sibling puppies that got traumatically separated from one another. When they find each other in the new life, something familiar and primal gets triggered in their subconscious, bringing forth all types of feelings and behaviors that mimic their previous relationship in the other life.

Dogs are extremely loyal to their master and their own brood. When sibling dogs are raised in the same household from puppyhood to adulthood, they develop a deep bond with their littermate, a bond so strong it becomes psychologically difficult for each of them to do things without the other.

The dogs share their waking and sleeping hours together. They take care of each other, licking each other's fur and wrestling playfully every day. If one leaves the presence of the other, both dogs become depressed, anxious, and withdrawn.

One of the pair eventually becomes the alpha lead while the other becomes the follower.

If one of the siblings should become deceased before the other, the surviving dog mourns heavily for their dead brother or sister, whimpering constantly, howling at all hours.

After the dogs have completed their canine life, they may reincarnate in human form. If so, their previous life's experience, emotional needs, and trauma are carried over into the next incarnation. It is no surprise then to find dogs, reincarnated as humans, subconsciously desiring to relive the bonds they had before.

It has been documented that people's closest alliances in one life continue into the next one. For example, your wife today might have been your husband—the one with the giant nose—in a previous life. Before that, he might have been strict cousin Luciana, and so on. It's a very long cycle that keeps repeating over and over again, but each time, with new faces, new genders, new ethnicities, and sometimes new species.

The likes and dislikes are also inherited from lifetime to lifetime as well, even when changing species. For example, the reincarnated person, as a previous dog, might have loved dog biscuits. As a human, he or she will still love biscuits, and will go for the human version slathered in gravy. If they were a real whiner as a dog, they will be a whiner as a human. The previous life has the strongest affect on the following lifetime because it is the most recent.

In a new body, it becomes hard to recognize an old brother or sister once they come back. If this concept is hard to grasp, think of it as going to meet a boyfriend or girlfriend at a huge costume party in a giant warehouse where neither of you know what the other is wearing, nor is there a way to text each other. That's sort of how reincarnation works.

Subconsciously, the co-dependent will try to relive that emotional closeness they had with the sibling every time they are closely involved with someone new. When they try to do this with someone who wasn't their former sibling but was really their former buddy down the street who regularly chased a ball with them in the park, the intense relationship they crave doesn't last very long, because the other doesn't feel the same way. It's sort of like throwing your arms around the wrong person at the costume party mentioned above.

When that former sibling finally shows up in the new lifetime, the former siblings recognize each other on a deep level which they can't explain, even if they had never met before in the new life. It's as if they could see through each other's costumes with x-ray eyes, enough to recognize dear old bro or sis. Once they find each other, no way will they let go (in case they get lost in the crowd again).

If you aren't convinced, just look at the similarities. Co-dependents must always know where the other person is, not unlike dogs that must always have the other sibling in view. If romantically involved, they feel free to lick each other's faces and body without abandon, the way littermates groom each other so easily. Co-dependents will never refuse a request from the other, even if it means jumping off a cliff; dogs are the same—they can never say "no" to their sibling's request. The co-dependent pair feels great anxiety when others insist on separating the two, just like sibling dogs when placed in different homes. There tends to be a dominant partner in the human pair, similar to the rise of an alpha dog in a litter. If the dog or the human dies the other is extremely lost, howling at all hours of the night.

RECOMMENDATIONS:

Past life regression would be extremely helpful for the co-dependent couple who wish to tackle the origins of this unconscious behavior. Together, the duo should seek a reputable hypnotherapist who can lead the two suffering souls into the previous doggy lifetime.

A successful session should be able to pinpoint the exact moment when the traumatic, unwanted separation began. Allowing the two individuals to express their fear and pain by barking, baying, howling, and growling can help heal the pain of separation anxiety.

Once the traumatic episode has been healed, the two can have a bit more independence from one another. They will also be able to have healthy relationships with others outside of their little circle and will cease to disgust all those who have to be in their presence.

The Competitive

aka: the challenger, the opposer, the rival

Shaquila wants to arm wrestle you. Again. It's only been thirty times and you're getting tired of saying yes. What's with her anyway? Why is she always trying to challenge you? It's strange. No one else wants to arm wrestle you as much as she does, not even close. It's not as if you're the strongest guy in the world, it's been a 50-50 split with half the times you winning. Muscle-wise, you're even, but it seems to be a thing with her, the desire to compete with you no matter the time or place—when you see each other in the break room, or if you're both having lunch in the same deli, or when you're at an employee meeting. That's because Shaquila is a competitive person.

A competitor is an individual who constantly challenges your ass (or another's) in a contest of speed, cunning, skill, or other measurable talent to show what a rock star they are.

Competitive types come in all shapes, sizes, and ages. That sweet little granny down the street with the sunny smile who says "hello" every morning might turn out to be a pistol carrying, crazy ass drag racer on a deserted highway waitin' for the chance to outrun some unsuspecting fella out for a quiet morning.

Sanctioned competition is something we all appreciate and enjoy, that's why there are so many beer guzzling dudes and dudettes willing to dish out anywhere from $50–$500 for a good seat at a baseball game.

Competition can drive us to do better, preventing us from becoming couch marshmallows for life. Imagine how a visit from an old high school cheerleader you lost your virginity to can change your hedgehog girlfriend into Miss Universe overnight. That's when competition serves a good purpose.

It's gets strange however, when the competition is over something banal or utterly stupid. You don't really care who's got the most ear hair.

CAUSE:

These seemingly aggressive people aren't as driven to win as you might think. In fact, their divisive antics may be a guise to express their sexual prowess.

When a person challenges another to a contest, a competition, or a race, they are really broadcasting their sexual availability and skills in a socially acceptable way rather than proclaiming it overtly.

In the earlier example, the granny who drag races a young male would have no other easy and appropriate way of engaging such a man in everyday life. But on the road—that's another story. The freeway is the great equalizer. On the road, Miss Granny can display her vitality, her sexual fortitude through her aggressive display of driving hard and fast. No words needed; actions say it all—what she does in the driver's seat, she can also do in the bedroom.

When a young man takes on the challenge of a drag race, they engage in a relationship, each driven by the other to perform their best. In a way, it's a safer version of a one night stand. Drag racing on the highway is a more socially tolerable way of sexually engaging others, without any moral judgment.

Young testosterone-filled men gun the accelerator with force, thrusting their foot down as if it were their dicks, showing each other what they can do. This symbolic display of penises can be seen as a form of foreplay between participants and bystanders.

Not surprisingly, race car drivers attract throngs of admirers that throw themselves at the speed demon's feet. In the case of granny, it shows everyone that she can handle a young stud.

The famed and popular hot dog eating contest is one of the most overt displays of sexual prowess in the form of competitive games. Hot dogs resemble erect dicks. Eating as many hot dogs under immense pressure in front of an audience is the most obvious form of sexual broadcasting ever.

By displaying their great oral skills—a very intimate activity in a publicly sanctioned and approved event—the male or female shows their ability, their readiness to perform oral sex under pressure in an acceptable and tasteful manner.

Nearly all forms of team sports require physical contact and/or handling of round objects, such as balls and/or phallic sticks of some sort, making baseball, football, hockey, volleyball, and so on, more than simple competition.

To plainly announce a desire for animalistic interaction would be considered crass and uncouth in a sexually repressed society. But by expertly handling a ball or stick, these players show off what they can do with their hands. Competing for a prize is a highly respectable way of saying "Hey, pick me! My pants are open for business!"

Physical fortitude is most obvious in the animal kingdom where competition is mandatory for mating; males of many species fight to the death for the chance to "do the dirty" with the female. Only the surviving victor gets the reward of ejaculation.

Humans are no different, except they use the ruse of competition and contests—sometimes without realizing it—as acceptable vehicles for expressing sexual fortitude, availability and skills.

RECOMMENDATIONS:

When someone challenges you to a contest, it may be a flattering roundabout request for a frisky physical engagement or a need to advertise their sexuality.

The correlation may not be obvious, but if it involves eating, racing, or any type of physical contact—arm wrestling or ball handling—there may be a sexual component involved.

If you are up for the challenge, your participation will make the competitor feel a whole lot better and help them out. Don't worry about winning or losing, it's not the result that counts but the physical interaction.

If you turn down a challenge, that is certainly your right to do. Sometimes you need to be in the right mood, unlike the competitor who always seems ready to go.

If a person starts to annoy you with their frequent challenges, give them a vibrator or a sex toy to use. If they are a friend, let them know you understand their libidinal urges, but you need time for other activities and cannot play right now.

The Conformist

aka: the conventional, the emulator, the follower, the unoriginal

Your little sister found the most darling dress in an old country western store. She didn't want to admit she loved it, primarily, because it looked like it belonged in a Little House on the Prairie episode. You offered to buy it for her, but she tells you she'd rather lick the floor clean than show up at school wearing something everyone would laugh at, because all the other girls dress like hookers these days, so she must dress that way too. You tsk tsk the poor thing who feels she must be a mindless conformer to fit in.

A conformist is a person who follows the herd, embracing a set of values, tastes, styles, and opinions that everyone in their peer group or society at large follows.

While this is hardly a terrible behavior, it does slide into the realm of meh, sort of like opting to be a piece of Velveeta cheese instead of a garlic jalapeño jack (apologies to Velveeta lovers. For you, a better comparison would be Velveeta or lard).

In grade school, kids learn quite early that standing out in a crowd is the same as having a big "kick me" sign glued to their shirt. If a boy goes to school wearing hoop earrings, he will get to see the bottom of a big garbage can from the inside.

However, there are many types of conformity, not all of them bad. There are some people who are naturally followers, who wear black muscle shirts because Drake wears them. For these folks, conformity is a good thing. Otherwise they'd be wearing vacuum bags.

There is also forced conformity, having to wear a uniform for school or work.

Sometimes a person has to behave in a certain way in a particular setting. Think boot camp—certainly not the time for a utilikilt.

Conformity can happen when a group of people require an initiation rite for acceptance. That almost always involves getting some young initiate into a physically dangerous situation, such as chugging down a bottle of whiskey while lying naked on a polar bear in subzero weather. Those who enthusiastically jump at the chance may not be the sharpest tool in the shed.

Conformity rites for a good cause would be beneficial to society, but unfortunately that doesn't seem to be a very popular idea. A hazing ritual where initiates have to teach Fermat's Last Theorem to juvenile offenders in 24 hours or volunteer at a T.B. ward for a day or take down an army of werewolves during a full moon would certainly be more laudable than choking to death from your own vomit.

CAUSE:

A conformist is created through student social interactions where a child can witness the terrible things that happen when someone is too different from the rest of a group.

There is a social pecking order among students where some are popular and some are despised. In between the two, there are cliques for the smart, the athletic, the artistic, the theatrical, and so on. If a student is lucky enough to find a group that they can belong to, they are damn lucky and will have many friends to play Nintendo with. If they are a lone potato, then they are in serious trouble, and you will need to hide the booze.

Take the example of Olive, the ten-year-old student from Borneo. She is in most ways like any other student in the world. She loves to play, she's social, she has dreams of who she wants to become some day, and that should be enough for her to make friends and fit in. But among a large student population, that's not enough. Olive is an orangutan and that is just the thing to set her apart from the rest of the students.

No matter how hard she tries to fit in, the fact that she has brown fur, powerful arms, and incredible tree climbing skills is enough to make her a pariah in the other students' eyes.

If she's the only student from Borneo, she is really screwed. Her days of loneliness and isolation may cause her to act out in ways that further alienate her. With her muscular arms, you'd expect her to be picked first for any team sports, but she is always picked last and unwillingly by the team captain.

A student who has the slightest empathy can sense the sadness Olive feels, but instead of befriending her, stays away in case their association with her spreads the non-acceptance germ.

Witnessing the social rejection of Olive can make a strong impression on a student, enough for that student to become the most conventional, sheep-like conformist for life.

RECOMMENDATIONS:

If you are a conformist and no longer wish to be one, you might want to spend time with a weirdo or spend time alone as practice for personal growth.

If you would like to develop your individuality but don't know how due to years of trying to be like other people, baby steps are encouraged.

Initially, try wearing a piece of clothing considered loud and outrageous, like a turquoise hula skirt or flashy pants.

Also, try voicing a different opinion from your friends as an experiment to see how it feels. If your buddies say they want a hot girlfriend, tell them you would be satisfied with a female-shaped scarecrow. If someone says strawberry is their favorite ice cream flavor, tell them artichoke is yours.

With time and practice, a conformist can become an individual with a unique perspective and a more eclectic wardrobe. If you can walk down a city street semi-naked with a string of fruit around your privates, you have defeated your conformist habit.

The Control Freak

aka: the anal, the micromanager

variation: the perfectionist

It's 11 o'clock, about the time you expect to see Mr. Micromanager come around the corner to check that you swept the floor in a north-south direction while singing the Star Spangled Banner in Latin at least twice, because the length of that song, repeated, is the right amount of time it takes to efficiently sweep the floor in the hallway. He knows, because he's done it and it has never failed him yet.

The control freak is a person who must inspect, harass, and criticize the way another person or group accomplishes tasks and duties, insisting that the other do it the micromanager's way, even if it's no better than what a one-legged kangaroo could do.

Control freaks are often found in the workplace, sometimes in positions of authority but could also be co-workers and underlings who are real nitpickers.

Under this twit's microscope, your days are cursed with being followed around, your work methods scrutinized and ultimately failing to meet the way the control freak wants it done.

This controlling type can also be found in the home with a parent obsessing over other family members' eating habits, dress, or recreational choices. Having a control freak in the home is a real bummer that drives their children to seek escape in Disney-themed movies where parents are much much nicer. That or heroin. Whichever is easier to get.

CAUSE:

The origin of this bad behavior seems to be rooted in childhood. A survey response supports my theory that almost all control freaks were forced to wear undersized diapers for the first two years of their lives.

Why would parents torture their wee ones with ill-fitting stool catchers? Using smaller diapers helped combat possible leakages from a child's butt. Parents who had expensive furniture were more likely to use this method of ensuring cleanliness around their precious upholstered fabrics. Tight diapers ensured no brown liquid could possibly escape onto any plush velvet or leather.

This surprising revelation also answers another mystery—how control freaks came to earn the not so flattering title of "anal retentive asshole."

A control freak's response to undersized, tight fitting diapers made bowel movements extremely painful, so painful that the child forced themselves not to shit in order to avoid the overly tight strain of full, soggy diapers, of which there was no relief from until the parent could smell or notice the excessive bulge coming from their baby's derriere.

When the infant could no longer hold it in due to abdominal pain and full bowels, it let loose a higher volume of crap than normal, enduring greater discomfort as the diaper became tighter from the excessive bulk.

Because the child pooped less frequently as a way of circumventing the ensuing discomfort, the parents checked their diaper less often, creating a vicious circle that culminated in the infant's tortured existence.

Crying could sometimes get a parent's attention, but if the parents were engaged in entertaining guests and a helper was equally engaged in party preparations, no one would be available for at least an hour or more.

Meanwhile, as a coping mechanism, the infant learned to fixate on other things. In doing so, the baby learned to disassociate from its body and instead, develop its mental faculties. But the infant's underlying anger would color their thoughts towards a negative hue, finding fault in the immediate surroundings as a way of channeling their anger. For example, a noisemaking shaky toy could distract the infant for a bit of time, but after too much time, the infant would notice the imperfections in manufacturing—a crooked seam line or poor design.

The baby developed the habit of judging the imperfections of their own parents, as well as the world at large, trusting no one to be capable of doing things properly.

This harsh assessment becomes habit long after the diapers have come off, extending into adulthood with the belief that only he or she is capable of doing anything right, that people must be fully managed down to the very last detail or they will fail.

The parents of control freaks could never have foreseen the psychological scarring and deleterious effects overly tight diapers would have on their children. If they had, one would hope these parents would have found a better method of protecting their precious home furnishings.

RECOMMENDATIONS:

As many people have learned, reliving a traumatic event in a safe environment under the guidance of an expert is one of the most effective ways of resolving past horrors.

Therapy for a control freak would include at least a year of wearing loose fitting adult-sized diapers and having bowel movements in them several times a day.

A well-paid attendant should be enlisted to change, wash, and apply talcum powder on the adult's buttocks.

This resolution of a childhood trauma would help negate the past and would psychologically benefit the control freak, breaking their desire to control other people's actions once they see they can be taken care of by others.

The Coward

aka: the chicken heart, the chickenshit, the prudent, the scaredy cat, the uncourageous, the wimp

"It's okay," you say. "There's no wind and it's not cold. We've got a life preserver right here. You will not drown. I promise you. It's not that deep. In fact I will go in with you," you tell your anxious former college roommate. She looks at you with hesitant eyes, uncertain of your sincerity. Finally, she offers her hand to you, entrusting you with her life. You grasp her wispy fingers and together, you step boldly into the bright green kiddie pool, for you must show courage in the face of cowardice.

A coward is a person who trembles at the thought of losing brow hair and is hindered from moving forward, taking action, making bold decisions or sometimes, even doing the right thing, behaving as if some bear will appear from nowhere and gobble them right up.

What truly constitutes cowardly behavior you ask? Isn't one person's definition of cowardice really another person's idea of prudence? Being labeled a coward is usually the result of a person unwilling to take risks that their peers or companion(s) deem safe. For example, a sober person refusing to go on a joyride with a bunch of drunkass dudes in a car might be called a coward by his buddies but might be called smart by his parents.

Cowardice is not the same as common sense. There is nothing wrong with self-preservation and a bit of caution. You can't plunge into a river to save someone when you can't swim. Doing something dangerous and stupid earns most people the label of "dunce."

However, there are some situations where a majority of the population might view a particular action or non-action as cowardly. For example, being afraid to eat a tortilla because you've only eaten white bread all your life might be considered cowardly.

So is staying in a relationship with someone who calls you "asswipe" and cuts you down on a regular basis. Someone who would rather put up with the abuse than leave—because it is safer than the unknown—might be called a coward by others.

So it would seem that a person earns the unflattering label when fearful of doing something considered safe by Cub Scout leaders and kindergarten teachers or fails to take reasonable action to improve a bad situation due to fear of changing the status quo.

CAUSE:

For the coward who seems to be afraid to make any sudden moves, there may be a good reason for their skittish behavior. A normal person can become a coward after an unplanned visit from the Grim Reaper, which can have a permanently scarring effect.

The Grim Reaper, the personification of death in poetry and movies, is actually a real guy—an immortal—who exists as a guardian of the underworld.

In the course of an average life, accidents are bound to happen. If the accident is bad enough, a person might "meet their maker" and die. But sometimes, a minor accident like a broken toe or finger might earn a ghastly visit from Mr. Reaper himself. Therein lies the problem. He's not supposed to leave his post unless someone really is—or soon to be—a goner. He isn't supposed to come around for minor boo-boos, because once he visits, it can really mess a person up.

The Grim Reaper is not an attractive dude. People do not want his company, so he doesn't have any buddies to hang with. The dead don't stay for long to keep him company. They are usually on their way to another destination: a fire pit, heaven, reincarnation, or disintegration. That means the Grim Reaper spends a great deal of time alone.

An eternal existence is a ridiculously long time. Think it sucks to wait for your phone to update? Imagine that wait time multiplied by a gazillion, except you have no cable or Taco Supreme or parties to occupy your time with.

Sometimes, in his eagerness for company, he can show up prematurely, making a house call when someone falls down and scrapes their knee. He is more likely to visit a person who owns some great gadgets in the home, for he is eager to try all the cool things not available in previous centuries when all anyone could offer was some wine, maybe some fine armor, or a torture rack. There certainly was no Final Fantasy in the old days.

The person receiving the visit has the bejesus scared out of them, as the presence of the grim reaper portends the end. And again, he's a very scary looking dude. One visit is plenty. A second one is most unwelcome.

For this reason, a person who has had a visit is going to do everything possible to prevent from getting another one. Who wants the company of an anorexic man who has no sense of humor anyway, a dude who seriously needs to gain some weight and doesn't have any good tunes to share.

The abject terror experienced by the coward makes them terrified of another visit. They would rather stay in a relationship with a real scuzzball or wench than face the prospect of going solo in the event the Grim Reaper comes around again. Having someone there with them in the reaper's company is much less scary than being alone.

RECOMMENDATIONS:

If a friend of yours is a coward, you could try to help them desensitize their fear of Mr. Grim Reaper himself by wearing a skintight all body skeleton suit, one that covers you from head to toe. But instead of going for the traditional hooded black cloak look, aim for something more festive to help turn around the bad rap old Reapy's got for being a gloomy guy. Try a baseball jersey of the coward's favorite team or a Hawaiian floral shirt. You could also wear a Christmas cape covered in baubles and gingerbread cookies. Don a clown wig. That'll help.

If you're a coward, don't fear the reaper. He's merely a skinny scary chump carrying a sharp, curved weapon who happens to have the ability drag you down into a very large dungeon of bleakness.

Reaper man won't really exercise that privilege, unless you're someone who does reckless daredevil stunts on a regular basis or owns a great entertainment center and boatloads of games in your possession. It's the adrenaline junkies who need to be afraid, but for some reason, a visit from Mr. Reaper only makes them more ballsy.

Continue your cautiousness, but try to think of the deathly dude in a different way. Check out Terry Pratchett's Discworld series where the grim reaper is featured as a friendlier fellow who can offer a good chat.

The Creep

aka: the flasher, the groper, the peeping Tom, the pervert; the sexual harasser

Packed into a subway train, you read the words for a Viagra ad a few feet away repeatedly, because you are jammed so tight in a rail car that if you turn left or right, you would be forced to share an intimate moment with a stranger's nose. That would feel awkward for both of you. It's at that moment you sense fingers slide across your butt cheek, creeping towards your precious privates. You try to turn around but can't, because you're surrounded by unfamiliar faces avoiding your gaze, all bunched together like asparagus wrapped in plastic. Then the car stops. People rush past you to escape that claustrophobic tin can and your groper is gone. You suspect it's that odd little man with the hideous plaid suit who glanced back at you with a self-satisfied grin as the door closed behind him.

The creep can mean many things to many people and is widely applicable to many unpleasant personality types, but is defined here as a person who gives others the willies by acting sexual in a situation that is absolutely not sexual, trying to impose a sexual favor from someone who does not desire or want the same, and/or doing clandestine sexual activities involving an unsuspecting person who would probably want to throw a big chunk of dry ice down the creep's pants if they knew what was going on.

Examples of creepiness include: a perv having a looky loo at an unsuspecting person undressing in their bedroom (a Peeping Tom/Tina); a person sexualizing or making innuendoes with objects at work (a loser); a groom or bride making unsolicited passes at various guests (bonehead).

For most people, rejection is a humiliating experience, enough to crush an ego into a tiny pinhole. A non-creep would desist in the face of rejection, but a creep keeps on going, as enthusiastic as the little Energizer bunny. Persistence when told "no" causes one to earn that unkind label.

Men are sometimes unfairly called creeps when they are perceived as disgusting or sexually repulsive for attempting to score with someone out of their league. In those cases, creeps can be the subject of much derision and ridicule merely for trying to get laid.

There are female creeps, but most often, people think of men when they think of the word. However, the creep label shouldn't really apply unless the person persists in displaying unwanted sexual behavior.

The label of creep can also be used when two or more people have a particular power dynamic; a powerful person (creep) is sexually aroused and able to impose their will on an underling (screwed) who wants to barf at the thought of "doing" their overlord.

The word "creep" has been used interchangeably with the word "pervert." Pervert is a popular word among teenagers who describe or associate innocent activities as perverted, peppering their sentences with the P word for things like eating bananas and adjusting underwear; many teenage brains are addled by hormones, making them see the world through a sexualized lens.

This would make teenagers natural perverts in theory but not so in practice. Many do not assert these tendencies, because they are so self-conscious and worried about what their peers think that the fear of looking uncool trumps any creepy tendencies.

It should also be noted that the creep is distinct from the sleazebag in that the latter will sleep with any consenting adult, including one in a gummi bear costume.

CAUSE:

Creeps may seem as if they were inherently pathetic, but the cause of creepy behavior is one that will astound—creeps have gotten that way due to spells by perturbed witches.

Witches of old and new are experts at spell casting and can be quite dangerous once pissed off.

In fairy tales, witches are seen as nasty old women with huge warts, but that is pure fiction. In reality, witches are average looking women and, on occasion, feminized males. Witches can also be attractive or ugly—no different than the general population.

Witches have the same type of emotions any normal person has with the exception of knowing how to do hocus pocus. They cannot change a person into a toad, but they can make anyone unappealing by throwing an aura of douchiness around them.

In the creep's case, an asshole has somehow crossed a witch by acting their rotten, jerky self. (Assholes often get away with their bad behavior unless their victim is a cop, a violent basket case, or an experienced witch.) When they piss off a witch, they've pissed off the wrong person.

The witch casts a spell under her breath as the asshole walks away. Later, she will strengthen the spell with a concoction of roots, plants, and more incantations while fixing an image of the offender in her mind. In a matter of days, the asshole graduates into the creep, finding romantic rejection wherever he, and in some cases she, goes.

Assholes are capable of having friendships and even popularity, but creeps don't as much. In fact, they are seen as wretched losers to be avoided.

If the asshole is a man and they turn into a creep, getting laid will be nearly impossible. If the asshole turned creep is female, getting laid won't be much of an issue, but the quality of the partner will suffer. When once upon a time she could land a real stud muffin rich dude, after turning creep, she might only attract horny pitbulls instead.

The morale of the story is not to be an asshole in general, so you won't be turned into a creep if you encounter a witch.

RECOMMENDATIONS:

If you meet a creep and don't wish to be bothered by them, you must shout out that a creep is in the house and is feeling up people at random.

The creep counts on you to keep quiet, expecting your silent acceptance of their roaming hands, but humiliation will help the creep back off. Screaming "no" will also draw attention to the creep and will make them scurry away.

If you are a creep but don't wish to be, you will need to retrace your steps and apologize to all the people you've insulted or irritated from the moment you started noticing widespread rejection of your sexual advances. It was probably around that time that you crossed paths with a potent witch with strong powers who turned you into the creep you are today.

If all your efforts produce no effect on your creepiness vibe, then you may have to find a witch who is willing to undo the spell of another's, but watch yourself. You need to be on your best behavior in case the new witch finds you offensive and strengthens the previous witch's spell by turning you into a creep with a severe rash instead.

The Critic

aka: the belittler, the faultfinder,
the hairsplitter, the nit-picker, the particular

"Nice car bro, it looks good, except for that color, kind of puke green. Why did you get a two door anyway? You know dad is gonna to have a hard time getting into the back seat. You didn't pay full price did you? I mean, that year sucked. Did you do any kind of research at all?" says the brother who makes you wish a FedEx truck would sideswipe his sleek SUV. No matter what you do, he always finds fault with it, because he is a damn critic.

The critic is an individual who, for a variety of reasons, finds fault with what you do, like the way you blow your nose, the way you feed the dog, the way you punch them in the face.

These folks believe wholeheartedly that they are smarter than you, and they have to remind you over and over again that they are smarter than you and do so by showing you how your ideas, your creations, your actions, your plans are lame in some way.

They are not giving you feedback in hopes of helping you—even though they might state that they are—really, it's to tell you what a fucking moron you are.

People who offer true constructive criticism have a way of delivering suggestions that don't make you want to smack them in the teeth, but rather, makes you perk up your ears and listen. Yes, you may feel embarrassed at first, and you may even feel defensive, but you know deep down you were given sage advice 'cause you really shouldn't be flipping that cop off with your junk, at least not to their face.

The critic, however, loves to hear themselves talk, and even more so when showing their wisdom by putting you down. They don't listen. They lack social grace and often possess a nasally voice.

CAUSE:

The critic became their nasty self from a really bad childhood where they had to endure hours and hours of caterwauling from an ambitious sibling or close relative gifted with the voice of a cat in heat, but believed themselves to be the next America's Got Talent winner waiting to be discovered.

In a critic's family, there was at least one sibling, maybe a parent or other, with a stirring passion for music but woefully lacking in talent.

The future critic, forced to listen to hours of a sister or brother's tortured howls, screeching violin strings, or piano bludgeoning have led to accumulated resentment and objections waiting to be heard.

Their parents were obviously no help with their own vicarious musical dreams; they forced the noisy sibling's daily practice while destroying the critic's eardrums.

Anyone who has watched a movie accompanied by a sister's soulful, off-key wailing in the background knows the damage such a scenario inflicts.

Attempts to shut the sibling up and to offer advice only resulted in annoying reprimands by the parent and a sneer on the sister's face. In short, the suffering sibling had to endure the torture and keep their mouth shut.

Not surprisingly, a person holed up in auditory hell can develop an arsenal of criticism waiting to be shot.

RECOMMENDATIONS:

One way to stop a critic in their tracks is to ask them about their childhood. Hijack their disparaging remarks by talking about your tone-deaf sister who sang so bad you had permanent ear damage. This revelation may get them to bond with you. It doesn't matter if you were getting chewed out over your poorly written programming code. The point is to take it in another direction.

The sudden change in topic might initially stupefy the critic, but might also ease the underlying tension in their heart, enough for them to forget their criticisms and stroll down memory lane to reflect on their own tortured past.

If the critic can somehow release their pent up anger and give that sibling the tongue lashing they deserve, they will become better people in the process.

The talentless sibling doesn't have to be present in order for the critic to receive some kind of benefit. It isn't so much about the need to tell off their annoying sister or brother. Having any willing listener is therapeutic in itself.

Note of caution, however. In a few instances, changing the subject so drastically might make the critic think you're mentally unstable or fucking with them. In either case, you might get into a whole mess of trouble. Blame it on some hot sauce you had at lunch and let them continue cutting you down.

The Cusser

aka: the blasphemous, the curser, the foul-mouth, the potty mouth, the profaner, the swearer

That really cute brunette you sometimes see when you go into the copy shop looked really hot yesterday with her sweet innocent smile. She's probably 20, maybe a little younger, a college student. She seemed smart; she had an advanced chemistry book in hand. She's way out of your league, but you somehow mustered up the balls to ask her on a date. Now, she's sitting in front of you with those beautiful brown locks, doey eyes, and glass of wine in hand. You toast the evening and hope—no, pray—to score tonight. Two hours later, the date isn't quite how you envisioned it. That cute brunette wasn't what you expected. Behind those red luscious lips hid the mouth of the raunchiest sailor you could imagine, one who says "fuck" and "shit" every five seconds and tells you stories you wouldn't repeat to a bunch of guys in a locker room. Unbeknownst to you, you landed a date with a real potty mouth.

A cusser is a person who can't get a sentence out without a couple of f-bombs and other taboo words deemed offensive to Miss Manners.

Cussing is a very common type of behavior found in most cities, states, and countries in the world. The offensive words are often spoken aloud with conviction, offering some type of emotional release for the speaker.

People cuss at objects, animals, people, and at themselves when they need to express something that is not offered in polite speak.

The people around them or the target of their cussing tends to react in one of two ways: agree, contributing more cuss words themselves; or disagree, possibly countering their cuss words with stronger language. Sometimes, people can also become angry and end the conversation abruptly with a blow to the face.

There are no universal cuss words, but there are universal themes considered offensive when combined in certain ways. For example, "mother" combined with any word referencing sex or animals seem to offend many people. References to a god or deity combined with the name of an animal or sex act is also viewed as offensive. References to dirt, an unpleasant afterlife, death, genitalia, anuses, and anus outputs are also regarded as distasteful in many cultures.

A few cuss words added in a sentence can help emphasize a particular verb or noun that a speaker wants his or her listener to pay attention to, as in "That damn bowling ball really fucking hurt my big fucking hairy toe!"

When does cussing become a bad behavior? When cuss words are used in a way that obfuscates the clarity of a sentence. For example, the sentence, "Who wouldn't love a root beer float on a hot day" becomes "Who the fuck wouldn't love a motherfucking, goddamn root beer float on an ass kickin' hot day?"

The second sentence contains many extraneous words making it difficult for a listener to comprehend, both in meaning and intent; it would be hard to decipher whether the speaker was angry, sarcastic, or just really loved root beer floats. Also, those within earshot of a cusser can be offended by the ferocity and meaning of cuss words.

CAUSE:

Cussers have a horribly foul mouth, because they secretly enjoy the taste of dish soap and hope to relive the comforting, semi-erotic experience of being forced by a dominant person to clean their mouth out with soapy liquid.

As children learn to speak, they learn by repeating what they hear, and sometimes what they hear is a swear word from an angst-ridden older brother or sister. Sometimes they hear bad words from a video or from a neighbor kid.

Wherever they learned the foul word from, they also learned the power of those words to make people behave in a certain way. When a little boy says sweetly to his mother, "Mommy, are you a cocksucker?" Mommy gets very upset, grabs the boy by the ear and pulls him into the kitchen. Once there, she squirts some dish soap into a bowl, mixes it up with water, and tells the boy to "wash his dirty mouth out right now."

The boy really doesn't know what he's saying. No one explained to him what cock-sucking was. If someone told him it was a sexually explicit act, he would not ask his mother such a personal and inappropriate question.

If the parents tend to be very busy people without much time for their kids, then swearing becomes the go-to method for a child to get his parent's attention. The child swears. Mom or dad stops whatever they're doing and spends 15 minutes giving the neglected kid lots of attention. It becomes a thing in the home, where the kid is unwittingly encouraged to swear by the response of his or her parent, repeating this ritual over and over again. Like anything eaten on a regular basis, the kid develops a taste for dish soap.

As many psychologists have stated, people are attracted to others who resemble a beloved family member in some way, either a similar hair color, eye color, facial tick, or communication style. Ultimately, we marry our parents. Isn't that lovely?

A person who swears a great deal is slightly turned on by the offended parties around them, because they remind him or her of an outraged parent or other family member's strong reaction. The more offended you are, the more you are turning on the potty mouth's juices.

Subconsciously, the cusser hopes you will grab him or her by the ear, push their face into the sink, and wash their mouth out vigorously with soap—preferably one with a lemony scent.

RECOMMENDATIONS:

If you are really put off by a person who swears constantly, the worst thing you can do is to show it, because it will only encourage them to say more taboo words.

Do not blink an eyelash if "shit" comes out of their mouth. The best way to behave is to not have any reaction at all. In fact, turn the other way and talk to somebody else for a while or start reading your phone. The dirty mouth will lose interest in communicating with you and seek someone else who might potentially wash their mouth out.

An older cusser won't easily change their ways. Having cussed for so long it becomes second nature well after the fetish for dish soap is gone.

There is still hope for a younger cusser through negative reinforcement; whenever they say an offending word, poke them in the groin with a skewer. This should replace their erotic feelings for dish soap with fear.

The Denier

aka: the escapist, the willfully ignorant

Jonathan has a giant woodlike toadstool growing from his eyebrow. It gets in the way whenever he tries to put on his sunglasses. His family and friends tell him that this is not natural and that he should seek medical attention for it, in case it is cancerous and could kill him, but he doesn't listen. Whenever they bring it up, he poo poos their concern, claiming toadstools are natural and will go away with time. No matter how much evidence he's given, he denies any kind of problem exists.

A denier is a person who refuses to face reality when doing so might actually improve their life, helps them move forward, and prevents them being called a "muttonhead" on a daily basis.

When the truth is butt ugly, people are sometimes tempted to put very dark sunglasses on to avoid looking at that unpleasant picture. That's fine if that ugly butt isn't something you have to ever deal with. But when that butt requires your handling, dealing with it might be your best option instead of hiding from it, hoping it will disappear. More than likely that butt will only grow in size until it is unmanageable.

People are said to be "in denial" when persisting in an endeavor beyond their capability or limitations. A person with reasonable sense knows to quit when positive thinking and persistence fails to pay off, but a denier would not.

The denier, as a result, frustrates those who depend on them or know them, because the denier insists on the impossible, refuses to face the truth, or defends fallacious logic.

For example, being human with the anatomy of a man or a woman means that one is not a bald eagle and will never become a bald eagle—at least not in the present lifetime (except in cases when extraterrestrial scientists are involved). No amount of positive thinking will help sprout ten foot wings, a razor sharp beak, and powerful claws. Insisting otherwise is rather difficult for all those who wish eagle man would shut up already.

Likewise, denying that a boyfriend—the one who banged the new intern at his workplace—is a first class slimeball will make your friends want to seriously grab you by the shoulder and shake you senseless until you see the light.

Yes the truth hurts. It hurts as much as a gaping wound inflicted by a rabid beaver. The sooner the denier accepts the truth, the sooner they can move on.

CAUSE:

A person can become a denier when they have few friends to play with as children and depend on storybook tales, myths, and happily ever Disney type movies which they take as real, not realizing that these stories were made up by starving writers hoping to become the next Tolkien or Rowling.

Unlike the skeptic who got their bubbles bursted early on, the denier could benefit from having some of their fantasies poked with a big long needle of reality so they can understand the crappy nature of life and the limitations humans have.

Unless we are the product of an alien experiment, we cannot fly to the top of a pine tree at will, we cannot play underwater hockey with a mermaid, and our BF or GF who is suspiciously gone for long periods of time without explanation is not really a secret agent but probably screwing someone that may or may not be hotter than us.

A dependence on "happily ever after" endings causes a person to believe that the ending to their gangrenous foot will be a good one if they ignore it. They believe that eventually, the dying foot can be magically restored to its healthy state by the help of a whimsical tree fairy.

When someone believes too much in the fantastic without a balance of common sense and reality, one can become a denier of the most tragic kind, the kind that ends up ass broke, left for dead on the side of the road, ripped off, or crying their eyes out.

RECOMMENDATIONS:

A dose of reality can be quite as startling as a bucket of ice cubes thrown at your face. Sometimes, that's what it takes. For a denier to face the truth, they may need to feel the chill of an ice cube against their cheek, letting it sit there until they understand that the unrelenting cold will result in a patch of numb skin if they ignore it. But if they can acknowledge that the ice cube bites and should be dealt with, then they are practicing baby steps towards dealing with reality.

Sometimes we need to admit certain truths. I'll start. "I cannot eat 50 Triple Baconator burgers all at once, because I am not a walk in cooler." And here's another. "Flashing my lonely meat stick to that crowd of pretty girls will not land me a date." Go ahead, try it.

Flatly accepting realistic limitations will help the denier face the unpleasant aspects of life they would rather sweep under a big thick rug where fleas often hide.

Otherwise, reality will jump out, just like fleas after a certain amount of time, to bite you on the stomach when you aren't looking and will cause an itchy welt that irritates the hell out of you until you are miserable.

The Destroyer

*aka: the defacer, the demolisher,
the devastator, the vandal, the wrecker*

variation: the arsonist

For the past two weeks as you whistle happily, you pass by a newly painted mural of jazz greats in American history—a piece of art that brightens your morning immensely as you go to work. One gloomy day, however, you pass by your morning exhibit to find the handiwork of some teenager with the IQ of a fork left on that marvelous example of artistry. In some young unformed mind, the quip "yo mama" spray painted over Dizzy Gillespie's face seemed like a genius idea. That's because a destroyer, a real dumbshit, came by recently.

The destroyer is an individual who destroys something considered valuable to the rest of society, acting as if they were some five-year-old who never got enough kisses on the forehead or enough cinnamon buns and now must play with spray paint, hammers, and matches to make up for it.

Destroyers damage things without any foresight or concern their destruction has on others. Examples include: smashing car windows, tagging someone's house, and throwing used motor oil in a lake.

The destroyer is known for having low intelligence, love of loud things, and often misspells their own name.

They can be found in urban cities as well as rural areas and can cause a great deal of financial damage, making their victims want to run after the destroyer's ass with a blowtorch.

CAUSE:

These destructive types cannot help but be what they are, having been born under some very unlucky planetary configurations which drives them to act the way they do.

According to astrologers, destructive people have one thing in common: Mars, named after the God of war (in ancient Roman mythology) in a stressful planetary angle to the planet Pluto, linked to the mythology of Hades. In other words, a person who lives to damage shit. ¡Ay, caramba!

With a combo like this, people born under this planetary influence don't contemplate the wonders of humankind. Rather, they wreck them as form of personal expression.

Spray paint, crowbars, sharp metal objects all fly out of a destroyer's backpack for action. This means a mural gets tagged, young trees get snapped in half, houses get burned down, and so on. Destroyers must leave their mark in some way, similar to a dog that pisses on objects wherever it goes. (Sometimes a destroyer will leave their pee due to urinary incontinence.)

These destructive peeps can't change their internal programming; it's the way they are designed. They have to deface, deform, destroy.

Generally speaking, these natural deconstructionists restrict their behavior to objects. In doing so, they are more able to get away with their handiwork. They know to leave people alone, because they still have enough sense to know that if they destroy a person, the police will search high and low for their ass. If locked away, they lose the freedom to blow shit up. In fact, they may have to blow things in prison they don't want to.

Destroyers might also be troublemakers (see *The Troublemaker*) if they've been dealing with sexual frustration for a long time.

RECOMMENDATIONS:

Although you can't do much about a destroyer's tendencies—they're innate—a destroyer's actions can be redirected to something useful.

The best job for a destroyer type would be on a construction site where they can blow up buildings, knock down walls, smash floors, and demolish concrete. This is where they feel most at home and offers them ample chances for self-expression eight hours a day until their little bodies are all tuckered out.

They should only be allowed to destroy, not construct, for that is counter to their natural abilities. If no construction work is available for them to work on, enlist them to beat up dirty old rugs or tenderize some steaks. Those feisty fists might as well be put to something useful.

The Diva / Divo

aka: the egotistical, the high maintenance, the prima donna, the princess/prince

Queenie walks into the room expecting the staff to take notice. After all, it is not every day a woman of her caliber enters the world of the riffraff. She takes a seat, noticing the ordinary folk milling around her. She hopes she won't have to wait long and won't have to talk to one of them. To wait at DMV for new vehicle registration couldn't be more beneath a diva.

The name of this unpleasant behavior had its origins in Italian opera where the star, well known for her singing talent, was considered a goddess, hence the word diva which is Italian for "female deity." Nowadays, a diva refers to a person who may or may not have any talent but who believes and acts like they are the star of the whole damn universe.

Divas and divos (the male version of a diva) do not think twice about imposing their will on others. They behave with the presumption that they are superior and more valuable than all else when, in fact, they may be a talented as a flowerpot.

This high maintenance person, who contributes less than their fair share at a potluck, will always take the lion's share of something good, like the dessert platter, and will weasel their way from cleaning up after themselves. The diva/divo does not understand the term "teamwork."

On the rare occasion that a diva/divo type does help someone, you can bet they will ask for twenty favors in return.

Divas and divos are selfish creatures with infantile needs. They also think they are above the law, deserving of exceptional treatment and shouldn't get that ticket for driving into that library.

When these pompous peacocks speak, they expect all those within earshot to fall to their knees in anticipation for the brilliant words that will tumble from their precious lips.

Divas and divos can sometimes be narcissists as well. If that's the case, you have a real winner on your hands.

These folks will never take responsibility for their bad behavior or admit to wrongdoing. If you ever get an apology from one of these baddies, make sure you record it so you can listen to it over and over again, because you probably won't get another one until you are gasping your last breath.

CAUSE:

A diva/divo is caused by an unusual mental condition called the Mary Ann Complex.

The Mary Ann Complex was named as such in 1968 from a Dr. Constance Shea Butter after seeing an episode of the old television series, Gilligan's Island. Gilligan's Island was a comedy about a group of castaways stuck on an island together for years unable to leave.

In season 3, episode 24, one of the island females, a sweet young thing named Mary Ann, hits her head after watching the performance of another castaway, the beautiful and admired starlet Ginger Grant. The head bump causes Mary Ann to get amnesia and forget her own identity, but brings to the forefront her deeply subconscious desire to be Ginger. For the rest of the episode, the simple country girl believes she is a sexy starlet, acting and behaving as such.

Divas and divos today suffer the same mental lapse caused by a severe head injury while being obsessed with celebrities. A person who reads everything written about their favorite star, who must see every movie their star is in and follows their idol's every tweet, are predisposed to getting Mary Ann Complex if they should fall and smack their head badly. (Luckily, I didn't have this issue when I hit my head hard or I'd be struttin' around thinking I was Jack White and you wouldn't have the good fortune to be reading this right now.)

In knocking their noggin, they may forget their own identity and believe themselves to be Lindsey Lohan or Charlie Sheen. As a celebrity, this gives them license to be a prima donna, a VIP—a desire they may have buried deep inside somewhere that gets unleashed when they get a strong smack to the head.

RECOMMENDATIONS:

If you know someone who is a diva or divo, suggest they see a doctor to get their head examined. In time, a person's memory should return and can be helped with vitamin B12.

However, if life as a diva/divo under the assumed celebrity's identity is more fun for the person, they may not wish to return to their lackluster existence and will unconsciously repress their true self. If this is the case, you can help them by making life as a diva/divo unbearable. Whenever they deny your attempts at the truth, tell them that their career is over and tell your friends to boo and hiss whenever the diva/divo is around.

Showing the diva/divo a photograph of themselves compared with an image of the celebrity they have assumed, is useless. When a person suffers from this complex, they see what they want to see.

You may want to seek out the Gilligan's Island episode to show the person in question what they are suffering from. It may or may not work, as the diva/divo may be too stupid to connect the dots.

If you happen to love following stars, stop it. Spend less time admiring someone else and take up new hobbies that help increase your mental activities. Try word scrambles and memory games.

In the end, it may take another knock to the head before the diva/divo regains their senses. If the diva/divo becomes an unbearable ass, the likelihood of another knock to the head is pretty strong.

The Downer

aka: the depressed, the disparager, the doomsayer, the frowner, the gloomy, the pessimist, the sad, the weeper, the woeful

You're in Vegas baby with all your girlfriends in a strip club for the bachelorette party of your life. Everyone's having a blast except for the bride's sister. She's been the only one who seems out of place and self-conscious. You don't really know her, you just met her in fact, but you hear she is kind of a wallflower. You decide it's your duty to become her best friend during this trip, so you saunter over to the corner where she's been hiding while your girlfriends make cat calls to the naked male bodies gyrating in front of them. After 30 minutes with Ms. Wallflower, however, you find yourself remembering the worst moments of your life, like the time you were told you had zero talent in grade school and the time you were turned down for a waitressing job at a truck stop, because your tits weren't big enough, and the love of your life who said being with you taught him how much he wanted to have sex, with men—it all comes tumbling down to the forefront of your mind as the many pains of rejection coalesce to this moment of false happiness. Spending any amount of time with a downer can throw a few brown spots on those rosy-colored glasses.

A downer is a person who seems to be constantly sad, who says negative things and whose company makes you feel so bad that you decide to wear the same dirty boxers for the next 50 years and forego all showers, because you will die anyway so why bother changing?

Downers are also the street name for tranquilizers that knock you out, but that is outside the scope of this discussion. (But if you wish to get some downers, I may know a number you can call. Talk to me later.)

Unlike some of the other bad behaviors that have a way of sparking knee-jerk reactions, downers tend to garner sympathy, because they seem so pathetic.

Downers are terribly unpopular; get dumped an awful lot by lovers and friends; and generally wind up talking to a lamp. People have a way of turning the other direction once they realize they're talking to someone who could off themselves any minute.

Try as you might, you can't seem to lift the mood of these sad folks. A downer can, just by being in their energy field, knock you from the high you thought you were on, down to a pit where poisonous snakes bury themselves in your soul.

As a result of constant rejection, downers keep a low profile and are generally tolerable if you can overlook their glum outlook.

CAUSE:

Strange but true. The cause of downer behavior is not just bad luck; it's really underwear, specifically GMO cotton underwear that was sourced from India.

GMO cotton seeds have destroyed Indian farmers' livelihoods due to the disastrous financial returns that GMO crops have produced. This, in turn, has caused a surge in farmer suicides.

Those who don't commit suicide are nonetheless quite depressed about working so hard for slave wages. Their desperation and sadness energetically transfers from them to the crops they produce. Any individual wearing such products absorbs the hopelessness, frustration, and fear of these poor farmers.

Simply stated observations become misconstrued as proclamations of doom or hopelessness for any person wearing undergarments made from this cotton. For example, telling such a person that they "look a little tired today" could be absorbed as "man, you're an ugly ass fucker and always will be."

Without GMO undergarments, news of any kind is recovered from much more quickly. But with that sad cotton against a person's private parts, the smallest of slights is felt as a monumental slap across the face never to be healed from.

RECOMMENDATIONS:

When dealing with a depressed soul, it is of utmost importance that you buy them a pile of fair trade, organic cotton or organic hemp based underwear. Choose happy colors of pink, magenta, and green. Avoid blue. It will take a week or two for that energetically happier cotton to take effect.

Meanwhile, expose the downer person to slapstick comedies. Kung Fu Hustle, White Chicks, Scary Movie are a good start. Also dumb knock knock jokes. Consider tickling if no laughter seems forthcoming despite your best efforts.

The Drama Queen

aka: the attention whore, the exaggerator, the melodramatic, the sensationalist

"You cannot believe what I went through! The way I was handled, ordered like a criminal to put my hands up in the air so I can be examined like a piece of meat by some remote voyeur who is probably saving pictures of my body to put on porn sites. It was horrible! They went through all my belongings, examining my bags as if I was a common thief. There was no respect, none whatsoever, but that's not the worst of it. The worst is when they told me I wasn't dressed properly, shaming me in public like that. It was uncalled for and completely disrespectful. I'm going to file charges against those bastards," says Johnson, your overly excitable cousin. "Johnson," you respond. "What do you expect if you go to the airport in nothing but a see-through thong?" "But it's so hot outside, I have to be comfortable if I'm going to take a six hour flight," he says, feeling slighted by your unsympathetic words. Johnson is a drama queen, and no matter what you say, he will turn the story around to suit his needs.

Drama queens are labeled as such for their exaggerated response over stuff like ingrown hair and wrinkled t-shirts, making these melodramatic douchebags difficult to take seriously.

These types of folks incite a great deal of crisis and drama around themselves, using their crisis as a means to capture attention from and bond with their listeners. Once a drama queen has a captive audience, they will continue in a narrative that best engages that audience into focusing all their attention on the drama queen's problem.

Drama queen behavior tends to be seen more frequently with women, girls, and some gay men, though not exclusively. Straight men can also be drama queens but are rarer to find, because most men are trained to punch refrigerators or whine when they want attention.

Drama queens can be found in any region where life is relatively comfortable and easy. You find fewer drama queens in ghettos, because life really does suck when you're poor. But when there is too much cash and too little activity, drama queens can be found in greater quantity.

CAUSE:

Those with a life of ease and boredom are more prone to becoming drama queens if they snack on large quantities of cherries that contain pesticide-resistant cherry fruit fly larvae.

The cherry fruit fly, a big pest of cherry trees, is very common and extremely difficult to eradicate. Due to increasing amounts of pesticides now needed to rid the world of these damaging pests and the resulting resistance to chemical inundation, a new strain has emerged called "Super Fucking Fly," named as such by the perplexed farmers who can't seem to get rid of this little winged shit.

The Super Fucking Fly is a tenacious insect that cannot be destroyed. It does not even get destroyed when meeting hydrochloric acid in a human stomach. It not only survives stomach acid but actually flourishes in the caustic solution, allowing it to breed formidably along the intestinal tract.

When the larvae hatch into the inner sanctums of a stomach, they wish to take flight. The little flies will move upward, up the esophagus and up the nasal passages. The exaggerated head contortions of a drama queen along with the accompanying sweeping hand motions are, in fact, the fruit flies collective attempts to go airborne.

Inside a body, the Super Fucking Fly doesn't have many meal choices. It will start chowing down what's available, which means the host's organs and various body parts, including the vocal chords, making the host sound more excitable and shrill.

If the drama queen is lucky, the Super Fucking Fly will fly out of the mouth and be on its merry way, but if unlucky, the unfortunate human host becomes the main food source.

Flies need to be high up in the air and not on the ground. For this reason, the brain is the inevitable place where these flies will gravitate towards. Once there, they will feed on this gelatinous organ, causing severe brain damage. This is why drama queens act so foolish.

When a body is riddled with these little fuckers, expect every minor incident to be handled as if it were an emergency with the words, "I could have died" at the end of each sentence.

RECOMMENDATIONS:

When a drama queen begins the expected dramatic performance or starts to make a scene, swat his or her head with a flyswatter. Let the Super Fucking Fly know who is boss.

If the drama queen gets all upset and in your face, explain the dangers of harboring pesticide-resistant super insects in a body. Tell them to be silent, but ask them to keep their mouth open so the flies have a way out.

If no winged ones are forthcoming, dangle some cut cherries in front of the drama queen to entice these little fellas out.

Even when the body is rid of these tenacious flies, there is no guarantee the drama queen will return to normal as the newfound attention might be addictive to the partially eaten brain. If that is the case, a couple of aspirins will help you relieve the headache you get from being in the drama queen's presence.

The Drunk

aka: the boozer, the inebriated, the juiced up, the liquored up, the lush, the sauced up, the tanked, the wasted

"I will have the banana pancakes and a side of hash browns," you say to the friendly waiter taking your order. Across the table from you is an old friend you haven't seen in a decade. He tells the waiter in a slurred voice, "I'll have two more Bloody Marys and an Irish Coffee." You're surprised. He sounded fine this morning but by the time you showed up at his chosen restaurant, he was belting out "God Bless America" to the next table. You ask him why he ordered so many Bloody Marys and he responds, "Gotta eat my veggies." There's a strong possibility your friend is a drunk.

A drunk is a person whose behavior is affected by consuming excessive amounts of alcohol, which causes notable physical and behavioral changes that make them the life of the party or the dude you steal from when they are passed out.

There are various levels of drunkenness—based on the amount of alcohol in the bloodstream—corresponding to different types of behavior; one drink to help relax those crazy thoughts, to ten drinks for a passionate night of loving up the toilet bowl. Anything in between can amuse or horrify, depending on the person, the company, the situation, and the place.

Drunks can be fun, except when they are mean, behind a steering wheel, violent, rude, stupid, a show-off, or generally just an unlikable ass. Three gin and tonics can transform any uptight ape into Mr. Happy, giving endless hours of pleasure to all those with cameras in hand. But in extreme cases where the drunk can actually do something incredibly stupid, like feeling up a wall hanging or worse, killing someone—that's when it falls into the realm of really awful behavior.

If a person simply must drink booze to get by in life but can function in a normal capacity, well, that's not the end of the world. It's between them and their liver. But if a drunk causes devastation, financial ruin, and leaves their kid in a shopping cart, then a drunk may have a hard time getting smiley emoticons from family and friends.

CAUSE:

Some in the medical profession blame a gene mutation as the root cause of alcohol addiction. That may be so, but there is also another explanation. After decades of dealing with drinkers of all shapes and sizes, I believe persistent alcohol consumption may be the drunk's inner most subconscious, unfulfilled desire to be a sea mammal of some sort, perhaps a sea cow or a seal, or some other pinniped.

During my visit to the West Coast a few years back, I had the opportunity to observe sea lions that had beached themselves approximately 200 feet away from where I was staying. It was during that time while I was observing the behavior of these wonderful creatures that I had an epiphany. What I was seeing in front of me reminded me of how my bar patrons acted when completely soused. It was at that moment I understood my customers deep emotional needs better than ever.

I could not turn a blind eye to the obvious connection. Being completely sauced up mimics the sensation of floating on water, even while collapsed on a cement floor or a wooden bar top. Due to high alcohol blood content, the drunk is allowed the freedom to crawl on all fours without explanation, similar to a sea mammal forced to crawl on land. Sea mammals spend their life in a horizontal position—so too does the drunk.

Conversation is garbled with a drunk, just as it would be if having a conversation under water. Clothes become a hindrance, allowing the drunk to strip naked on a stranger's bed. A sea mammal would definitely do the same if forced to wear apparel in a warm ocean.

The drunk also sprays a great deal of saliva when they speak with conviction, much the way a sea creature sprays water with its flippers when excited. Finally, a drunk shits their pants without inhibition when enough booze is consumed. So too do sea creatures while swimming in the ocean.

Furthermore, the daily chores and responsibilities of a human life, mundane stuff such as taking out the trash or working in a tedious job, are impossible to do as a marine mammal.

The intense desire to be a sea creature, to live freely in a large body of water, is what drives the drunk to stay in a perpetual state of inebriation.

Plain and simple—drunks do not want to be walking upright on two legs. Their need to be a dolphin or some other large sea mammal explains why drunks spend so much time in a horizontal position swimming in their own vomit.

RECOMMENDATIONS:

Taking a momentarily sober drunk to a warm ocean at least five times a week would help the poor soul fulfill their innermost need to swim and move fluidly in water.

Make sure the drunk does not have any alcohol in their system while in the water as that might cause drowning.

If possible, allow the drunk to spend time with seals, dolphins, or whales in a controlled environment where conversation between the two species can be had.

With time, the drunk may become conscious of their issues and will want to address it with the help of a marine biologist.

A drunk must never be shown any footage of fishing expeditions and documentaries on whaling, seal clubbing or poaching as that may drive the drunk to cry endlessly, causing them to drink even more.

The Entitled

aka: the privileged

Two whole hours. That's how long you've been standing in line waiting to get into the bicycle ballet show. You and your friend are twenty feet away from the entrance when two faces you recognize from a TV show head straight for the front of the line. The ticket seller, an older cowboy with a gruff expression, tells the duo they can't cut in, but one of the pair tells the cowboy they are famous vampires on a hit show. The cowboy takes another look at them and says, "Famous vampires, eh?" He reaches inside his coat pocket. "Well I got some silver bullets loaded up in here and I'll be happy to use them on you two idiots if you don't get to the back of the line." The two roll their eyes and leave. You decide to tip that cowboy.

An entitled person is one who believes they are deserving of special treatment, because they are famous, have an important position, or can fart out Jingle Bells perfectly.

Entitled behavior can be seen in celebrities, politicians, rock and rap stars, the very rich, the super thuggy, spoiled brats, and so on. Anyone who has been worshipped by others has a greater tendency to act like a snot bag.

Sometimes, the opposite is also true, when the very poorest and most marginalized, maligned group in society feel entitled to some type of compensation for their suffering. That sense of entitlement could be justified or not, depending on the situation.

Finally, there are also ordinary folk who feel entitled to special treatment because they believe they might be the next Prince.

This bad behavior can appear at any time anywhere and is not appreciated by guys in biker gangs.

CAUSE:

Why would one person feel entitled while another with the same circumstances does not? Because the entitled individual endured the childhood horror of watching their beloved toys destroyed in a cruel way, causing that person to become a disturbed individual forever.

Children get very attached to Mr. Teddy or Miss Panda. It's their best friend in the dark of night, keeping monsters at bay. They form a bond with their stuffed buddy as strong as with any person.

But if a rotten sibling, neighbor kid, parent, bully, or teacher takes the adored stuffed animal and dismembers it ruthlessly in front of the child's eyes out of spite, anger, or impatience, the little one can be forever traumatized. Watching their beloved buddy's limbs ripped from a torso, their head snapped off while cotton polyester guts spew from a neck—it's all too much for a little nipper to handle.

If this unkind act is repeated several times during the formative years between ages two and seven and there is no recourse against the perpetrator, a deep resentment against the world can develop. This lack of justice makes the child feel as if their suffering, their grief, is unimportant. Therefore, they are not important.

As the young one grows, they carry this inner pain like a debit card in the wallet of life.

Some, in a desperate drive to negate their childhood insignificance, try much harder to make a name for themselves. But others will try and fail which is doubly painful for them.

Both types, regardless of their success, expect you to understand their need for attention and special treatment. You and all others become the surrogate authority figure who should have done the job of punishing the cretin that ripped their Pooh Bear's head apart. But you can make up for your lapse right now by giving up your spot in that long line for the bathroom, thus acknowledging their value.

RECOMMENDATIONS:

If someone you know is an entitled person, you can help them ease their childhood pain by offering a new stuffed animal in hopes that it will heal their heart. Better yet, if you can find out the exact stuffed toy that was murdered, you can get them a replacement.

If the entitled person is someone you don't know but meet in a public place, they might piss you off with their self-important attitude. If it's no skin off your back and they're not asking for much, you might think about giving in to their demands. It is their old wound which compels them to act so dickish.

If you are an entitled person and you didn't realize it before, you may want to look honestly at yourself and ask, "How did I become such a douchebag?" Then go to a toy store and get a bunch of new bedtime companions to make up for the past. Stop pissing everyone off with your inner angst.

The Exhibitionist

*aka: the exposer, the flasher,
the flaunter, the show-off*

Selena wakes up to songbirds outside her window. The dawn of another day finds her well rested and cheerful. She dresses quickly in her dark room. She wants to pull the blinds up to let that bright sunshine in, but she is scared to. She resents having to keep herself sealed up, but what choice does she have? Its either that or watch the hairy old fart in the next house do his penis stretching exercises in front of his big windows.

An exhibitionist most commonly refers to a person who exposes their body to anybody who happens to be around, whether that'd be a UPS driver or the skunk roaming around the yard.

Exhibitionism, when seen as a negative or disgusting behavior, is dependent on the circumstances in which it is displayed. At certain events and settings, acts of exhibitionism may be very appropriate and acceptable. For example, at a love-in, traipsing around with your ding dong swinging wildly to the left and right is no problem, but giving all a good view of your hairy crack during church services would not be cool.

Exhibitionism makes non exhibitionists and prudes feel extremely uncomfortable and concerned about the sanitation of an uncovered butt while in a restaurant or a patient waiting room.

People who have the luck to be accosted by the sight of a person's genitals on their way to the hardware store are either pleased or repulsed by the spectacle, depending on the physique and appearance of the exhibitionist. A naked Sophia Vergara or Zac Efron might be a welcome sight. The dude with the cluster of pustules on his back is not.

CAUSE:

Like the scene stealer, an exhibitionist was mistreated (see *The Scene Stealer*) by those who failed to recognize him or her for the person they really were. But unlike the scene stealer, the exhibitionist-to-be was not seen as a living organism but rather, as a common kitchen scrub brush and treated as such.

Sometimes, people are born with the inexplicable luck of resembling household items. Also, some parents have a neurological disorder that makes them see others not as people but as inanimate objects. One or the other can cause a child to be seen as a cleaning tool and not as a live being.

Attempts would be made, from a very young age, to put him or her in the sink with the dirty dishes, and to use their arm or their head to sponge off gunk from pots and pans. The hair would be used as a good scrubber for those very tough spots if the child was blessed with a thick mop on their head. All in all, it's a lousy beginning to the rest of their life.

Like the scene stealer, the need to make themselves stand apart from a scrub brush runs deep. In order to show that they are not, in fact, a handy household item, they need to publicly display themselves in an overt manner.

Drastic misperception calls for drastic measures. It is very hard to ignore someone's genitals at the checkout line when they are staring right at you. Because genitals and breasts are so seldom displayed out in the open, they become the first thing our eyes zero in on when in view.

Seeing another person's privates, outside the usual parameters of a bedroom, alerts the world at large that the exhibitionist is most certainly not a cleaning tool with a straight plastic torso and hard brushy fibers on their head but an honest to goodness human being.

RECOMMENDATION:

Do not mention dishes, dirty countertops, or cleansers to an exhibitionist. This is a very sensitive topic for them, one that might get them doing backflips and shimmying while naked. You do not want to see those private body parts hurtling next to your face.

Do tell them that they have nice skin, good hair, and a great personality. Emphasize how wonderful they are and how you appreciate their existence.

Don't invite them over to your house for lunch for it might get weird when it's time to place dishes in the sink. They might have some anxiety around dirty dishes. One way around this is to use paper plates or go out for a bite. With time, the exhibitionist will get over their need to flash the world.

The Fanatic

aka: the believer, the devotee, the extremist, the zealot

Don't you know when a carrot is ripped from the ground, it screams quietly inside. When a leaf is cut from its stem, it hurts the same way a nail ripped from our fingers would hurt. In the presence of a flame, the zucchini plant's electrical pulse quickens, terrified it'll be burned to a crisp. So next time you thoughtlessly stuff a piece of lettuce in your mouth, remember it's no different than chewing live monkey flesh, because plants have feelings too! Stop eating root vegetables now! Brought to you by your local plant rights fanatic.

A fanatic is a person who is absolutely and uncritically devoted to a particular thing or cause to the point of hysteria. And they need to convince you that you are wrong wrong wrong and to convert you.

Sometimes, that means you will end up wearing excruciatingly painful shoes made from shampoo bottles to stop an animal rights friend from torturing you with graphic videos of pigs crying and screaming during slaughter.

Fanatics are nearly always subjective and come in many flavors: harmless, crazy, guano nuts, and fruit loops insane.

These very impassioned souls can never be dissuaded from their belief system, because it gives them meaning and purpose to get up every morning and use that toothpaste, the way a delicious plate of nachos with a heavy heaping of guacamole and a little sour cream does for yours truly. Hell, I'll get up extra early if you throw in a tasty tamale too.

The most blatant acts of fanaticism can be seen in any daily news report over the last few decades: ISIS beheadings, cult colonies, ethnic cleansers, and so on.

The less blatant acts are scattered in everyday life, like the friend who wants to save you from eternal damnation or the pal who shames you for owning fur boots.

It's really hard to discuss issues with a fanatic, not too different from talking ideology with your pet gerbil—they don't get it no matter how hard you try to reason. The only thing a gerbil understands is an extra stalk of celery (not to be given in front of the plant rights fanatic).

CAUSE:

Of all the personality types listed in this collection, the fanatic is by far the most complex and squirrelly. Why? Because the source of this baddie changes frequently depending on import and export laws, international trading partners, the folks in power in various countries, insect counts, air pollution, and a whole host of other factors. That said, it can be stated with some certainty that the cause of fanaticism within the last 25 years has something to do with the Taliban. Opium, smuggled into the U.S. as various forms of narcotics, may be the cause of fanaticism in America when it is grown by fanatical growers such as the Taliban who spit and piss in their fields.

The Taliban is a group that formed from the Mujahideen. The Mujahideen was an Islamic group that fought Russian invaders in Afghanistan during the 1970s. The U.S. helped fund the Mujahideen to push those aggro Russians out. When the Soviets got booted, the Mujahideen beget the Taliban, and the Taliban are pretty gung ho about their religious beliefs.

Opium comes from opiate poppies. For some decades now, Afghanistan has been the main country of origin for opium production with the Taliban in on the game.

Although the Taliban has publicly badmouthed opium, they know the stuff buys them exploding devices and big guns. Some, but not all Taliban members secretly participate in opium poppy growing when not otherwise gutting and decapitating infidels.

The substance able to bring down an entire empire can also provide great relief for that backache that won't go away or when you want to melt into a puddle. Opium gets smuggled into many countries pretty easily.

Spitting and peeing is inevitable when dirt gets kicked up into a worker's mouth and when there are no port-o-potties around. When a Taliban member, a fanatic of the extreme kind, leaves an essence of himself on a growing poppy plant soon to be harvested, he spreads his passionate spirit into that plant; anyone coming in contact with that plant is affected, even after it gets processed.

As the opiates from the poppy get transformed into different narcotics—heroin, morphine, and codeine to name a few—they can reach a wider group of buyers. Therein lays the danger.

Once the Taliban-tainted products get smoked, injected, or eaten by a user, the Taliban's passionate zeal releases into the body of the receptive user's mind.

Opiates already reduce the willpower of a user, making that user an easy receptacle for suggestion. Mix in the violent fanatical nature of a Taliban member and a new fanatic is born.

However, because the Taliban's fundamental beliefs and interests are not native to many Americans (beer, bratwursts, and boobs are not okay in Sharia law), the user's own belief system suddenly gets amplified a hundredfold. For example, if a person had a predisposition for saving dolphins, after popping a codeine pill made from a poppy laced with Taliban spit, they might become a pro-dolphin terrorist, shooting down great whites and other predators to save those smart swimmers.

In the case of fanatics who commit destructive homicidal acts, time travelers may be involved (see *The Killer*) with implanting insane thoughts into unstable minds.

RECOMMENDATIONS:

The cure for such a detrimental (dis)ease is through intervention.

A fanatic needs to be placed in a warm empty room with pink light and fuzzy chairs. A comfortable, plushy bed should be available to lay them down gently so they can relax. Play the Bee Gees' "Too Much Heaven" nonstop until the fanatic denounces whatever hardcore beliefs they hold.

After two days, check to see if the fanatic has been cured. You can do so by contradicting their beliefs and egging them on. If they insist on the righteousness of their cause, offer them a bathroom break, but then resume music therapy. This time try Icona Pop's "I Love It (I Don't Care)" for 24 hours on a loop.

If after this second attempt, no progress is evident, then your fanatic friend has gone off the deep end. Abandon all hope and send them to a remote location in North Dakota during winter.

The Fickle

aka: the disloyal, the flighty, the unfaithful

Phuong was utterly flabbergasted when her doting new boyfriend, who told her how much he loved her after a week of dating, didn't seem that interested in her after two more weeks. He stopped returning her calls, emails, and texts without any explanation. It was as if she didn't exist. Her girlfriend made her feel much worse when she told Phuong her boyfriend was seen fawning over another gal with the same ardor he had shown her. His fickle behavior was heartbreaking. She wished she had gone for his friend with the mohawk instead.

A fickle person is one whose feelings of affection, love, passion, loyalties, and friendship goes from hot to cold for no apparent reason, making their victims feel cheap, confused, and wondering if they somehow entered a parallel world where everyone they thought they knew turned out to be escapees from a circus show.

People can be fickle about their dentists, websites, food choices, and even about their shoes. This kind of fickle behavior causes no problems. You won't find someone wailing like a banshee because you suddenly hate stripes. But when a love interest or friend is easily dumped like a torn rubber, well, that can bring on some pretty bad I want to bite your nose off and feed it to the cat feelings.

Fickle behavior can be spotted in grade school with children who seem to get romantic crushes lasting for a few hours to a few days. Friendships among the very young can change on a dime, depending on whether the friend gives them a piece of bubble gum or lets them copy their homework assignment.

It is expected that as a person matures, they are capable of having relationships lasting longer than an hour, based on common interests and activities.

When someone fails to act consistently in a relationship, much anguish can result for the person who is tossed aside without a second thought. Explanations for their unpredictable behavior are never that satisfying, the same way eating a plastic bag could never fulfill that craving for a caramel. You're better off replacing the flighty fool with a loyal pup.

CAUSE:

Due to a visual hallucination called facial recognition transference, a seemingly stable and kind person can act fickle, causing much grief for those who thought they had a relationship with that person.

Facial recognition transference causes the person with strong feelings for another to transfer the mental picture of their loved one on to another person's body. For example, if José loves Phuong passionately, he will think about her all the time. He holds a picture of her beautiful face in his mind's eye, and this is where the problem comes in.

He has such a strong visual attachment to Phuong that his mental image of her gets transferred onto the face of the next attractive female he sees. It is not completely transferred, maybe about 50%, but he will suddenly feel affection for this new female, which he cannot explain, especially if this new female matches the height and hair color of his current beloved.

José will then romance and charm the new female, believing her to be the next "it" gal for him.

In time, the new gal's face will replace Phuong's face in his mind. He will forget Phuong altogether, unless she shows up and screams vile words at him. This act might jar his memory and he may regain his old feelings for her.

Sometimes, having two or more attractive people in the room can cause serious problems, as the person with this diagnosis may get very confused and strip down, expecting an orgy with everyone they are attracted to in the room.

In friendship, it works the same way but with less urgent emotions involved.

Facial recognition transference causes big problems for the sufferer and is a very tricky ailment belonging to the annals of unexplainable medical conditions.

RECOMMENDATIONS:

A possible but untested solution is to have the fickle person wear extremely dark sunglasses or a blindfold when out in public. Of course, this presents other problems, such as injury from street signs, getting hit by cars, and robbed by nearby criminals.

The lover of a fickle person doesn't have many easy options. If the fickle person is worth trying to hold onto, one possible remedy is to carry placards with life-sized head shots of frightening characters from horror flicks. Think Freddie Krueger and Chucky.

When an attractive person is within range of a fickle person, quickly place the placard in front of the fickle person's face so their view of others is obscured, but they can clearly see Chucky and Freddy instead. The image of horror stars will naturally cause an adverse reaction and keep their love of you safe, even with facial recognition transference. However, this is not an easy practice to maintain and will draw much attention from the general public.

Admittedly, none of these options are great, but it beats locking the fickle person in your closet.

The Flaker

aka: the latecomer, the no show, the uncommitted, the undependable, the unreliable

You've got tickets to the World Series. Your new friend at work begged you to take him. You said okay, as long as he picks you up and buys the beer, hotdogs, and fries at the game. On the day of, he calls you, says he's running late. He'll be there in a half hour. That's cutting it closer than you'd like, but okay, you get all your stuff packed up and wait. And wait. And wait some more. Two hours later, you have punched holes into the wall you're so darn mad. It's nearly impossible to drive now with the intense traffic out there, but you'll try. You've got the game streaming to your headphones as you head out. Your friend hasn't answered your texts or calls. You fantasize revenge—maybe roofing tar in his gas tank? All you know is you're pissed off, and you never would have said yes had you known what a flaker he was.

Flakers are highly unreliable people who continually blow off appointment times, don't show up when they promise to and always make you miss the first half of a movie when you go with them, forcing you to sit in the only remaining seats up front guaranteed to give you neck spasms after 15 minutes.

Flakers tend be free-spirited and quite inspirational when you can actually get them to show up. Life tends to be "in the moment," which is wonderful if you are stoned shitless, but a real bummer if you need to get to the O.R. quickly for a liver transplant.

Strangely enough, flakers have ample opportunity to practice flaky behavior time and time again. For some reason, these individuals tend to attract hordes of people; they are strangely popular. Perhaps their appeal lies in the lackadaisical way they flout schedules and timelines others seem so enslaved by, the way you can't be mad at a cat for not coming when you want it to.

Flakers may seem the same as irresponsible people (see *The Irresponsible*) but aren't necessarily so. They can possess common sense and fulfill obligations once they arrive. You just have to have patience.

These poor planners are distinctly different from the apathetic, who just don't give a shit.

A flaker generally disappoints friends and fails to meet commitments with a variety of excuses: they were accosted by little silver dwarfs, they were too hungover to remember, or they dropped their phone in the blender.

Sometimes, flakers are the super rich who purposefully flake on poor people, to remind the poor that they are peons for others to kick around.

Whatever the reason, the bottom line is this—you will wait and wait some more. It's nothing personal unless you are an absolute bore. In that case, many people will flake on you.

CAUSE:

Most causes of flaking can be can be traced back to elementary education when the flaker missed a portion of classroom instruction dedicated to understanding, reading, and evaluating time on traditional and digital clocks.

Due to an extended illness, hooky, detention or some other reason, the flaker did not learn how to use time personally and effectively. They also failed to learn how time can be used as a social exchange between two or more people in a community.

Because understanding time and reading clocks are a core part of any child's basic education, missing such an important aspect of this everyday function can become troublesome to employment, friendship, relationships, sex, and pet ownership.

The flaker child, having missed this vital instruction, does not realize the full impact of this important function until they are older, when they are required to manage more of their own time as opposed to having their time scheduled and managed for them by parents and teachers.

When they finally realize their lack, they may be too embarrassed to ask for remedial instruction and fake it, pretending to understand the clock's movements throughout the day when in reality, they misinterpret the representation of time.

Telling a flaker to meet you in 30 minutes might be misinterpreted as 30 days. Meeting at noon might be confused for meeting at midnight. Asking for a call back in four days may be understood as "some time this century." Because the flaker failed to learn the meaning and definition of time, they may not understand why others become so irate when they don't call or meet at the time specified.

RECOMMENDATIONS:

When dealing with a flaker type, let them know that you know they never learned how to read a clock properly and that it is "all right." Offer to help them learn what each hand of a traditional clock represents and how to read a digital clock. Explain the difference between A.M. and P.M.

Be gentle with your words. Flakers are highly touchy about their educational lapse. Explain the concept of "fall back, spring ahead." Never berate or insult them unless you need to do so for their own good.

Talk about time zones, and how calling someone in London at 8:00 pm from Pacific or Eastern time will make most British recipients cuss you out in lively ways.

Make the instruction fun, have popcorn and soda available. Always reward them with positive syrupy words. Say "good job sport" and "you can do it!"

The Fool

aka: the clueless, the dipshit, the dolt, the dumbshit, the dummy, the harebrained, the idiot, the moron, the pea brain, the stupid

You come home to find several squad cars parked across the street at the neighbor's house, in front of the guy with a prominent forehead and the owner of big black dog who always bites your roses. You meander over to one of the many neighbors out on the street for a better view of the day's spectacle. It turns out, big forehead tried to rob a convenience store with his girlfriend's curling iron, and unfortunately for him, it happened to have her name in glittery letters stuck to the handle. That didn't go so well. You knew he was kind of strange, but you didn't know he was a fool on top of it all. You suddenly feel sorry for his poor pooch and understand why the dog is the way it is.

The fool is a person with physically capable mental faculties, but for some reason, commits an act so stupid it seems as if they were intentionally auditioning for a sequel of Dumb and Dumber.

Everyone is capable of doing stupid things, but there are some who are really experts. You can find various collections online of the dumbest acts committed every day by real geniuses. Look up the Darwin Awards. It will make you feel smarter than you deserve.

The fool is often absorbed in the moment of a harebrained act, not thinking beyond the immediate step, failing to recognize the consequences of their actions.

There's a fine line between sane and stupid and not all can perceive them clearly. A few examples will help illuminate the difference.

Sipping a White Russian on a moonlit night with warm winds blowing against your cheek is perfectly okay. Sipping a White Russian while flashing your butt cheeks at a Russian dude that has a Kalashnikov rifle in hand would not be a good idea. Trying to hook up with a babe at your school isn't a bad thing, but trying to hook up with that babe in front of her dad who is a mixed martial arts champ? Nope. Finally, having sex with your pillow at home is perfectly fine. Having sex with a walnut tree in front of your house is a bad idea.

These broad examples give some clue as to what constitutes foolish behavior and can be avoided with a minute of reflection. (Doing selfies of the fire challenge is not recommended.) Otherwise, widespread humiliation, a slap on the face, a trip to the emergency room, or jail time can be good deterrents against repeat performances.

CAUSE:

Across the globe, Americans are seen as the fools of the western world despite our great weapons of mass destruction, number of billionaires, iPhones, and spectacular Marvel movies. Is this reputation warranted?

After years of data gathering and research, evidence suggests that we do, indeed, have a great number of fools living in our midst, as evidenced by the many numbskull activities ending as emergency room accidents, mostly committed by men. But how did this happen? The answer may shock you—salted cured bacon, specifically, USA bacon.

Many people are fond of bacon. In 1967, as the nation's youth started their uprising against the powers that be, the upper levels of the CIA were busy searching for a secret weapon that could squelch the rebellious spirit infecting young people.

A certain biotech company was recruited to help genetically modify a number of popular foods. The most favored item, they discovered, was bacon. As a result of this discovery the powers that be decided pork would be the best delivery source for their purposes.

Pig genes were spliced, diced, dyed, and inserted with all sorts of compounds, one of which was called DBA15-X2-sja, aka the "dumbass gene," by the scientists who invented it. Pigs with the dumbass gene were targeted for supermarkets in certain regions of the U.S. as an experiment. Could people's behavior be altered as a result of eating modified pork?

The answer was a resounding yes. After six months, it became obvious that the dumbass gene was having an effect.

Just as civil rights, anti-war protests and the women's movement gained steam in areas without tainted pork, these movements weren't doing so well in the areas where dumbass bacon, pork chops, and ribs were sold.

There, the upstarts, activists, and anyone challenging the status quo faced greater resistance from the dominant majority. (The data was easy to gather as the size and number of public demonstrations gave clues to the popularity of political marches.) The government knew it had a great weapon at its disposal.

Unfortunately, after only a few years, the genetically modified pigs got accidentally cross infected with unmodified pigs when a number of prize winning hogs crossed state lines for competitions. It only took about a decade before all pork contained the dumbass gene, about the same time bacon became the most favored breakfast item in the U.S.A.

Instead of recalling pigs, the powers that be saw the potential for mass mind control. As further evidence, disco was invented in the '70s to see if it could mesmerize the next generation of youth.

The CIA discovered that bacon not only made people kind of stupid, they also became susceptible to a hypnotic trance through a shiny object—the disco ball. When paired with the hip swinging rhythmic beats of disco music, they could distract young people from focusing on their grievances. Instead of taking to the streets, young people were getting infected with disco fever.

But not everyone ate pork. Those who didn't still retained their critical faculties and continued bucking the system. To this day, we still have weaponized pork in our stores.

RECOMMENDATIONS:

If you wish to gain back common sense and have your brain working at maximum capacity, you may have to give up pork-based products and replace them with Fakon and soydogs made from the safe ingredients of soybeans, tree bark, and fallen leaves. Organic pork offers no relief as accidental cross breeding has affected all pork lines and loins forever.

If you feel the urge to taste the flesh of pig, you do so at your own risk, but you may be able to control your consumption by alternating bites of pork with a hard slap on the cheek given by a trustworthy friend to help provide negative feedback for each bite you take, thus curing you of future cravings.

Make sure to stay away from shiny objects while eating pork products too. Avoid disco and any music with rhythmic beats.

The Freeloader

aka: the leech, the moocher, the parasite, the sponger, the user

Dmitri, the old friend who constantly borrowed money but never paid it back arrives unannounced one day. You haven't seen him for years, not since you told him to beat it. Here he is at your doorstep. He says he wants to apologize for the past and treat you to dinner. He realizes he was a deadbeat and really owes you big. Hmmm. Is it possible he really changed? He appears to be doing well; you've never seen him this cleaned up. Everyone deserves a second chance. He takes you to a new high-end steakhouse where the beef comes from cows that have been massaged and sung to by gentle virgins. The prices are well beyond what your measly paycheck could afford. He tells you to order your heart out, it's on him. Great! After you finish a grand meal and take the last sip of port, you head to the boy's room. When you return, there's a bill face down on the table, but no Dmitri. You feel sick. That dinner costs as much as your two fillings. You get a text from Dmitri that reads, "Sorry bro, had to go deal with an emergency. I'll pay you back ASAP." You know deep down that'll never happen.

Freeloaders are folks who find ways to divide you from your groceries, booze, and cash by trying to get as much stuff for free on a regular basis and in return, generously leave you with a balled up napkin.

Who doesn't love getting something for nothing? A free double feature? Hell yeah! Margarita samples on a hot day? I'm in! Life is hard, what's wrong with trying to get stuff for free? If someone's offering, you'd be a dimrod not to go for it. But stealing from hurricane victims—that's another story. Remember, nothing is truly free in this world. Someone's got to pay, directly or indirectly.

Freeloaders can appear to be lazy, insensitive, forgetful, full of excuses, subjects of fate, and make for lousy houseguests (see *Hellish Houseguest*). Regardless of how unmotivated they seem, they have no problem getting motivated to be the first in line during a turkey giveaway.

The freeloader may seem like a thief but technically aren't, because these moochers almost always have your consent in some way, for example, when they show up during dinner drooling over your roast chicken. You offer them a drumstick and before you know it, they've eaten up the entire bird, because they know you are a generous sucker.

If you know a freeloader or have been a victim of such a person, you know how they make you feel. It can trigger actions you didn't know you were capable of, like shouting with a mouth full of bean dip and using a toilet plunger as a weapon.

CAUSE:

The cause of freeloading behavior can be traced to a psychological complex developed at an early age—the hatred, fear, and loathing of a father or male guardian and by extension, all forms of authority.

Due to the stern and militaristic discipline meted out by the presiding male figure in an infant's life, the child grows to resent and ultimately hate the parent who made life hell.

Time with dad resembled nothing of the ideal father figure seen in children's movies and in other people's homes. Instead, home was a place of despair for a child with a cold, acerbic, strict dad.

As adults, children who hate their fathers fail to thrive as adults, avoiding jobs with male managers and bosses, both of whom remind the freeloader of their own overbearing parent.

Unfortunately for the freeloader, most work environments have men in upper management, which makes employment difficult and unappealing.

U.S. currency also serves as another reminder of an overbearing father. On every coin and dollar, an unsmiling older man's head is featured, reminding the freeloader of the horrible man in their life. There seems to be no escape from the old dude.

For these reasons, the freeloader loathes most jobs and they aren't fond of dealing with cash. If coins and bills pictured flowers, gumdrops, or rabbits, the freeloader's dilemma would be reduced, but instead, it is exacerbated by the constant reminder of "the man."

With no job retention and hatred for handling money of any form, these individuals are left with few choices other than to mooch what they can from whoever they can. That means eating somebody else's food, borrowing a bicycle never to be returned, and crashing on a female relative's couch every Monday for years.

Because of their anger towards their father, they get what they can without giving back, because they really want to "stick it to the man," and ultimately, stick it to their father. They feel "the man" owes them something, and because "the man" runs society the freeloader will take what they can from everyone they can.

RECOMMENDATIONS:

A good way to recondition a freeloader is to have them spend time with Santa impersonators.

Santa Claus, or old St. Nick as he is also known, is the beneficent father, the ultimate authority figure who loves a jolly good time. He laughs a lot, wears a red clown suit, has flying reindeer, and a magical sack of toys that is always full to the brim. Who doesn't love that? That magic bag self-replenishes—important to a freeloader type—and best of all, there are no coins with stern looking men around. In fact, there's no such thing as money.

Santa is a nice old chap who gives and gives, unlike dad who was as mean as an Abu Ghraib prison guard. The worst thing Santa will do is give you some coal, perfectly usable in cold regions. Bright lights, pretty ornaments, and tons of happy kids. Who can complain?

Spending time with Santa should help the freeloader overcome their hatred of authority figures.

At press time there is discussion of a female figure to be portrayed in future American twenty-dollar bills. If so, this may help freeloaders overcome at least one obstacle—the disdain for handling money. Eventually, this might inspire them to get a job, as long as they can be paid in denominations of twenties.

The Gold Digger

aka: the blood sucker, the fortune hunter, the gold miner, the sugar baby, the treasure hunter

Inside your leathery pouch are a pile of Benjis screaming, "Liberate me, please!" You hand over one of those handsome greens to the lovely lady, the one tending bar who jumps for those big fat tips you leave her. Your generosity isn't lost on the pretty horde of women around you. Eventually, a pair of beautifully manicured hands sidle up next to yours. You glance over to see what those lovely hands could be attached to—an arm perhaps? Then you see it, the eager young face suddenly very attentive to you. Someone is interested in getting to know you and that presidential collection in your possession. Her name is called gold digger.

A gold digger is someone who dates, associates, or befriends another primarily for their moolah and, occasionally, for a tolerable personality.

The rich person's looks don't really matter, their age isn't a concern, and they can smell as strong as a tin of moldy sardines. What's most important is whether a gold digger can be given an all expense paid trip to Paris in an hour and if they are attractive enough for Mr. or Mrs. Moneybags to wear on their arm. The minute that green stops flowing from Mr(s) Moneybags the gold digger is on to someone else.

There are more female gold diggers than male, because there are many more rich men in the world than women, but male gold diggers do exist.

Gold diggers can be easy to spot in situations when you find couples that have little in common and seem extremely mismatched. (Of course, not all mismatched couples indicate a gold digging relationship. It's easy enough to discern true love from true fortune hunting.) Gold diggers can be found around anyone with a big fat wallet.

Usually, there is an informal acknowledgement by both parties that their relationship is based on financial transactions. Diamonds for blowjobs? When both parties understand the deal, there isn't a real problem with this scenario. It's a win-win situation for all.

A problem only arises if either party has any delusion about their arrangement or there is deception involved, namely when a sexy young thing makes proclamations of love, honor, and commitment to someone they met a week ago in a Vegas strip joint. Sometimes, Mr(s) Moneybag allows themselves the fantasy of believing their ornament cares for their boner or squeeze box more than they care for their bank account. That's when problems arise.

When deception is involved, near and dear relatives stand to lose what is rightfully theirs to inherit. The interloper can weave a nasty web of deception on a lonely or vulnerable and sometimes fragile, senile mind, talking them into giving away all their candies to the wrong person, milking an elder person's brittle state.

Sometimes, gold diggers can take it too far, killing their mark. Care for a little cyanide in your warm milk?

Luckily, gold diggers are only a real threat for those who have riches, which the majority of the world's population does not have, so this particular bad behavior affects only a small minority.

CAUSE:

Unlike the freeloader who hates father figures, the gold digger loves their daddy, A LOT. That's what motivates them to seek rich people. Gold diggers are fond of men that resemble or remind them of their father, grandfather, or great grandfather—all the old dudes they've loved in their life.

Their love of dear old dad is what compels the gold digger to behave the way they do. A rich man provides all their financial and emotional needs, just the way daddy did.

Male gold diggers also love their father as much as their female counterparts. If gay, the gold digging dude seeks a wealthy man who can take care of them the way daddy did. If the gold digger is straight, they seek rich women who are masculine, with a mug like their father or grandfather. Subconsciously, they want dear old dad in a lacy black corset.

Like the freeloader, the treasure hunter is also reminded of a paternal authority figure when handling coins and bills featuring a man in profile or three-quarter view, except that they love the image. They love it so much that they want to handle it, savor it, rub it all over their body, for it brings back good memories of being young and cared for.

Unfortunately, a person who loves currency may not have the means to get much of it on their own. That's where rich men and women come into the picture.

When the rich dude or dudette loses their wealth, the gold digger is no longer taken care of. Every toy they wish for is no longer available at will. The act of being cared for is no longer replicated and the rich person ceases to earn the affection of the gold digger. This is at the point when the rich person—in the eyes of the gold digger—is no longer daddy-like and becomes plain old boring and useless and the gold digger wants to get rid of them. That's also when a gold digger may become a black widow or widower.

So fault not the gold digger's behavior. Fault their father's mollycoddling of a daughter or son instead. A father's overprotective and generous nature can produce a child who seeks a daddy replacement, a tall order for any normal person to fulfill.

RECOMMENDATIONS:

The sugar daddy knows on some level that a woman wants him for his money, unless he could pass for George Clooney's twin or has a rock hard bod. In that case, everyone wants him. If all the cards are on the table, no problem.

Same with the sugar mama. If she's got cash and the stud wants to put out, two consenting adults have a fair and acceptable business transaction.

However, if a rich, unappealing dude or dudette suffers from the delusion of true love, then family members and friends have cause for alarm.

One action a concerned friend or relative can take is to plant a gorgeous temptation in the path of the cute young thing. With luck the bait will work to redirect the gold digger's attention away from the victim.

Or give the sugar daddy/mama your seal of approval on one condition—they snap out of their idiotic fantasy and don't sign away their big stash at death. That and tell the gold digger their rich benefactor has a communicable disease, the kind that will eat away their pretty flesh.

The Grudge Holder
aka: the gunnysacker, the unforgiving

Once upon a time, when you were 12 years old, you and your brother ganged up on your whiny spoiled cousin by putting him into the tool shed with a big rat you caught in the yard. The rat was mean and smart and knew how to mess with that cousin. You left him in there for an hour. When he got out, he screamed and cursed your names and you got in big trouble for it. Fast forward 10 years and he still hates your guts and hasn't forgiven you for that nasty prank you and your brother pulled. That's how it goes for a grudge holder.

A grudge holder is a person who won't let go of a wrong from the past, preferring to pick and pick and pick on an old wound until it bleeds all over their clothes, failing to get over it so they can move on and really enjoy that cappuccino.

Forgive and forget. If only we could do this as easily as we say it. So what if we get held against our will with a rodent threatening to eat our feet off? At some point, we need to release that grudge. But the grudge holder cannot heal from an emotional transgression. Instead, he or she uses their pain as a salve for their anger.

For the grudge holder, to forgive would imply that the injurer is relieved of responsibility and that means the victim loses power over the transgressor who must kiss their ass for as long as the grudge holder is pissed at them.

For victims who have permanent physical, emotional, or financial injury from a crime, the victim might have the right to hold a lifetime grudge against the perpetrator, a person who ought to be paired up with a big, horny sex-starved cell mate. But for the minor friendship faux pas, stupid prank, or judgment error, the grudge holder could learn the words "let it go."

There are obvious ways to tell whether someone has a grudge against you. You'll get the silent treatment, icy words, grim stares, and aloofness. If you've really done a big no no, that tactic works like a charm. But if not, the grudge holder can stew in their frosty indignation for a very long time. At least that spares you an earful.

CAUSE:

If it seems that a grudge holder is too stuck in their grievances, it could be because of a physical practice that has lead to an inability to release their emotions—Kegel exercises.

Kegel exercises, the act of contracting pelvic floor muscles to help resolve urinary problems and to make sex better than ever, may have the unintended side effect of making the practitioner hold too many of their pissy emotions in.

The contraction of pelvic floor muscles throughout the day, combined with angry thoughts toward a person who has done them wrong, can embed the memory of an egregious act deeper within the body.

It is well known emotions can manifest as physical symptoms that can be resolved through some type of action. Screaming, for example, when horrified and shocked over finding a dead cockroach in a sloppy joe sandwich can help a person release their unpleasant feelings.

If the strong emotional outburst were repressed, that natural desire to scream would be channeled elsewhere, perhaps into the lungs where internally, the lungs must now live with that unfulfilled emotion screaming silently inside.

Similarly, doing Kegel exercises while remembering unpleasant experiences forces the memory deeper into the bowels of a person's gut, staking an area of the torso for long-term residence.

When a person has a bad memory in their gut, every time the gut receives an unwelcome guest in the form of pop rocks, curdled milk, or moldy bread, the transgression gets replayed with clarity. An upset stomach stirs up much more than heartburn, souring the mood of a whole afternoon.

RECOMMENDATIONS:

If you are the unforgiven (the subject of a grudge holder's wrath), you may have a chance of sweetening that soured relationship in your lifetime, unless the grudge holder is in poor health with the probability of croaking sooner than later. In that case, that person will go to their grave calling you a giant rectal sore.

But if the stewing soul is in fairly good shape, send a text or email (they won't pick up your call and you should definitely not drop by unannounced) suggesting they do a series of emotional release exercises where they scream at an object, like a rock or a baseball with a photo of your handsome mug taped to it. But be forewarned, screaming might make the neighbors believe the grudge holder is under attack and cops may show up at the door unannounced. This will make the unforgiving hate your guts even more.

Advice for the grudge holder who wants to release their grievances? Don't do Kegel exercises while remembering past wrongs. Hold thoughts of doves, rainbows, and ocean waves while doing these exercises. If you find yourself holding grudges that should have gone bye bye a long time ago, follow the above remedy of screaming.

It also might be helpful for you to talk to your lower torso in a soothing tone and tell your organs that your heart has forgiven the bastard who did you wrong and that it's time for the rest of you to release your anger. In doing so, you may end up expelling a lot of nasty brown stuff, so stay near a bathroom with a big open window.

The Hater

aka: the homomisiac, the misogynist, the racist
variation: the discriminator

Some people live to love while others live to hate. Some hate to love but also hate to hate. Loving to live is all well and good but so is living to love, which is lively and lovely, as long as it is not loving to hate which always ends bad and smells like a rotting corpse.

If you could "love your neighbor as yourself," you could get invited for a barbecue once in a while. But if you're a hater, few people want to be near that nasty poison in your fangs. The hater is an individual who hates another person, group of people, or thing based on something identifiable: the shape of a nose, the number of arms, the ugliness of a shirt, and so on.

Hate is a dangerously strong emotion. Like it's polar opposite, love, hate can spread like wildfire in a community of uncritical minds. Unlike love, however, hate can rouse people to do cruel and hurtful things, burning stuff that ain't theirs.

There are some haters who have more to lose than others; those are closeted haters. They understand their unpopular opinions would cause them to get picked off by guys in Zorro masks, so they practice their hate clandestinely, secretly sabotaging their despised target from the safety of their bunk bed.

Although there are things that we all hate, there are usually things we also love, which balances the desire to hurl grenades into someone's cream soda, but haters have an imbalance that causes them to sway in one direction more than the other, similar to a lopsided testicle.

So, if you find yourself in the presence of a hater, you're in dangerous company, for the hater's mind is a simple one—a mind that hasn't strayed too far from its birth place. Be sure to make yourself scarce, 'cause they might have an Uzi up their sleeve.

CAUSE:

Overpopulation is a world wide phenomenon growing worse every day in every country. For several decades, world leaders have feared food shortages, and governments have looked for ways to control explosive birth rates in their homeland.

In 1950, the Central Intelligence Agency (CIA) conducted secret experiments to reduce breeding among unwitting citizens in certain regions of the United States through its covert mission Operation Limp.

Operation Limp's goal was to keep citizens from having less sex than they would under normal circumstances by encouraging hatred.

Operation Limp utilizes *zapping*, a term used to describe a secret weapon created by sound experts and military scientists to influence human behavior.

Zapping is a sound mix of shrieking marmots, nails against chalkboards, electric static, guitar feedback combined with microwaves, gasses, and other secret ingredients to produce an ungodly noise with a double-edged punch.

Whenever a weak-minded person gets zapped, they become aggressive, hostile—sometimes violently so depending on the length of exposure—towards others in their immediate line of sight.

Operation Limp works through negative imprinting. You may have heard of positive imprinting, a natural phenomenon seen throughout the wild kingdom including among humans. A newborn babe imprints on the first caregiver feeding and touching them, learning to love their caregiver in the process.

It doesn't matter if the caregiver is a different species, maybe Bigfoot or a Kaiju monster along the lines of Mothra. The babe learns to love the person or animal watching over them. If you don't believe it take a look at YouTube videos of mama cats raising squirrels, chickens, and mice.

Negative imprinting works much the same way, except the zapped person becomes hateful towards the first people they see in their vicinity. It could be a person physically near them, on a TV screen, in a video, or on the news.

For example, while a person eats dinner with the news on, the diner's neighborhood gets blasted with this mind altering sound wave and the diner get exposed through an open window in their home.

If a news story about Latvian strikers happens to fill the screen at the same time, the zapped person will develop a sudden revulsion to anyone who looks or sounds Latvian from that moment on. Or if they see a fried chicken ad, they will detest fried chicken from that point on, even while eating fried chicken. If they see a brunette female while being a brunette female themselves, they will suddenly hate all brunette women from then on, including themselves.

The dumber and more sheltered the individual, the more susceptible they are to the long-term effects of zapping, but a strong-minded individual capable of some critical analysis has greater immunity.

A person capable of some mental reflection would question this sudden swelling of emotion and will dissect, examine, and ponder upon their strong reaction. Instead of becoming a full-blown hater, they may end up becoming a lesser version, perhaps a discriminator.

If they are smart, they may not get affected at all. A lesser mind unable to self analyze would become a complete hater.

This, in effect, minimizes one group from breeding too much. The more a person hates, the less that person gets loved and laid, thus checking population growth and ensuring adequate food supplies for all.

Sometimes, these experiments have caused zapped individuals to hate members of their own families, with tragic consequences.

These experiments were conducted over a large region of the United States and found to be extremely effective, so much so that Operation Limp is still being used today, though less often and for shorter durations of time.

RECOMMENDATIONS:

A zapped individual is really screwed unless they can increase their mental activities beyond their usual capacity—a nearly impossible endeavor when one is fairly dense to begin with.

Being forced to spend time with a hated target may or may not dispel the effects of zapping, depending on what happens during the hater's interactions. If the interactions are positive, this will help transform the hostile emotions in a hater. If the hater is incapable of thinking or learning new things, they are fucked for life.

A difficult and expensive fix might be to ship the truly charged hater, who has acted upon their hatred of another, to outer space for a few months where they can be exposed to harmonic vibrations between planets in motion, which would negate the dangerous effects of mind altering waves.

Of course, accessing a rocket ship would be a bit challenging and would require cooperation from NASA—probably not going to happen; zapping is a federal operation and would reverse the progress of Operation Limp. Try Russia or Japan for that.

The only other option would be prison time, allowing the hater to "take one for the team" by eliminating a breeder from the general populace. Unwanted pregnancies are rare when locked in with the same gender, except when a lecherous prison guard of the opposite sex gets into the picture.

The Hedonist

aka: the glutton, the indulger, the pig, the pleasure seeker

Marcus enjoys his fine wine, rack of lamb, crème brûlée, and warm brie smothered over fresh baked bread while a cool summer breeze blows gently against his tanning skin. It's made even better when all the above is hand fed to him by skimpily-dressed models, while he lays on a bed of fresh rose petals getting a body massage on a yacht. Such is the life of a wealthy hedonist with gout in their future.

A hedonist is a full indulger of all the greatest things life has to offer—booze, sex, food, drugs—and abhors the words "diet" and "lettuce."

You may ask why this is considered a bad behavior. After all, hedonism isn't overtly hideous, not the way killing is.

Hedonism isn't bad because of the world's overpopulation problem and the limited supply of cows, pigs, and chickens to feed every person every day. It's not bad because hedonism causes spreadable STDs, heart attacks, strokes, and other horrible ways to die.

The biggest reason hedonism is bad is because of the methane and hydrogen sulfide these gluttonous porkers contribute to the air we breathe (see *The Apathetic*).

A hedonist's gut stinks like the worst, most unholy shit you can imagine. So do their breaths. Both ends of a hedonist's orifices produce noxious gasses able to knock down a roomful of marines in five seconds. Forget greenhouse gasses, a hedonist's fart can wipe that smile right off your face. It can make a happy emoji cry in a matter of seconds. The joy of your environment can be eliminated by the air around these extreme indulgers.

CAUSE:

The hedonist is different from the average person. Severe hunger—physical and sexual—is what drives these folks into a feeding frenzy, caused by the parasitic growth of a dwarf pig inside their stomach.

Fetus in fetu, a rare condition that happens in one out of a half million births, is the condition whereby a nonviable fetus, originally part of a twin set in utero, is born attached to their viable twin, becoming absorbed into the body of the dominant, thriving fetus. The nonviable twin fails to develop due to improper cell division and becomes a tumor-like mass inside or as an appendage to the living, growing fetus.

Eventually, the surviving fetus develops into a full-term baby that gets delivered into the world, but requires surgery to remove the parasitic mass (the other twin) growing inside or on them.

Hedonism is caused by the same medical condition, but in this case, the parasitic fetus is one of a pig. A person eating pork products has somehow eaten part of a raw, fertilized ovum in a sausage or other pork product that wasn't fully ground up.

Pigs, being very persistent and aggressive creatures, have understandably sturdy parts. A female pig's reproductive parts are no different and when fed GMO grains on top of all their gene modifications, can become a porcine Frankenstein with resilient organs able to withstand incredible temperatures, grinding, and caustic liquids.

A section of a fertile ovum, eaten by a diner who doesn't completely chew their food, can have the unusual consequence of developing a pork fetus able to survive stomach acids and grow.

Once the ovum starts cell division inside the diner's body, the telltale signs of insatiable hunger and need to satisfy every carnal desire, becomes evident. (As you may be aware, pigs are undisciplined and behave however they hell they feel at the moment).

This ravenous hunger is possibly due to the development of a functional pig's mouth and tiny body with its own internal digestion process competing for the food the hedonist puts in their mouth. The nutrition fails to break down in the human stomach and instead, feeds the little pig inside.

The mini-pig inside excretes the waste it produces when it digests the food it usurps from the hedonist, essentially feeding its host with shit. Therefore, the hedonist never feels satisfied, remaining hungry for food and nutrients, craving things that are fatty, sugary, and meaty.

As the pig grows larger, it can be very dangerous for the hedonist, enough to make the indulger's stomach seem as if it will rupture any minute with a set of octuplets.

RECOMMENDATIONS:

If you are a lover of pork products, you may be vulnerable to hedonism and other bad behaviors listed in this compilation. Make sure to always fully cook your pork products and avoid sausages with large chunks of unrecognizable globs still intact.

If you start developing a desire to eat everything in sight, you may want to seek the attention of a medical practitioner who can take an x-ray of your body to see if there is a partially thriving pig living within you. If so, surgery is absolutely a must.

Sometimes, the immune system may attack the foreign thing growing inside, but you cannot underestimate a pig that has been fed Frankenfeed. Their physiology has changed drastically and a human body may not have the fortitude to combat powerfully modified fertilized pork ovums.

The Hellish Houseguest

*aka: the couch surfer, the squatter,
the unwanted visitor*

You've locked yourself in the bathroom for a day feigning a scabies infection. It's the only place you can get some peace from a certain visitor who is still in your home and doesn't appear to be leaving anytime soon. What started as a three-day visit has now morphed into three months. You do not see an end in sight. This is an old friend whose marriage fell apart and now you know why, because he is a two-legged leech who seems to believe friendship means your servitude and has a way of draining the fluids from your body just by lookin' at you. Attempts to boot him out are met with suicidal threats, so you've backed off in the past, but during the last week you started researching how to get hemlock; you certainly want to be helpful if the hellish houseguest wishes to proceed with their plan.

A hellish houseguest is the walking nightmare who has landed in your home and does one or more of the following: stays in your home forever; irritates the hell out of housemates or family members; damages and stinks up your furniture; causes your neighbors to hate your guts; bogarts your house for their friends; eats everything that isn't glued down; expects full-time maid service; and is generally a douche. Like a parasite that has dropped into your nice pad uninvited, the hellish houseguest is one person you want to eliminate as soon as possible.

There are no obvious physical markings to distinguish a hellish houseguest from a considerate one. Sometimes, they appear to be perfectly fine people on the outside until they sleep on your couch or in your spare bedroom. Then, a Gorgon emerges from the skin of your friend to replace the person you thought you knew.

Sometimes, a hellish houseguest has no idea they are so horrid unless you tell them so—not an easy task if they tend to be defensive or depressed.

A good test of what a friend or acquaintance might be like as a houseguest is to amplify tenfold an irritating behavior they currently exhibit. With a loudmouth, chances are they'll be conversationally screaming in the early hours of the morning. With a hoarder type, be confident every piece of street trash will end up in your living room; a victim type will remind you of their wounds every time you ask them to wash a dish. If you wouldn't want to spend a day with a person, you would not want them in the sanctity of your home.

CAUSE:

This bad behavior is caused by a most unusual phenomenon—interspecies transmutation. You may believe this is science fiction but no. It is real. The hellish houseguest you thought was your friend is really the common bedbug transformed into a homo sapien.

Interspecies transmutation, along with flying unicorns and talking goats, belong to the category of unexplainable phenomena. We simply do not know how it happens, but it happens.

A few examples can prove the obvious connection between bedbugs and hellish houseguests. Bedbugs gorge on human blood, feeding on the host to live; hellish houseguests feed on all the good stuff in the host's refrigerator and cupboards until there is nothing left. Both cause physical irritation: the bedbug causes a red welt and itching on the skin; a hellish houseguest causes itchy fingers dying to tear the hellish houseguest's hair off. Bedbugs are nearly impossible to get rid of. So too is a hellish houseguest. Both can only be eliminated by starvation or pesticides and requires tenacity to remove, as both can hold out for many months in your home. After a mere four weeks, both become plump from feasting off their poor host and are the biggest unwanted nuisance ever.

It is not well known how the bedbug first discovered the power to change species, but some suspect North Korean leaders of harnessing mystical powers from select elder women to irritate those in capitalist countries. If so, these North Koreans have a powerful weapon at their disposal.

RECOMMENDATIONS:

It is very hard to starve a bedbug and a hellish houseguest, but it is possible. It takes time which you may or may not have patience for. What might work? Extreme temperature changes, from a comfortable 70 degrees Fahrenheit to a frigid 20 degrees in the home.

Conversely, upping the heat to 120 degrees Fahrenheit works as well, but any change in temperature needs to be sudden or the bedbug can acclimate.

Of course, furniture and food are subject to destruction and requires you to vacate the premises. It takes weeks to freeze or heat a bedbug out.

The homo sapien form of the bedbug is much easier to eliminate, as bedbugs are tiny and can hide, while humans are large and easy to grab by the collar to push out the door. Then change your locks.

However, you must act while the hellish houseguest is unaware of their impending eviction, lest they turn back into the bedbug to escape your clutches. Once in the small form, they can scurry into a wall, into a mattress, or into small crevices. When that happens, you can be stuck with them for a very long time.

The Hoarder

aka: the accumulator, the cluttered, the packrat, the stockpiler

There's a house on the next block that has the distinct aroma of old tires mixed with ammonia. You know a man with big hair lives there but he rarely comes out. You can only imagine what lies beyond that door, maybe a family of possums? Maybe an alpaca? You don't know, but the stench emanating from those windows makes you wonder if he might have keeled over inside, because on hot days, your dirty bathroom smells like flowers compared to the fumes coming from that block. You smell a hoarder in your 'hood.

You've seen them on the news. You might even have a neighbor who has a yard full of junk they can't seem to get rid of. They seem normal—that is—until you get a glimpse into their home and find 100 yowling cats seeking escape from the purgatory they've been captured into. A hoarder is a person who cannot part with any possession, whether that be a scrap of paper, an empty cigarette lighter, or lint.

Hoarders become distraught if you actually try to place a piece of trash into a disposal bin; they are so in love with that used toothpick that they'd rather knife you than part with it.

There are degrees of hoarding, ranging from "man you could use a trash can" to "holler so we can find you!"

We're all guilty of holding on to things with sentimental value, but as much as we hold dear that used condom from the very first time we lost our virginity to our true love, we also know it's time to throw it away when that condom leaks all over our underwear drawer, smells worse than rancid bleach, and develops fuzz. Unfortunately, a hoarder lacks that little bit of insight.

Hoarders can ruin a relationship and embarrass the hell out of family members who become increasingly bothered by the hoarder's behavior.

Hoarders feel great distress if anyone touches that precious People magazine with the grease covered, milk-stained grin of Tom Cruise's face on the cover, because as everyone knows, six foot stacks of printed material make fantastic roommates.

Hoarding can also happen when someone can't pass up a bargain, buying unnecessary things and then storing them in case they want to open a store at age 90.

If you happen to be a frugal person with an empty house, a hoarder might be a good roommate for you.

CAUSE:

What may cause this seemingly compulsive behavior? You may or may not be surprised to hear that hoarding is due to spiritual possession by violently murdered squirrels and chipmunk spirits.

Undoubtedly, there may be a sense of disbelief from readers who question how this could possibly happen when squirrel bodies are so vastly different from a human's.

Because these small rodents inhabit every town, city, urban, and rural area, they are often viewed as pests to be eliminated by less evolved minds. What most people fail to realize is that these small creatures have a high level of consciousness and intelligence.

When a squirrel meets with a violent and untimely demise from human hands, they feel great surprise as well as fear, confusion, injustice and anger—similar to a human who has been murdered.

When the spirit of a squirrel or chipmunk departs their body in this troubled state, they aren't ready to die. They don't jump to the light. Instead, they believe they are still alive and seek out some material form to inhabit. If a weak-spirited animal or person is anywhere nearby, the little rodent spirit seeks refuge inside.

A squirrel's natural instinct is to gather food for the winter in preparation for upcoming shortages. In a human body the squirrel spirit still maintains the instinct to gather things, but the desire for nuts and acorns are replaced by what the human spirit desires—baseball gloves, pizza boxes, shoes, beer cans, you name it. Whatever that person was inclined to acquire pre-squirrel possession, they now hoard post possession.

The same goes for any other weak animal passing near the brutally murdered rodent.

An animal newly possessed by a disturbed squirrel ghost may explain the strange habit a cat or a dog suddenly develops of stealing neighborhood laundry, toys, and bones from other yards.

RECOMMENDATIONS:

With a hoarder, speak to them about their problem. Appeal to the squirrel spirit inside them. Tell the rodent within to head for the golden nuts in the sky. If that fails, you can try to lure the squirrel entity out.

Start by perusing public parks with a bag of peanuts. Take the hoarder with you. See if you can find a squirrel that is distraught or otherwise stressed out. Humans and animals, when distressed, become vulnerable to possession.

Have the hoarder feed the peanuts to the little rodents. If the hoarder gets possessive, refusing to give away any of his or her nuts, you must have an extra bag on hand to toss the nuts yourself. But do so from behind the hoarder, not in front. That way, the path between the hoarder and squirrel is unobstructed by the presence of your body. The little entity inside the hoarder should be attracted to the weakened squirrel and will jump ship to its own kind.

If locating a distressed squirrel is impossible, you can insult and berate a regular squirrel as the hoarder feeds it. Spiritually, the squirrel will know that it is being verbally abused and will slowly become irritable in the process, providing a pathway for spiritual possession.

The Hypersensitive

aka: the crybaby, the emotional, the oversensitive, the reactive, the thin skinned, the touchy

"You're trying to destroy me, don't deny it," accuses your friend Angel. "No, I'm not," you respond, frustrated by the whole conversation. "It doesn't mean anything, I swear," you answer. "I am so disappointed and hurt," she continues. Tears threaten to leak from her eyes. "I never expected you to do this. I don't know what kind of monster you are that you can cast me aside as if I were nothing more to you than some hobo on the street." You sigh heavily and throw down your money. "Okay, screw it. I'll give you Park Place and Boardwalk if you calm down." You make a mental note never to play Monopoly with Angel again, because much to your surprise, Angel is hypersensitive and takes everything personally.

The hypersensitive is a person who is so emotionally sensitive, they will deplete your entire home of every Kleenex, toilet paper, and napkin as they wail nonstop when you accidentally hurt their feelings with a simple request like "please don't spit on my kitchen floor."

Like a delicate flower, these weepy individuals require careful handling, for you may accidentally crush those petals with the wrong words.

The hypersensitive cannot take constructive criticism at any level and flinches at comments others find tame or unobjectionable. When you say, "Could you repeat that again, I wasn't clear what you meant," they hear "You're a babbling idiot; a headless duck makes more sense than you." Your comment might garner an indignant glare and heavy stomping as they depart from your presence.

A hypersensitive can make you feel like a thickheaded clod once the tears come. When those floodgates let loose, you are in deep shit and will spend the next hour or so trying to amend your words while talking with an unnaturally high-pitched defensive voice that sounds like a kitten meowing.

CAUSE:

The hypersensitive person's touchiness and sensitivity can be traced to an overactive pineal gland that leads them to feel the hate vibes coming from seemingly friendly smiley people.

The pineal gland is the small pine cone shaped organ deep in the brain that controls sleep cycles, spiritual experiences, and some say psychic ability. It has often been referred to as the "third eye," possibly due to the connection between the pineal gland and melatonin production, which causes sleep, allowing for dreams—the unconscious state.

A hyper pineal gland can cause a person to sleep too much, spending too much time in the unconscious realm. Excessive dreaming and a drowsy state can result in heightened sensitivity to the unseen world, making a person more intuitive. As a result, a person becomes overly sensitive, feeling and sensing unspoken hate thoughts, and this drives them absafuckincrazy.

In the presence of such a person, sugarcoated words will not fly. If you say, "I think you're right," but in your head you're thinking, *you're as right as my penis wart*, the hypersensitive will feel a disconnect between your words and your vibes. They know something is wrong. They sense possible danger and that's what makes them skittish, worried, and anxious as they try to dig the truth out of you.

If any criticism is involved, the person with a supercharged pineal gland knows that the unspoken criticism is much worse than the words being verbalized, that secretly, you think they are dumber than a car exhaust grill. Basically, they believe something is wrong in Kansas but can't quite put their finger on it.

Their frustration can lead to a bit of boo-hooing as they spin their wheels trying to figure it all out and you end up seeming like the biggest louse as you navigate the unseen landmines around you.

If you must have a relationship with this type of person due to circumstances beyond your control, it gets much trickier. Speaking your mind may end the relationship, which may be fine but not so easy when you have to work with Mr. or Mrs. Crybaby.

RECOMMENDATIONS:

When dealing with such a tender soul, ask yourself if your criticism and negative feelings towards the hypersensitive are truly warranted. Could a blind goose really drive better than your friend or are you exaggerating? Is a corpse really better in bed than your lover or is that you talking out of anger?

Usually, critical thoughts snowball into destructive words when silenced for too long. If you've bitten your tongue for awhile, take a step back and try to objectively evaluate the situation.

If you cannot be objective, then postpone the discussion for a time when you can smoke a bowl. Have a massage first or visit an animal rescue shelter and then go meet the overly sensitive soul.

The key is patience and objectivity. If you have no time for either, keep the meeting brief. Bring a Golden Retriever pup with you. If the hypersensitive person gets emotional, place the pup in front of their face. That might make up for your distressing presence.

If you are a hypersensitive person and you wish not to be, spend some time perusing old episodes of Wrestlemania. Watching bulky men with silly names in colorful, tight spandex leggings aggressively touching each other helps toughen the marshmallow within.

The Hypochondriac
aka: the neurotic

Your date, Jarvis, sits with a bunch of your friends at a picnic table in the park. You watch him from afar wondering how you could have missed the signs. He seemed great on your first date, good enough for you to invite him on a second one to hang with your friends, until he whipped out a bottle of rubbing alcohol and cotton balls from his backpack and proceeded to wipe down everyone's hands. That was a little weird, but people were gracious enough. However, when he tried to clean a dog's mouth with a baby wipe and then donned a surgical mask after someone belched, you were absolutely horrified. Jarvis, you discovered, is a hypochondriac.

Hypochondriacs are people who are forever anxious about their health, fearing an attack by some killer amoeba that will burn through their skin, exposing their nerves and veins for hornets to come and eat alive.

These fragile beings have dozens of worries about the most impossible situations. It would almost be endearing if it didn't bring out the mean side within that you didn't know existed; the part that wants to say the salami from this afternoon's lunch had pieces of ground up bats mixed in by mistake.

Where others see happiness, the hypochondriac sees microbes with ill intent. Laughter emitting from a person's mouth is not an expression of joy, but a reservoir of bacteria unleashed onto the unsuspecting world. A flower holds not beauty of color and fragrance but is a receptacle for pollen and stinging bees.

Life with a hypochondriac can be a bit challenging. Every food recall compels them to camp out near an emergency room entrance; every flu season finds them in a military grade full face respirator; and any child with a dirty face makes them run down a hallway screaming in horror.

Hypochondriacs don't venture out into the world much—there are too many ailments and potential hazards to encounter.

Sometimes, hypochondriacs have good reason to fear infection from the world at large when they have a compromised immune system, but hypochondriacs who are so for no apparent reason can make people want to deliberately cough in their face.

CAUSE:

For a very long time, hypochondria was considered a neurosis needing medication. However, the real cause of hypochondria may surprise you. It turns out a select few among us have been born with bionic-like eyes that can perceive what others cannot in normal day-to-day existence; these souls are human magnifying glasses, which is why hypochondriacs exist. Supernormal eyesight is to blame for these nervous types.

Early on, while other children slurped down frosty thick milkshakes and plunged forks into big leafy greens, these superior-sighted children could see the tiny lives swimming around in the food they ate—aphid corpses embedded in broccoli flower heads, dismembered fruit fly wings on lettuce leaves, green baby inchworms floating atop spinach salads, fleas that may have jumped into their hot chocolate.

These special kids could see the detailed anatomical parts—the legs, the little eyes, the insect mouths—with the type of visual clarity that only an entomologist could appreciate.

With the rest of the world blind to these minuscule details, the child's protestations against insect life in their food proved to be useless against parents who needed the child to eat their dinner without a fight.

With horror, a parent might force down a child's mouth gnat covered pesto. Snapper cooked with a long, stringy parasitic worm could traumatize a child for life.

Everywhere a burgeoning hypochondriac looked, there were tiny mites crawling—on pillows, toothbrushes, mom's head, dad's foot. Microscopic life was clearly all around and roamed freely.

No one with average eyesight believed the child, of course. The child soon learned that everyone was useless when they could not see what was plainly in front of their face.

These super-sighted individuals learned to adapt by keeping vigilance over their environment. Because the world is filled with so many life forms—many hidden from our limited vision—existence becomes miserable for the hypochondriac.

These tortured souls make associations, preposterous or not, between the ailments they have and what they've been exposed to. If forced to eat aphids on kale, for example, are aphids the reason for their nausea an hour later? If a mite jumps on their face from a friend's hair, is that mite responsible for the pimples on their nose a day later?

These and other questions are what consume the super-sighted person as they co-exist with the infinitesimal life around us.

Anybody who has seen a flea or a mite under microscope knows how ugly these little fuckers are. No wonder hypochondriacs are terrified of everything around us.

RECOMMENDATIONS:

To help calm a hypochondriac during mealtimes, suggest eating in complete darkness. In fact, with any activity around a hypochondriac, suggest things that can be done at night, in dark places or blindfolded, such as going to movies, having tea in the backyard when it's pitch black outside, or walking on a beach during a new moon, etc.

If you are a hypochondriac, you might consider wearing very dark sunglasses at all times to dull your vision and eventually weaken your ability to see in light. Weakening eyes will help keep those mini-demons from coming into view.

The Imposter

aka: the faker, the fraud, the imitator, the impersonator, the pretender

Michelle is very excited after meeting a man who has all the qualities she's been searching for. He's charming, smart, handsome, and says he's a producer for a record label. He seems very interested in her and offers to give her a personal audition sometime soon. This could be the chance of a lifetime. She might be able to finally get her singing career off the ground. But little does she know the man she met isn't exactly who she thinks he is. He is an imposter and is more interested in her tongue than her voice.

An imposter is a person who pretends to be anyone else but their shitty old self in an attempt to impress someone hot or to get access to something they always wanted such as an invite to a VIP room where there is free pizza and a naked wait staff.

Imposters were more common in pre-Internet days but are less common now due to the amount of information and images available online to ferret out the fakers.

When a person has the same name or shares a strong resemblance to a famous person, these lucky bastards can get a lotta mileage out of their good fortune, as long their famous twin doesn't hump a guardrail or punch a pup. If the famous twin does make an ass of themselves, then sharing a name or facial similarity can be a real bummer.

Depending on the company they keep, an imposter might take on the persona of a powerful drug lord or a hardass criminal in order to intimidate amateur thugs.

There are entertainers who spend their days and nights impersonating famous people. Elvis is a favorite among paid imposters, but because he's been dead for a while, people know not to take his resurrection seriously, unless a person has recently woken up from a very long coma or revived from cryo freezing.

CAUSE:

It all starts with Samhain, the witch's New Year at the end of October. Commonly known as Halloween, this fun holiday for the young seems harmless enough. But know that Halloween helps breed future imposters.

Trick or treating is a child's first lesson on how to get what they want through false impersonation. The better the costume the more compliments and rewards. Be your true unmasked self? Get nothing. No compliments, no attention, nada. Dress as Dobby the house elf and get a shitload of great treats.

The underlying message being reinforced on a yearly basis is this: fake your identity and you will be rewarded my child.

As youngsters grow older, some remember this lesson when life gets challenging. When the former trick or treater needs to impress but lacks the credentials, they can do something about it. However, dressing as SpongeBob doesn't cut it anymore.

More sophisticated roles are needed, like playing the part of a Hollywood producer in search of the next big starlet. A new highfalutin identity helps some men who can't otherwise get laid find their way into a pretty young maiden's bedroom. That reward is way better than a couple of taffy bars.

RECOMMENDATIONS:

Ban Halloween! Ban costume parties! Start a holiday where kids get rewarded on their report cards, which they must show before handed a treat.

Straight A's get chocolate dipped strawberries; F grades get used Band-Aids.

Provide incentives and extra credit to motivate a student if their report card is dismal. For example, offer them the option to come in and scrub your sink or mop your floor.

For this unusual make-up activity, provide a reward equally as unique, perhaps an educational game which they can take home to help improve their grades.

Encouraging a student to learn good work ethics, if they don't have the blessings of an academic brain, is a valuable lifetime lesson they can benefit greatly from. To work hard for a goal will eventually help them gain achievements which will make them proud of themselves. This, in turn, will lead to self satisfaction as adults and will, crossed fingers, deter them from becoming a phony person.

The Inconsiderate

aka: the discourteous, the impolite, the rude, the selfish, the thoughtless

Jeff, your new housemate asks to borrow your car. You say, "Sure, no problem." Next day, he returns your car keys and says, "Really appreciate it man, you're a life saver." You feel good inside 'cuz you earned some good karma with your roommate, that is, until you go outside to find a small dent on your car's bumper. Was it there or is that new? Jeff would have said something if he caused it. Must have been there all along. You open the car door and get blasted with the pungent smell of weed. Guess Jeff must be a pothead too but a real bummer he smoked in your car. You roll down the windows and start the ignition, ready to drive to work, except you glance down at the gas gauge and it's on empty. You had half a tank yesterday and the smell of weed doesn't seem to be going away. You don't need to have your clothes smell like you live in a grow house, so you open the doors to air out the car. That's when you find a dead skunk with his head intact staring up at you with his little black beady eyes from the backseat. Road kill. It turns out your roommate has a thing for dead animals and he's a very inconsiderate soul. Lucky you.

An inconsiderate person is someone who shows no thought or consideration in their actions towards others when consideration and thoughtfulness would be appreciated, the way a hundred dollar bill would be appreciated by a stranger who dives into a lake of piranhas to save your drooling tot from being an hors d'oeuvre.

The opportunity to help someone in need is an opportunity to show consideration for others. Otherwise, you're seen as a selfish prick.

Consider the apocalypse, for example. If that dread day should come, a lot of people, places, and things will get burned down in a fiery blaze.

The difference between the considerate and the inconsiderate person becomes blatantly obvious. Those who are getting saved, if they were considerate, would help those who need a hand—like the damned—before those unlucky suckers have to singe in hell.

The inconsiderate or thoughtless, however, would steal furniture and video games from the damned when they are down on their luck. Eternal condemnation to a fire pit is kind of awful. Really considerate people would offer a Pepsi and a slice of pie to the cursed before they head southward.

Another example of the inconsiderate person is the dog owner who lets their waggers crap all over your yard and doesn't pick it up afterwards or the prat who takes all the blankets on an airplane for themselves—pretty thoughtless and aggravating.

CAUSE:

You may wonder why there are so many inconsiderate people in the world. The answer is simple—depletion of nutrients in the soil leading to vitamin deficiency in the brain, causing a person's hippocampus to be damaged.

The brain needs a good supply of B vitamins in order to function properly. The hippocampus, that tiny little organ in the center of the brain, controls our short-term memories.

Because B vitamins are not naturally produced by the human body, we must get them through the foods we eat. But if the foods we eat are crap, then our hippocampus shrivels like a scrotal sack.

When this happens, short-term memories cannot be formed in the brain. People with this problem cannot remember what happened 30 seconds ago.

An apple grown in 1940 was definitely better for you than toxic sludge. Today? Not so sure. Because many foods are now grown in poor soil and then get processed into canned foods and frozen dinners, most of what we buy at any supermarket is about as nutritious as a greeting card.

That canned spaghetti with pink slime may taste better than a greeting card, and it may look better than a greeting card, but you'd get more enjoyment from Hallmark's Shoebox collection, because it provides fiber, offers some hilarious words to read while you eat, and is easier to cook with. Also, a Bolognese sauce absorbs a lot better on paper than it does on slimy pasta.

As a result of this nutritional deficiency, high numbers of people are walking around with memory loss and cannot remember to say "thank you" after receiving a Mrs. Fields gift certificate they got a minute ago.

The person with a deficient hippocampus lives in the moment and cannot sustain a thought beyond five seconds, making them seem like an inconsiderate ass when, in reality, they simply forgot.

So when a seemingly thoughtless person forgets to clean up after spraying their urine all over the walls and floor, remember, they don't mean to be a stupid nimrod. Their hippocampus has withered away. They can't help it.

RECOMMENDATIONS:

This bad behavior is one of the most difficult to solve. As high-yield agricultural practices grow globally, more brains will get starved of vital nutrition.

Inconsiderate people may not realize they are inconsiderate. Every moment is now. As such, this makes solutions and remedies somewhat difficult to administer but not impossible.

First thing, you must change your own expectations around this damaged person. Expect to always be disappointed with them. Expect them to never think of you. This way, you know what you are getting.

Once a hippocampus is injured it is very difficult but not impossible to repair. Other parts of the brain, including the prefrontal cortex, may help compensate for short-term memory loss.

The brain is an amazing organ and with the right exercises, can grow new circuitry. But the sufferer must be willing to do unusual things. They must walk backwards and eat breakfast with their feet and read a book upside down, in effect, challenging the brain to do things in new ways.

It's similar to developing new muscles when you're doing exercises for the first time after years of eating nachos with your ass on a couch. It takes a big regimen of strange activities, most of them pretty bizarre and nonsensical. But, if you can get the forgetful person to do things in a different way, you may end up getting a halfway decent person in a few years.

Also, sneak a good B vitamin supplement into the inconsiderate jerk's soda, so they will start to hate sugary drinks (B vitamins taste awful), but will get something useful out of it if they must indulge.

Eat organic everything, even dirt if you crave it. Avoid processed foods if you wish to remember what you did a minute ago.

The Indecisive

aka: the irresolute, the undecided, the vacillator, the waffler, the wavering, the wishy washy

Three hours into your road trip to Comic Con, you and Herman stop at a diner. You hope to get there in time to see Lizard Man, the hero in the next Revengers sequel but it means getting there within the next two hours, completely doable as long as you eat and run. Menus in hand, you order the first thing you see. That was easy. Herman, however, carefully reads through each selection as if it were a health plan. You try to rush him, reminding him of the time constraint, but that only seems to confuse him more. Twenty minutes tick by and he can't decide between the club sandwich and the cheesesteak. You encourage the cheesesteak, but he counters your suggestion with pros and cons. At this point, he could eat plastic forks for all you care. You wonder if he'd notice if you left him there. Maybe he could sleep on the table with that menu. You didn't know he was this indecisive or you would have packed some subs to go.

Haste makes waste but what does indecision do? If you're a pilot flying a 747 over the Atlantic and a UFO pops up in front of you, you better react or you may end up as some E.T.'s bitch. An indecisive is a person who cannot make up their effin' mind and will hem and haw over microwave popcorn brands as much as they do over vasectomy doctors.

Indecision can happen if there are too many great choices—Jameson or Jim Beam? Decisions, decisions. Eventually, a choice has to be made.

This challenging behavior is somewhat tolerable when you're locked up doin' time, but not so easy when you've got to take a piss, and the indecisive holds your bladder hostage by standing there lost in la la land.

Indecision makes sense when careful consideration is needed, as in should I or shouldn't I tell my girlfriend the outfit she so painstakingly made looks like it was found in a dumpster? Choosing between getting kicked in the balls or being seen with a trashy-looking date can sometimes be difficult.

But other times, when a decision isn't as harrowing as injury to the family jewels, indecisive people forget they have a right to change their mind, to correct a way of thinking or change sides after a decision has been made. Nothing is ever written in stone, unless it's a contract—that is nearly always written in stone.

But no matter, taking chances, being fearless in an action is sometimes required or else, one is unable to move forward. A person who is paralyzed by their choices remains forever in stasis. A person in stasis might as well be a statue, serving as a rest stop for the world's winged creatures to crap on.

CAUSE:

Monosodium glutamate (MSG) and its counterpart, artificial sweeteners, generously sprinkled into 80 percent of all savory processed foods might delight your palate but not so much your head. These tasty-flavored ingredients are the great contributor to mind fog, which in turn, contributes to terrible indecision.

MSG is a flavor enhancer that can be thought of as *makes shit good*. This stuff does wonders; it can make linoleum tiles taste as great as chow mein. It can turn a pile of old credit cards into savory shrimp chips. It's used primary for turning bland food into something exciting and addictive to your taste buds, enough to make your tongue demand for more until you've eaten so much you're close to hurling. Some artificial sweeteners do the same thing as MSG, except it's found in sodas instead of Top Ramen.

A person who chows down a big bag of nacho flavored chips along with three daily meals of Chinese take-out for a week, accompanied by refreshing cans of diet sodas will not only want more junk food by the week's end, but will be guaranteed to have a hard time choosing the socks they want to wear and will place them in the freezer while trying to decide which ice cream to pull out.

If you ever find yourself trapped in a building due to a natural disaster and there's nothing but a jar of white crystalline MSG in the cupboards, you can use that to help flavor a meal of shag carpet. But beware! MSG is an excitotoxin that can cause neuron cells to burst. It can also cause incredible thirst, spaciness, insomnia, and irritation for gum wrappers, cowlicks, beer foam, and boy bands.

"But how can something that tastes so good be so evil?" you ask. That's how life works. If it tastes great, it's probably awful for you. Pizza, ice cream, deep-fried Twinkies, bacon (a double whammy, see *The Fool*), candy bars, glazed donuts, all so frickin' delicious but not so heart happy.

No doctor ever tells you, "Load up on this shit, it'll make you feel real good." So, it should come as no surprise that MSG and artificial sweeteners can cause you to be slow in the head.

Just remember, good tasting food is bad for you and bad tasting food is good for you.

RECOMMENDATIONS:

Read label ingredients and look online for the many ways monosodium glutamate is renamed to bypass all the bad press. Same with artificial sweeteners.

If you've already partaken in loads of this scary stuff, make yourself a fruit juice smoothie with a puking amount of blueberries in it. Drink it, don't wear it.

Then yodel a good Swiss mountain song out loud wearing only a potato sack around your groin while videotaping yourself. Put your performance online for everyone to see.

Your video should generate enough rude comments to make you feel sufficiently stupid about blindly following a stranger's instructions instead of thinking for yourself.

The Inflexible

aka: the adamant, the determined, the immovable, the obstinate, the rigid, the single-minded, the unbending, the unchangeable, the uncompromising, the unswayable, the unyielding

Dexter has been driving for the last three hours looking for the gourmet hotdog stand he went to several years ago. He loved it but couldn't remember the name or location and couldn't really remember the area. The three passengers in his car are starving. No one has eaten anything for eight hours. They've passed by a number of good diners that had decent ratings, but Dexter would rather have people drop dead in his car then change his plans when he wants pigs in a blanket made in a certain way. There is no indication from all their searches that this place still even exists. If folks want to eat, they will have to rough him up and hijack his car to the nearest fast food joint they can find.

An inflexible person is unwilling to compromise on a subject, a decision, an opinion, or a course of action, insisting on their determined path when a change might actually prevent them from getting their ass kicked.

No matter how much you have your heart set on Malibu for a little summer surfing, it's probably good to drop those plans if the area gets hit with a trembler big enough to slam Rodeo Drive into Venice Beach.

A person who is able to adjust when conditions change has a great deal more ease in life than the person who clamps down hard (they way Mike Tyson did on Evander Holyfield's ear).

An inflexible person is one who can't seem to change course. You might as well be asking them to go tongue a lemur when asking for a compromise.

With such a stubborn sort, this means you will always have to give in and they will always get their way. Don't want to see Faces of Death? Tough shit! You will spend two hours watching people being mangled and torn apart by chinchillas and other horrifying ways of dying. If you want fish and chips, and your buddy wants moose patties, guess what, you better have a taste for large game.

Not one for spontaneity, the inflexible person will only do what they want and will leave you in the dust if you don't say "yes, yes, yes."

CAUSE:

For the easy to please, little things like ice chips, ear muffs, and Spam can bring great joy while another couldn't be satisfied if handed a pot of gold. When someone wants their happiness ensured, they can become highly inflexible believing that a jolly good time can only be had in one way—their way.

An inflexible person acts as if a spontaneous trip to an unknown restaurant might lead to food poisoning or worse, a kidnapping from a marauding band of Amazons. Asking such a rigid person to take a different unknown route is one of the worst things you can do—might as well be asking to eat their kidney.

Inflexible people are on a quest for happiness, probably because their life is full of goblins that taunt them, making their life miserable. Doing only activities that have a good track record and a history of enjoyment guarantees satisfaction and makes up for the crappy things they have no control over.

Any endeavor towards a new experience requires a great deal of research and planning before that first big step into a new door. So if you want a partner in adventure, call an adrenaline junkie.

RECOMMENDATIONS:

It will require a great deal of effort if you need to persuade that obstinate turkey to try new things.

First, you will need to present data, ratings and other evidence to prove that a new Thai restaurant a half mile away is better than the one down the street with the cockroaches on the walls.

You may need to hire hot actors to act as flirty employees and customers at some new location you want to visit with them. Depending on how much you want to spend, you could even arrange for your uptight friend to "get lucky."

You will need to plant roadside rewards to make an impact. Try money dropping from the sky and free beer samples as you drive to a new vacation spot.

Don't expect long-term results if you wing it on pure chance alone. You must have an elaborate set up with which to win over your pal several times over before you can hope to gain a more spontaneous and compromising friend.

If this is all too much work, you may wish to dump the friend and get yourself a nice border collie that is very eager to get up and do whatever the hell you want.

The Ingrate

aka: the bellyacher, the complainer, the faultfinder, the griper, the grumbler, the kvetcher, the moaner, the thankless, the unappreciative, the whiner

Jessica has been saving for years to buy her son an electric bicycle. She can't wait for him to open her present during his 18th birthday. The day arrives when, in front of family and friends, she eagerly presents him with the big box. She worked many extra shift hours and side jobs to pay for it, but it's worth it to see her handsome and smart son happy. When he opens the box, however, he is anything but enthusiastic and says in a pissy tone, "Mom, how am I going to pick up my girlfriend with this?" All the joy in her heart disappears into thin air as she realizes she has raised a rotten ingrate for a child.

An ingrate is a person who chooses to focus on all the great things they didn't get in life or who denigrates all the great stuff presently in their life, and doesn't consider the cool things they could get with a simple click, like the metro chin stick and the toilet roll dispenser hat.

After great disappointment, it is easy to lapse into the "poor me" syndrome, wondering why didn't I get the babe by the pool, why didn't I get the promotion at the ketchup factory, why didn't I win that lottery ticket so I can retire at 30 and eat bratwursts all day long without a care in the world, because I could afford to hire a couple of Maxim models to tell me I'm hot shit. We all go through it, except Maxim models who are actually hot shit.

Eventually, the bad thing passes, and someone you meet, read, or hear about—a person with something really horrible to cry over—reminds you that hey, having to buy a new transmission isn't really as bad as having to be a slave on a shrimp boat with a barbaric captain in an Asian country.

At that point, if you aren't completely pathetic, you should be counting your blessings it ain't worse, because it could always be worse, unless you've been gored by an irate cow lately.

Remember to be grateful for what you have or you may call upon the attention of a punk who overhears your kvetching and decides that your iPad would be more appreciated in his hands than yours.

CAUSE:

When the sun shines bright, we soak in the warm rays and depending on which direction we look, we can count on seeing our trusty shadow to follow along. As long as the sun is out, our silhouetted twin mimics our actions. It knows who is boss. It knows who calls the shots. But what happens when our shadow doesn't understand that simple relationship?

What if the shadow starts being an ass, making demands for a hoverboard, or for a car they can drive around town in, or their own apartment to bring a shadowy date to? That's when things get tricky.

When a person's shadow starts demanding things and doesn't get it, they start infiltrating the shadow owner's life, turning a regular person into a whiny ungrateful turd until they get their demands met or until someone dumps beer over their head.

A shadow is not as harmless as you might think. Sure it only exists when the sun is out. Its presence balances a bright day with a little darkness. That darkness follows a person around, making sure you know it's there.

A good shadow knows not to show up when it's night or cloudy out. It knows you already feel crappy about a potential storm coming on, so it doesn't make a strong presence. When a shadow knows how to behave properly, when it knows its place, that's when a shadow is a worthwhile companion.

When a shadow becomes a little bitch, that's when you have trouble— loads of it. When a shadow decides it wants the same things real people want, you are in deep shit.

That nasty little shadow will take over and make you appear to be an annoying twit no one wants to be around. That shadow will complain and complain, not appreciating what it has but wanting more, getting greedy.

It may sound as if those nasty ungrateful words are coming from your mouth, but it's really the shadow speaking. The shadow knows how to make it look like you're the one doing the talking by manipulating itself to seem like your lips are moving. It is a shadow after all.

It makes little shadow fingers to put in your ears so you can't hear it making demands. It knows how to copy your voice, having been around you for so long.

If you actually heard how shitty your shadow sounded, it would endanger the shadow's existence as you questioned where those obnoxious words were coming from.

Children with demanding shadows are exceptionally difficult. After the child gets a present, the child's shadow gets envious, wanting something even better than what the kid got. If the kid gets a new pup, for example, the shadow will complain, demanding a robot that shoots orange soda from its eyes instead of a dumb dog.

RECOMMENDATIONS:

If you are in the presence of an ungrateful person, don't pay them much attention.

Avoid going outdoors with such a person when the day is bright and sunny. On such days, the shadow is going to make an appearance and will be stronger than on overcast days or at night.

If you must be in the company of an ingrate, go out around noon, when the sun is high, making the shadow a little shorter and smaller than it would be near sunrise and sunset. You don't want these figures to take over.

You may want to carry around a shadow catcher, a device that will keep them under control.

If friends have called you a whiny bitch, your shadow might be making you an extremely unpopular figure.

If you sense your shadow taking over, make a shadow of a hook with your finger to yank them by the neck and keep them in their place. Let them know you can whoop their ass if they don't behave.

The Insecure

aka: the self-conscious, the self-doubter, the unconfident

Yesterday, your friend Flora got a big raise and a promotion at work for a project well done. She seems to be the picture of confidence, until you get her alone during lunch. While picking at her Caesar salad, she proceeds to tell you her fear that she isn't as smart as everybody thinks, and her supervisor is going to find out and call her a fraud and demote her, and she'll be publicly humiliated and forced to do a chicken dance in front of the staff. You don't understand where all this is coming from. She's always been successful, yet the way she's talking now makes it sound like she never graduated from potty training. Flora is a highly insecure person who needs a lot of reassurance that she is okay.

The insecure is an individual that lacks confidence in their own ability, believing themselves to be worthy of onion peels when they are worthy of gold stickers.

When insecurity strikes, a person can be plagued by so many self critical thoughts that it requires a yelling session of aggressive compliments, like "you are fuckin' wonderful," and "your wit can light up this hellhole," before the insecure realizes how stupid their fears are.

Insecurity is a more pervasive problem among women than men, probably due to the pressure women feel to look like Sports Illustrated models, while men can look like iguanas and still be paired with hot babes in movies and ads.

Insecurity can be a temporary phase when a person is given a new task or must deal with a big challenge. For example, it would suck to be the boyfriend of a woman whose ex constantly shows up in cologne ads wherever they go.

And then there is the chronically insecure person who needs constant reassurance and hand holding to move forward. After a while, you end up wanting to give them a big fat bill for your time.

CAUSE:

Insecure people lack a good strong foundation from which to hold their head high, free from self doubt. From an early age, they discovered they were very different from everyone else. Unlike other children that had a firm stance on the earth beneath them, insecure kids had detachable renegade feet that tried like hell to escape from them. A child with such unusual anatomy is highly prone to insecure behavior.

Where other children had shoes to put on, insecure kids had trouble putting on shoes over their rebellious feet. Their feet didn't always stay on when the kid ran and jumped, and in fact, seemed to have personal preferences for other places than with their owner: the dog park, the ice cream shop, or a gaming store.

When the child lost their footing and their balance, their face often met a cement floor. If someone never knows when their face is going to slam down on a hard surface, it can make them feel very unsure about themselves.

A child's renegade feet would also cause tension between them and their parents. If dad said to little Cindy, "Time for a nap," but little Cindy wanted to go play on the slide, her feet would run off on their own—sans owner—to the nearest playground, while the rest of Cindy had to somehow crawl to her bedroom. Her father would be steaming mad at her runaway parts, chasing after them with a large net in tow.

Of course, Cindy would get scolded for disobeying, but she had no control over those heels with their own agenda. Those feet would rather be out having fun jumping on a trampoline or roller skating in the park than stuck indoors on a sunny day.

The lack of a solid foundation and of a body's betrayal is always in the back of an insecure person's mind, causing uncertainty for those who constantly have to second guess various aspects of themselves.

RECOMMENDATIONS:

Foot binding, that centuries-old tradition before it was outlawed in China, might have been an early attempt to reign in renegade feet, but it was done in such a shoddy manner that it became a form of punishment by mangling the foot instead. Better to strap those lowly extremities with some good duct tape and sturdy waist high boots.

The feet need to be rewarded on a regular basis by the hands which should work to massage the feet to keep them interested in staying with the owner. The more the feet stay with an insecure person's body, the more secure that person will eventually feel.

Self doubts will disappear as the owner learns to trust their feet to give them support when they need it.

Once feet have the incentive to stay, they will stay for good as the years roll on, when the feet must face other problematic issues—bunions, warts, and fungus.

Having a good foundation leads to greater confidence and self-assurance, the perfect remedy for an insecure person.

The Insensitive

aka: the coldhearted, the crass, the hard-boiled, the hardhearted, the heartless, the stony, the thick-skinned, the uncaring, the unfeeling

Shireen's beloved aunt was hit by a cauliflower truck and now she's in the emergency room undergoing critical surgery. Unfortunately, Shireen is the only one available to work the cash register at the Chunks R Us Butcher Shop. She asks her boss if she could leave early go see her aunt in the hospital, but he says "no" with a firm face. He tells her if she leaves, she can kiss her job goodbye, because he is an insensitive prick who cares for no one and nothing except his own meaty profits.

The nemesis of a hypersensitive is an insensitive jerk that says and does things without regard for another person's feelings or situation. Think Joffrey Lannister (*Game of Thrones*) as headmaster of an orphanage.

An insensitive can also be considered a person with damaged nerve endings who has lost the ability to feel physical sensations, but who gives a fuck about that?

It is easy to blurt putridly harsh words at a time that calls for delicate phrasing. This is quite true for people who haven't gone through many of life's trials. However, with experience comes wisdom and the expectation from others that you'll have the intelligence to speak in a way that doesn't make somebody want to step on your toes with combat boots.

When there is a need to be sensitive, there are usually clues that only a meth addict would miss—signs such as tears, depression, anxiety that a person in distress openly displays.

A person who misses the obvious not only needs to get their ears and eyes checked but deserves the penalty of a tattoo with the words, "I am an uncaring asshole."

Ironically, insensitive people can sometimes be the biggest wusses when it comes to their own pain, bawling like babies when stabbed by life's sharp daggers.

However, there are a few insensitives who are able to buck up and take the emotional blows without flinching. These people have emotional walls of steel and may be psychopaths.

For most of us, however, an insensitive is not who we want in our presence when tragedy strikes. We want to lick our bleeding wounds, not have someone stab a fork in it.

CAUSE:

One cannot help but pity the poor insensitive. How they became so is due to the neglect they underwent as a child. These hardened souls didn't get swaddled in nice warm cotton blankets with sweet sounding coos and "ahhhs." No warm cuddles and nose nuzzles by a devoted parent. Instead what they got was a babysitter that was really an upside down mop in a dress. Such a sad neglected child grows up to be a cold-hearted adult.

These unloved tots repeat what they know and what they know is a stringy haired, unresponsive hard wooden pole with a glued on face of a pretty woman—a figure who neglected their cries for love and attention.

It is not surprising that these abandoned children would become as stiff as the caretaker who watched over them. The babysitter's face would be unchanging, forever frozen to the moment their picture was taken.

When a real person did show up, the contact was brief. The baby would get a quick smile and maybe a pat on the head but left the child wanting. Not enough time would be spent with the wee one to help them learn the different types of expressions on a face and what it means.

When the child was scared and sad, no one came along to play "this little piggy" finger games and peek-a-boo. It is a lonely start that begets an icy person in the end, a person who fails to recognize the emotional needs of others.

RECOMMENDATIONS:

The insensitive person may not realize they have a problem, until they get cussed out and lose friends. After a hailstorm of insults, the insensitive may come to realize they need to change their behavior.

One way to heal such a thickly-walled person is to educate them in the meaning of facial expressions. Videos of people in various troubled states can help show the range of human emotions available. With each expression, show the insensitive the proper response to that emotion. For example, for a person in grief, show the insensitive the proper body language to adopt and the right words to say. Tell them that certain actions, in the way of hugs or a willingness to listen or an offer of an ice cream bar and so forth, would be appropriate things to do for someone who is in despair.

In rare cases, an insensitive may be hopeless and for that, there's not much that can be done. It is best to surround that basket case with mops positioned upside down, for these are the right companions for an unfeeling type. (See *The Antisocial* for other possible origins and treatments.)

The Irresponsible

aka: the flighty, the harebrained, the reckless, the thoughtless, the undependable, the unreliable, the untrustworthy, the useless

Jeremy needs to leave town in an emergency, but he has one big problem; there's no one to help take care of his dog Munchy while he's gone. The kennels are all full, and he's got a plane to catch soon. As he ponders his options, he remembers hearing an acquaintance mention something about needing a place to crash for a few weeks. He locates this person immediately, a woman named Marsha who is a friend of a friend. Marsha eagerly agrees to feed Munchy and take him out on walks. Jeremy leaves the key under his plant outside and heads out feeling relieved that his dog will be cared for. Two weeks later, when Jeremy returns home, he finds 20 strangers in his home guzzling beer and puking on his front steps. Munchy is nowhere to be seen. Angrily, Jeremy boots everyone out the door and tries to find out where his dog is. Marsha gets bent out of shape that her party ended so abruptly. Jeremy is worried sick that his beloved pooch is dead somewhere, and he is pissed to be left with a pile of shit to clean up. He never should have trusted Marsha with his place.

An irresponsible person is one who cannot be relied on to resolve matters as if they had any common sense or to show up when they are supposed to (see *The Flaker*) or to take care of tasks and duties without seeming as if they were Mr. Potato Head or to recognize when they screwed up in a big way. In other words, irresponsible people are as useful as a paper cut.

Some people are naturally more responsible than others. Highly motivated individuals who exceed expectations make you feel like you're in good hands when they are in charge. But an ambulance driver who detours to an In-N-Out-Burger for a basket of animal fries in the middle of you bleeding out in the back wouldn't make you feel so good. Yes, animal fries are delicious and they are covered in a creamy mayo sauce with melted cheese. You've got a point.

Children, lacking maturity and experience, are expected to be worthless while adults, having to cough up money for rent, bills, and food, are expected to act as if they have a functioning brain. However, things don't always work as expected. In a messed up world, children can sometimes be more responsible than their idiot parents. This is a shame.

Irresponsible people are flakers, but flakers aren't necessarily irresponsible; many flakers can hop to it once they arrive. Not the irresponsible.

Undependable people irk those who aren't. In a work situation, these poor performers—to the relief of other employees—usually get terminated quickly, unless they are screwing the boss.

If the crappy worker is screwing the boss, then they are screwing everyone else over too. Eventually, the lame-o worker's picture will get a moustache drawn on it and it will then grace every employee's home dartboard.

CAUSE:

If you think irresponsible people are uncaring asses, you would be highly mistaken. They only appear to be lousy, thoughtless, immature buttheads but in reality, are highly intuitive souls who possess some type of psychometric talent; they can feel the history of an object or an article of clothing in contact with their skin and this is what drives their irresponsible behavior.

Some item an irresponsible person is regularly in contact with, for example, a piece of secondhand clothing, jewelry, a recycled smartphone, or a coin, was once possessed by a person or a number of people who went through some great injustice or wrong.

The irresponsible person feels overwhelmed by the previous owner's troubles but doesn't understand why or where those feelings come from. The person in possession of the item, if highly sensitive, cannot cope with the emotional pain they feel, so they end up shirking their responsibilities.

Take, for example, the common quarter in a pocket. If that quarter came from a cashier who previously received it from a depressed bloke made homeless by a she-devil wife who squandered their life savings and dumped him for a Ferrari salesman, then that homeless man's feelings of anguish is a residue left on that quarter.

The sensitive person who receives that quarter becomes haunted by some faint indistinguishable feeling of someone getting fucked over somehow. This causes the possessor of the quarter to feel really bad.

Given a choice between having to do something unpleasant—adding to the burden they already feel from contact with the sad object—or doing something that makes them feel a whole lot better, the irresponsible person goes for the option that is much more fun.

The more enjoyable activity counters the negative juju from touching the haunted object. Playing Guitar Hero all day, for example, is a whole lot better than going to a crappy job getting yelled at by angry customers. Running off with a hot stripper is a lot more appealing than coming home to screaming kids with measles. Leaving a tumor-filled cat out on the street is a lot less painful than paying for surgery.

If you were burdened by some terrible unnamed sense of wrong and despair, you would do everything possible to make yourself feel happy again, and what could make you feel better than to be carefree, skipping down the street doing whatever the hell you want. If that means dumping your kid at the local Walmart, so be it.

RECOMMENDATIONS:

If you are dealing with an irresponsible person, suggest a vacation where they can strip down in public without getting any jail time.

Unless you plan to have a discussion in a hot tub or a nudist beach, you are stuck dealing with these individuals until they are rid of the offending object—a challenging endeavor if the irresponsible person happens to love secondhand shops and antique jewelry.

If you've been accused of irresponsible behavior, throw your clothes to the wind. Stand naked with nothing but sunbeams caressing your skin and a gentle breeze kissing your ears.

If within five minutes, you have the sudden urge to pay a bunch of past due bills, you'll know a tainted object is the problem. You may need to reintroduce each item to your skin to find the culprit.

The Jealous / Envious
aka: the covetous, the possessive

Jolene gives a big hug to her brother Nathan who just arrived in town for an accordion convention. As they walk to a nearby diner, Peter (Jolene's new boyfriend) comes running up behind. He takes them by surprise. "What the hell Jolene? Who the fuck are you?!" he screams, visibly upset. He puts his fists up in the air. When Nathan and Jolene are too stunned to answer, Peter throws the first punch. Luckily, Nathan is a kung fu black belt with quick reflexes. In three moves, he has Peter down on the ground. Jolene snaps to. In an angry voice, she introduces him to her brother. Peter calms down and apologizes. He even puts on a friendly demeanor. "Nice to meet you, bro!" he says, as if nothing out of the ordinary just happened. Jolene shakes her head. This is definitely a red flag for her.

A person can be "green with envy," but what about the other nasty sibling, jealousy? The two are often confused with one another due to the crazies both of these gremlins can evoke. Sometimes they can be found as companion emotions. The jealous person is stricken by the fear of losing a poor sucker trapped in a relationship with them, while the envious person greedily covets the goodies someone else has.

Both emotions can drive a sane person into doing very insane acts with very sharp things.

Jealousy is a toxic emotion and if you've got a lover who likes to share their pleasure parts with random people, it's natural to want to throw raw chicken gizzards over their head and glue a tracking device to their neck, but the chronically jealous is another story.

The extremely jealous person, with no obvious reason to be, must monitor every movement, friendship, text, and phone call of their loved one's life, worried that if they let their guard down, their BF or GF will jet off with the next set of genitals walking down the street.

Envy doesn't usually drive a person to do crazy things, unless the envy involves something that is entirely within reach and can be gotten without detection. However, envy can sometimes make a person loony when they desperately want someone they can't have.

Generally speaking, jealousy tends to trigger bad behavior more frequently than envy; people seem to be more motivated to act when fearing loss than for want of gain.

For example, Dave may desire neighbor Tyler's fancy racing bike, but Dave is probably not going to go through the hassle of dressing as a ninja and donning infra-red glasses to break into Tyler's garage for the expensive two-wheeler in the middle of the night. Unless Dave is mental. If he is, all bets are off.

But if Tyler keeps flirting with Dave's booty call, the desire for Dave's fist to meet Tyler's face can be fairly strong and Dave might actually complete the act if Tyler doesn't stop acting like an ass. Dave freaks over the thought of losing something so valuable to him.

The poor unhappy sport who gets possessed by jealousy or envy is one you don't want to get on the wrong side of, because when they are in the blood rage state, they're just as nasty as a thirsty vampire let loose in a hospital ward. There will be casualties.

CAUSE:

The chronically jealous or envious person has a difficult issue nearly impossible to resolve—distorted vision due to the way their brain processes images seen through the cornea with reflected light. Basically, they can't see their own reflection clearly and instead, see a big warthog when they look in the mirror, causing them to fear being alone stuck with their own frightening company, which drives them to behave crazy when they find someone to latch onto.

When someone sees themselves as a hideous wild porker with horns, it can be a frightening sight. In reality, the jealous/envious type does not resemble a wild pig at all and should not be afraid of themselves. It is only their fragmented self-perception.

When some wonderful new person comes into their life, the jealous person forgets about their own appearance and has a whole other person to fixate on. With their new love interest, they find relief in the form of sex, laughter, joy, and so on, which they cannot do in solitude.

The fear of their own presence drives the jealous person's cloying and possessive behavior; they are terrified of losing their personal savior. The jealous person's inner struggle is a sad personal statement of self fear, a terrible curse to be stricken with.

In the case of the envious person, their visual perception is a bit less distorted and they resemble less of a warthog than perhaps a cute little piglet.

Instead of complete self terror, they are instead, dissatisfied with one or more aspects of their porcine appearance. They may wish for a smaller cute nose, smaller ears, longer eyelashes, and an oval face but aren't quite as motivated to act—generally speaking—as a jealous person. That is, unless that envious person really can't stand their life and becomes consumed with wanting something that can improve their situation immensely.

For those dealing with momentary bouts of jealousy or envy, temporary visual distortions can also be caused by alcohol, killer weed, expired food, and LSD.

Once the mind altering substance clears out of the system, the person regains visual clarity and can see themselves without distortion again.

However, the chronically jealous/envious should stay away from all mind-altering substances; their hallucinations can become more severe, turning their warthog reflection into a demonic one with cockroach eyes, flaming horns, and melted lips.

RECOMMENDATIONS:

If you have a chronically jealous or envious person in your life, remove all mirrors and reflective material from the home.

On vacations, avoid trips to lakes and any bodies of water. Don't let the jealous person drink plain water, for they will catch an image of themselves on the side of the glass or in the water's reflection.

It can be a full-time job to keep a jealous or envious person under control.

Healing is possible only under the guidance of a therapist (one who doesn't wear glasses) who can help these jealous/envious people look at their own image without fright. In time, the visually challenged person can learn to feel good about the person staring back at them in the mirror.

In the event you are unable to remove a heavy mirror, make sure there are no sharp objects in the room in case the jealous type tries to kill its image in the mirror.

With time, it is hoped that a medical cure will be found that can help these passionate souls see themselves clearly again.

The Judge

aka: the moralist, the preachy, the sanctimonious, the self-righteous

On your arm, you sport a tat of a large fire breathing dragon. It took eight hours to needle that image into your tender skin, but it was worth it. You proudly display that body art on your upper arm, thinking you're too cool for this tedious world. You're traipsing about minding your own business when you encounter a Brady Bunch type family. They're obviously tourists. The father stares at you with disapproving looks. He pulls his teenage daughter close to him, in case you sprout a tail and start molesting her. You're stunned by their reaction. You want them to know you have a PhD in physics and you make gobs of cash and have all sorts of fancy credentials after your name, but that tat on your arm marks you as a fiend by judgmental types who don't know better.

No one likes to have their life summarily dismissed by outward appearances, but try telling that to a judge. The judge is a person who makes instant conclusions about another person's life, deciding someone might be a tool, a snake, a sleazeball, a wackjob, or some other negative character based on superficial evidence or circumstances, for example, judging someone with a green goatie on their chin or a portrait of Ozzie on their chest to be a miscreant.

There are many types of judges out there. There is the judge in the legal system who has practiced years of law and spend their days presiding over court cases and slamming down a gavel to shut everyone up, but that's not the type of judge referred to here.

Certain guns are also referred to as "Judges" that mete out justice the old fashion way—gunning someone down. Not talking about that either.

The type of judge referenced here is the person at work, an acquaintance, a person you have just met, or a relative who thinks the actions you take and the choices you've made are the result of you having the intelligence of polluted seaweed.

The judge may or may not verbalize their thoughts, but you definitely feel their moral eyes on you.

Like the critic, a judge can have strong opinions. But a critic is more apt to focus on a particular subject they disagree with; they don't think you are necessarily pond scum as a result of it. Not so with the judge. You are definitely the scummiest pond with a bunch of mosquito larvae.

If you have any good qualities, they're not notable enough to warrant you a pass as a human being. You might as well crawl back into the hole from whence you came. That's how the judge sees it.

No one is perfect, but the judge forgets this. Judges believe their lives are above scrutiny and feel free to cast the first metaphorical nail-studded two by four in your direction. That's not very polite.

On occasion, however, you may meet the judge who has the opposite opinion, one who believes or is fooled into believing you are a better person than the stinker you really are. In that situation, most would enjoy being judged, but how often does that really happen?

CAUSE:

As anybody on the receiving end of a judge's verbal disdain knows, much finger wagging is involved when a judge delivers a platitude. Those waving that finger in the air right under your nose are prone to acting self-righteous because of a distal intelligence embedded at the tip of an index finger—the second brain.

The second brain, called the "little boss," is not a fully functioning brain but rather a partially functioning one that was invariably separated from the big boss in the skull.

For men, there is also a third brain but that one does no thinking, often gets the owner into a shitload of trouble and resides with the second head down yonder.

The secondary brain, generated from a migratory or misdirected neural stem cell, is what causes the finger to go airborne into a back and forth motion when a judge decides to verbally express how you should behave. The slow wagging or wave of the finger is the little brain working hard to keep others at a distance.

The secondary brain lacks a hard reservoir—a skull—to safely contain and cushion the little boss and is quite cramped being near a bone.

In fact, the little brain does not like it when the finger does activities as high impact as volleyball and clapping.

During these high impact moments, the little brain gets rattled around into agitation.

The big brain doesn't necessarily understand why, but it is engaged in a battle with itself as the two brains struggle to control the finger's movements.

The little boss, even though less complete by comparison to the big brain, is smart enough to know self-preservation. It knows that it must engage the big brain in some way to lessen the physical impact on the finger. This is where judgment comes into play.

When the eyes initially sees someone who it deems as unpleasant, unappealing, fear inducing, appalling, or kinda stupid, the index finger is quick to perk up, sending strong distress signals to the main brain, knocking out potential reason and analysis to force the main brain into snap judgments so the body and main brain can be engaged in negative opinions. This results in aversion behavior, namely distancing the self from the judged person by creating a psychological barrier.

The finger knows not to stimulate the pleasure or happy centers of the main brain, which would induce touching of others and celebratory gestures. Think high fives, clinking mugs of beer in the air, or clapping—all of which impacts the brainy index finger.

Judgment separates people, resulting in boring times, sparing the index finger of trauma. The little boss is quite smart.

RECOMMENDATIONS:

If you are judged by a judger type and receive a lecture on your vices, you might want to bite the air with an audible clack, loud enough to scare the judge's brainy index finger into submission. The fear of being bitten off would stop the judger's moral evaluation, displacing judgment with surprise and fear.

If you find yourself easily dismissing others without many valid reasons, you may be a judge unconsciously controlled by your index finger.

You can test yourself by seeing how you feel when you wave that finger in the air. If that act makes you feel morally superior with the sudden urge to scrutinize and sneer at the people around you, then Mr. or Mrs. Finger is behind the wheel.

In order to prevent your finger from isolating you into a life of solitude and moral disgust, consider wearing doll-sized finger pillows to comfort that little mind in your digit.

The other option is amputation, a drastic measure, but a necessary step if the little finger gets too devious to control.

But first, try dipping your fingers into a bowl of valerian tea, sedating the little boss into an agreeable mood.

Amputation is the very last resort and only after a lifetime of battles, with the approval of a professional therapist and a surgeon.

The Killer

aka: the black widow, the homicidal maniac, the mass murderer, the martyr, the serial killer

Natalya gets a text from her husband while she's in the middle of getting her eyebrows dyed, a text that shocks her to no end. His message reveals that the downstairs tenant, the quiet one who keeps his curtains closed and burns frankincense every day, is actually the mullet murderer, a person wanted by the police for gunning mullet heads in cold blood, then brutally cutting off their offending hair and leaving behind the chilling note, "Mullet heads do not belong in the 21st century." Natalya can't believe her eyes. A killer has been living right beneath them this the whole time. She's so thankful her husband is bald.

To slaughter, shoot, or destroy another individual until there's no longer a pulse is numero uno in the bad behavior department, but for the killer type, whose answer to life's problems is to obliterate anyone that gets in their way, killing is how they deal with problems. In turn, this makes the victim's family and friends want to burn the killer's face off with a hundred steaming Hot Pockets.

Killing differs from manslaughter; manslaughter is the unintentional killing of a person, as is the case of car accidents or dog attacks. Killing is quite intentional and premeditated, sometimes with a hired hit man found through Craigslist or through word of mouth.

This baddie is universally maligned with good reason—there are no take backs, no way to repair the damage done. You can't apologize or say "Oops, my bad, sorry bro" and expect things to be copacetic. It doesn't work that way.

A killer kills for a number of reasons. A common one is during a jealous rage—that's called a crime of passion—when someone finds their significant other in bed doing the nasty with someone else and shoots them both on the spot.

Then there is killing for profit, the slaughter of a group of people who protest the destruction of their land, water, and resources by a bunch of greedy bastards who want to cash in on valuable metals, minerals, oils, or gasses in the area.

There is also the dispassionate killer who kills to get what they need or desire—that's the psychopath (see *The Psychopath*).

There's the mass killer who deals with their mommy issues by taking it out on others.

Then there are those who kill for sport; hunters who pay large sums of money to shoot an endangered animal minding its own business gnawing on the ribs of some zebra, harming no one, sitting in the sunshine enjoying a nice day.

Sometimes, killing happens in self-defense.

In most cases, with the exception of accidents and self-defense, killing is inexcusable, unless it is the act of killing pests: cockroaches, mosquitoes, flies, and slugs.

Most people don't like killers and wouldn't want them over for a game of hoops, because they are scary SOBs.

Strangely, over time, the word "killer" has accumulated other meanings and uses that are associated with positive attributes. For example, someone who says "that's a killer beer" does not mean it literally—that the beer is laced with arsenic—but is expressing their high recommendation for that beer.

To avoid confusion, it is best not to use "kill" in a positive or encouraging way.

CAUSE:

Environmentalists warn of food shortages beyond our imagination, as grain prices have soared in many countries causing food riots. So what does a race doomed to destruction do if it has a chance? It tries to change the course of history if possible. Not surprisingly, the increase in killing overall along with the increase of mass murders done by mentally deranged people and religious zealots globally can be blamed on time travelers from the year 2522 coming back to a pivotal point in Earth's history to cull the population.

Historically, people have killed for a variety of reasons, almost all of them involving religion, politics, food, greed, passion, and power. Yeah yeah, killing still happens for all those reasons. Not much has changed in modern times, except for the increase in mass murder during the worst time in Earth's history (most people and worst pollution ever), unless you count the time a big meteorite obliterated the earth.

Murder, in general, has gone up as resources dwindle and numerous animal species starve to death.

Depressing isn't it. Makes you want to have a strychnine cocktail. I don't advise it. Strychnine tastes really really shitty. Not that I know what shit tastes like, it's only a guess.

Time travelers from the future implant crazy thoughts into various men—the easiest candidate for mind control—to fulfill the mission of preserving earth's precious resources by helping us kill each other off. Think of robot wars, but replace the robot with a wacko who can purchase a semi-automatic rifle on a coffee break. Think also of the lunatics that command bands of maniacs to kill others at random.

Doing so lowers the number of breeders from producing children who will beget more children exponentially.

These time travelers are motivated by self-preservation, coming from a period when there is mass famine, disease, pollution, and advanced electronic gadgets, like the talking iron and the airborne desk chair, to distract from hunger. They blame the idiocy of past generations for their hardship.

As preservers of the human race, they come back with the sole purpose of saving the future from destruction, having learned how to reverse time by traveling faster than the speed of light in vehicles invented by hybrid human/AI machines.

During this pivotal period of bizarre weather patterns, species die-offs, and crop shortages, these time travelers will up the ante, generating more killers in our midst.

So the next time you read about a deranged terrorist blowing a business up, know that these insane people have been made so by the guardians of the future and don't let it make you despise the human race, leading you down a road of despair and hatred.

RECOMMENDATIONS:

If you value living and plan to contribute something useful to the planet, than be on alert in public places where a deranged person with a weapon might be hanging around—in malls, theaters, skating rinks, and so forth.

If you are a breeder who pollutes the earth to no end and beats up little children and tortures animals, you may want to spend more time in public places wearing brightly colored clothes and tall hats.

If you wish to stop these time travelers from conducting their mission, keep an eye out for individuals wearing clothes that can do what we think of as impossible, like deflect bullets and serve as a mattress when needed.

These time travelers come from a future when technology is so advanced a person can watch a movie while showering and cooking at the same time. So however despondent you might be over the senseless violence you read or hear about, remember there are guardians here controlling some of the people around us.

The Killjoy

aka: the fuddy duddy, the party pooper, the spoilsport, the stick in the mud, the wet blanket

Miranda can't wait to get home to watch the game with her buddies. It's Super Bowl time! She's got the pizza, chips, and salsa waiting on the table. The doorbell rings. She opens the door. Patty stands before her with a case of brewskies, Linda's got the peach pie. Game on! Miranda slams down her first refreshing can of beer. Ahhh. Suddenly, the power goes out. The big screen shuts down. What the hell? Jason, her spiritual roommate comes storming in. "I told you no parties when I'm meditating. You can't be making all this noise!" he snaps. "Super Bowl only happens once a year. Can't you please meditate somewhere else today?" Miranda asks. "You know the rules," he retorts. "Take it elsewhere!" She and the other gals reluctantly gather up their things. She doesn't have a choice. He can kick her out if he wants. Grrr. Jason is a killjoy whose quest for spiritual enlightenment makes her want to shove patchouli oil up his nose.

A wonderfully scented flower can suddenly smell like a puddle of diarrhea in the company of one of these fun folks. A killjoy is a person who seems to resent other people's enjoyment and throws a chainsaw into an otherwise grand time by acting sour, complaining, sabotaging a fun situation, or bumming everyone out by being around.

On your happiest of days, when you're getting praise for that big promotion or Jennifer Lawrence's twin walks into your life, a killjoy can find a loose thread somewhere in your narrative and yank on it, unraveling your enthusiasm right before your eyes.

Suddenly, that promotion seems like a giant spiked chain around your neck and that soulmate just grew a pair of testicles on her forehead. Your zest for life is suddenly gone.

At first glance, the killjoy may seem the same as the downer, but they really aren't. Pessimists truly see the world through a lens of doom whereas killjoys seem to take all the fun out of life.

Killjoys aren't appreciated for obvious reasons. Killjoys tend to be repeat offenders and are easy to identify, making it easy to steer clear of these party killers.

CAUSE:

The killjoy's seemingly fun murdering behavior isn't based on malice, but is due to how their ears perceive sound. They suffer from audiomosis, a condition that translates the joyful sounds of laughter, bird calls, sing-a-longs, and other pleasant things into shrill sounding, sharp pinpricks against their auditory nerve.

Music involving higher chords, stringed instruments, bells, and other joyful tones sound the same as wailing fire trucks to a killjoy.

However, deep bass tones, slow droning hums, mournful sighs and the like, offer some bearable and even pleasant relief for the compromised individual.

The condition is somewhat rare—1 in 10,000 suffers from this disease. It is unclear whether the condition is hereditary, caused by trauma, or a bacterial infection.

The person with audiomosis, as a coping mechanism, learns to adapt as best they can as there is currently no cure for this illness. They do so by discouraging the possibility of a situation that can generate laughter or exclamations.

Seemingly negative, the audiomosic person does not really wish to cause misery or destroy your fun but are motivated by self-preservation, a need to prevent extreme nerve pain.

They don't want to be in the company of revelers. That's why they'll discourage you from having a birthday bash and bemoan the misery of an outdoor concert. Asking them to see a performance of harpists is the same as asking if they wouldn't mind having firecrackers lit inside their ear.

Audiomosis can be a source of vulnerability for individuals who would rather be considered a killjoy than be at the mercy of anyone with a good stereo system and a boisterous laugh. They may not want to admit the real reason behind their stick in the mud attitude.

RECOMMENDATIONS:

The discouraging words from a killjoy's mouth are really attempts to prevent ear-splitting pain. Do not take their cranky words personally. It's not about you.

You can prevent them from ruining your enthusiasm by feigning a heavy sigh of disappointment and casting your eyes downward.

Warn them that a party will soon take place but denigrate your joyous occasion with unkind words. Tell them you expect guests to cry all night and possibly commit hara-kiri. Beat them to the punch. Gently warn them that soon, some samba music is on its way, but you know it will be a real bummer and someone will probably break their leg. Give them an out by saying it will be a real shitty time and the killjoy isn't obligated to come.

This way, the killjoy gets to keep their vulnerability secret and you've prevented the seemingly resentful person from spoiling your fun.

Your melancholy demeanor shows that you share the same sentiments as the killjoy and are only putting up with the party out of obligation, but you'd really rather be in a dark room thinking deeply on world hunger.

The Know-It-All

aka: the smart alec, the smartass, the smarty pants, the wise ass, the wise guy

variation: the condescending

Chauncey is headed to a big family reunion tonight. He's looking forward to seeing everyone except for one person, Cousin Percy. Percy grates on everyone's nerves, because the words "I don't know" is not a sentence he can say. He has an answer to everything and sometimes Chauncey wonders if Percy makes things up to sound smart. Chauncey decides to do a test. He reads up on the blobfish so he can introduce an unusual topic to test whether Percy really knows it all or is really full of shit.

The know-it-all is a person who is an expert on every topic conceivable and needs to make sure everyone in the room knows he or she has a higher IQ than a coat rack.

Sometimes, a smart person can be perceived as a know-it-all in the company of people who are insecure about their intelligence, are less knowledgeable in a subject matter, or have spent the last decade alone in a cave somewhere in a remote part of Montana. But a know-it-all can also be an egomaniac who adores the sound of their own voice and believes they have mastered every known subject in the universe.

Know-it-alls may be able to deduce how many jellybeans are in a 16 ounce jar and may be great at trivia or at accumulating facts, but may lack the common sense to do something as simple as give advice to a buddy whose fiancée insists he gets his dick pierced or she will dump him. In other words, they may know a lot of shit, but don't know shit about things that truly matter.

There are situations when know-it-alls are easy to spot. When a person feels it necessary to correct the grammar of a dying person's last words, that's usually a big clue that an obnoxious smarty pants is in the room.

CAUSE:

This tiresome behavior is due to encyclophalitis, a swelling of the brain due to information overload from reading too much of an encyclopedia or too many Wikipedia pages at one sitting.

That big organ inside the skull is a huge energy hog. When learning new material, about 10–16% of the human brain actively fires up, sends signals down axons and across synapses to help the mind function. Or something along those lines.

Meantime, the other approximately 84–90 percent of the brain is busy automating bodily functions without us knowing it. Imagine that a Lilliputian is living inside your head calling the shots.

We could not have the billions of cells in our brains firing all at once or we might spontaneously combust.

Think of a picnic with only 100 hotdogs and 100 guests, just enough for one hotdog per person if they sit around and guzzle beer for two hours.

But then, 20 of them decide to go off and play ultimate Frisbee. After some hours, those Frisbee players return to the table and they're going to be very hungry and vicious if they don't get at least two or three hotdogs in them soon. If they hurry up and eat, they may have the stamina for another game.

Some of those sitting guests, wanting the Frisbee players to shut up, anonymously give up a hot dog to the hungry players. The players don't necessarily know who generously gave their juicy dog up, but they don't need to know, as long as they're fed enough to quit whining and get back to the field.

Of course, if someone wishes to get off their lazy ass and go get more wieners, the problem would be solved, but that requires leaving the fun for an hour and who wants to do that? And what does this have to do with the brain firing signals? Nothing. Hotdogs just sound really good right now.

In the case of encyclophalitis, more than 16 percent of the brain is sending electrical impulses at one time causing a person to rattle off all kinds of details, because it is in the forefront of their mind from a cramming session of material they've read sometime in the past.

For instance, you mention something about moustache wax. Those two words will trigger a synaptic connection in the know-it-all's brain, and they will automatically start regurgitating everything they know about the subject, which is plenty if they've done any reading on it. Moustache wax might very well be an interesting topic, but may fall kind of flat after an hour.

In very rare cases, when a person has too much going on in their head, strange things are known to happen. A person might start singing in Pig Latin or their brain synapses could affect radar signals overhead. They might even become a temporary radio tower or be able to cast their voice from another room.

However, this is not an equal opportunity affliction. It only affects those who have an obsession with gathering facts and trivia.

RECOMMENDATIONS:

A person with this condition will have a strong urge to discuss the composition of sea foam and offer lengthy pros and cons on the use of paper clips, so if you enjoy learning new things and aren't a great conversationalist, a know-it-all might be a good companion for you.

Otherwise, know-it-alls can be stopped with the help of chickens. Chickens, with their incessant clucking creates an audible disturbance that will make the know-it-all wonder why the hell you would want that kind of racket in the background.

You can try to be direct and tell smarty pants they are a nuisance, but it is not going to be heard in a positive way. Nor will that drive them to change their behavior.

But chickens, they can do what no human can. They can make a know-it-all puzzled and confused, momentarily stopping the know-it-all's lecture.

If you can't get a hold of chickens easily or don't want the mess, you can play a recording of chickens in the background.

You can also pose abstract questions to a know-it-all where there are no definitive answers. For example, *What does it mean to wear a green turtleneck* and *Do fruit flies prefer mangoes over oranges?* These types of questions are a good exercise for the know-it-all; it helps them enter the realm of abstract thinking. If this fails, blasting loud music can quash all discussion.

The Liar

aka: the dishonest, the exaggerator, the fibber, the tale teller, the truth bender

You wait at a cafe keeping an eye on the door, waiting patiently for the woman of your dreams to walk in. You met her online in an ad that screamed perfection. She was everything you hoped for, a beauty of rare treasure, a comedic personality, a lover of outdoor sports, and best of all, she enjoys driving an ATV on the weekends. So it is with great surprise when in through the door comes an extraterrestrial of the hideous kind, with platinum rods for hair and three fish eyes equally spaced across its forehead. This highly unusual customer scans the room for someone, and that someone turns out to be you! Someone lied in their personal ad when they said they were born in California!

The truth is out there somewhere but probably not on the lips of a prolific liar. The liar is a person whose words should never be trusted, because what comes out of their mouth is mostly bad sewage.

Whether it's over small stuff—the shoe size they wear—to really big doozies, like the eight kids they don't have waiting at home, liars hope what they say might impress, perhaps enough to get them special handling from that eye candy who wouldn't normally look their way.

There's probably not a person alive who hasn't told a teeny lie in some form or another. Only saints and dull people are immune. Once the truth is out the reality is never as good as the made up story.

There are many types of liars. Most do so for personal gain, but some lie because they don't have a handle on the truth and some enjoy reinventing reality.

Sometimes, lies are told to protect a person's feelings—a rather noble reason to fib if one must. If retired Uncle Charlie knew his family really thought his passion for painting on poodles was weird, it would do him no good to give up his one enjoyable pastime.

There's also the compulsive liar who regularly tells lies because they are compelled to do so, motivated by a desire to appear more impressive than the loser they really are. This type of liar is easy to nail, because they don't really remember anything about that private jet they said they owned two weeks back.

There are also amateur liars who blush, blunder, and stumble through false words, who lie because their head would be chewed off and put on a pole if they spoke the truth.

There are professional liars who do so for financial gain. They are gifted with the ability to make up credible scenarios and possess good memories in order to tell more lies to keep the ruse going. Liars of this kind are one of the nastiest. Their lie becomes obvious once they've cashed out and an investor is left penniless. Unfortunately, the punishment for this type of lie never equals the loss and doesn't satisfy as much as having the liar's eyeballs eaten out by crows.

Lying is not generally recommended for most people, unless you're in a hostage situation or forced to eat something disgusting your in-laws lovingly cooked for dinner.

CAUSE:

The moon is a powerful luminary in the night sky capable of influencing behavior on Earth. When she shines bright, everything is illuminated and you can't get away with things so easily. But when she's eclipsed or waning, it gets harder to see and that includes the honest to God truth.

In some metaphysical circles, people believe the moon's phase can make us behave differently than we would at other times, that she can bring out the prince or the pig in all of us.

The moon is popularly credited with affecting certain things: the tides, blood pressure, cardiovascular systems, madness, and werewolves. But what about honesty?

When the moon is full, people are known to go crazy committing acts that make no sense. That's because the truth is easier to see, because we can perceive ourselves and others more clearly. When this happens, reality can hit us like a punch in the goiter and make us go berserk. Suddenly, we realize that a fence post gets more action than us, that we're flat broke and always will be and no one really likes us, because we kind of suck.

In many religions the moon is associated with a female deity, and as we all know, women rule with an iron fist. When she's bright and strong, she makes sure you are on the up and up.

When the moon's light is weak such as during an eclipse or as a sliver in the night sky, that's when people go heavy with the lies.

In darkness, we can delude ourselves with greater ease. We can reinvent reality and tell ourselves things we and others want to hear, things, such as "I'm not married, we can hook up if you want," or "I have a disease only a blow job can cure," or "I crashed my Lamborghini yesterday but I'm getting a new one next week." When the moon's light is weak, it's similar to how kids sneak cookies from the jar when mom is out of the room.

During her presence, even into the daylight hours, she has a strong influence on whether we are likely to fib or not. This is true especially for overcast days and during wintertime.

However, when a person is outside on a hot sunny day, this can affect size of a lie and the numbers of lies told. The sun makes a person happier and when happier, less lies get told. When the sun is too strong, it makes a person so sweaty and miserable that thinking becomes difficult and lies are not as forthcoming; lying does require some effort.

RECOMMENDATIONS:

If someone you know tells you a blatant lie and you want them to stop, wait until the moon is strong, when it is full before having a conversation. However, be careful if you suspect your friend to be a werewolf as your life might become endangered, making conversation damn near impossible.

With compulsive liars, you are dealing with multiple issues beyond the moon's luminous strength, including malevolent elves and sewer monsters that may be out for a bit of fun and games, prodding people to behave poorly.

Happy, content, and satisfied people are less apt to lie than the miserable flop that can't stand themselves.

During an invisible moon, you might want to hang around people who smile a great deal and exude a strong pink aura. Stay away from the unhappy lot who seem desperate to escape their sucky lives.

If you must have an interaction with a suspected liar, bring a very bright lamp into the room and tack up a poster of a full moon behind you. A lamp and a picture are poor substitutes, but it's worth a try.

The Litigious

aka: the ambulance chaser

Anya bites into a taco and cries "ouch." Apparently, her thumb got caught in her molars, having slipped into her mouth at the moment her jaw clamped down on the edge of her crispy hard-shelled bean taco. Now she's suing the restaurant where she bought the taco. It turns out, the guacamole, being smooth and creamy, was the offending agent that caused her thumb to slip into her hungry mouth and now someone must pay for her pain.

Litigious people are folks who make up or exaggerate harm from an incident for which they use as the basis to sue the pants off of an individual or a business for shitloads of money. Wendy's anyone?

These cantankerous cretins are experts at squeezing money out of unusual situations and are very imaginative. Sometimes, they come at you when you least expect it.

Once a litigious person has entered your world, watch out! That tootsie roll you put in your mouth can be viewed as sexual harassment in front of the litigious person across the street. That unibrow on your face might cause a litigious person emotional, psychological, and physical distress that has to be remedied with a $25,000 check.

If you are a victim of one of these nasty sorts, you are in for a fight. Litigious people are experts at legal filings, having had sexual relations with dozens of loose law books in their day. They know how to work the system. Finding ways to make you pay feels as good as foot massages for these quarrelsome people.

CAUSE:

As children, many of these individuals were taunted as weaklings by bigger, more muscular students in school; schoolyard meanies are really to blame for creating a future monster by grabbing the young victim, flipping them upside down, and shaking them by the ankles until all the candy and change flew out of the poor kid's pockets.

Being helplessly strung upside down gives a child a skewed perspective on humanity. Blood pools to the head causing great discomfort alongside public humiliation amongst their peers.

After five minutes, dizziness, nausea, anger, and frustration can result. If this torment occurred on a regular basis, the victimized child can become bitter and angry.

As the child grows older, a sense of righteous indignation can develop, fueling the desire to make other people pay for their childhood pain.

This bad attitude is reinforced when no adults or other students come to the aid of the victimized child and there is no relief from the constant bullying and torture.

This leads the young impressionable child to harbor great resentment towards others overall, and especially those resembling their former bullies in physical appearance, height, voice, or name. Unable to match the brawn of others in society, the litigious learned to hit others in the pocketbook whenever possible.

Vengeance is the motive behind each of these lawsuits, with defendants acting as the unwitting surrogates of all the past tormentors in the litigious person's past. If this contentious type doesn't ever receive the emotional help they need, the extent to which they will destroy others knows no limits.

Not every child who is bullied turns into a soul-sucking dick, but for the litigious person, financial payback becomes sweet revenge.

RECOMMENDATIONS:

To cure the beast within the litigious person's soul is a very difficult task. It requires the person to revisit the ugly past, back to the students who taunted and robbed the person of a happy childhood, and to forgive the small little assholes for their mean behavior.

Children do not know what they do. Asking the litigious person to willingly go back to that ugly past is a bit like asking a chicken if it wouldn't mind volunteering itself into a pan of hot oil. It requires the litigious person to admit they have a problem and to seek help. It also means losing a good source of income for them.

This vengeful person views all others as hostile beings so working with people is out of the question, while going to court and suing the pants off a neighbor is much easier and gives them a great deal of time to play badminton and eat donuts.

You can only hope that a litigious person will change or have some type of emotional breakthrough. Sometimes it helps if you talk to them through a ventriloquist dummy so that you can entertain them, putting them in a better mood than they would normally be. Or it might make them afraid of you, thinking you're going to stab them in the spleen when they aren't looking.

It's a hard call. Unless you can get them to have a change of heart, you will see them in court.

The Loudmouth

aka: the hollerer, the obnoxious, the screamer, the shouter, the yeller

"Them penis pumps work great! You should try it! It'll help your erectile dysfunction!" says Bubba in an overly loud voice. Eyes glare in your direction. You wish Bubba would shut the hell up but no such luck. "Could you keep your voice down?" you ask impatiently. You should have left Bubba at home, because he is a loudmouth and should not be at a memorial service when unable to speak in a whisper.

There is no such thing as an "indoor voice" to a loudmouth, a person who speaks at high volume without discretion about anything. They must tell you about the time they had a cup's worth of mucus lodged in the back of their throat and how thick and green it was when they finally coughed it out, while you're trying to enjoy your key lime pie.

The loudmouth embellishes stories with disturbing details at the worst possible times. During your work party, they need to tell you how they wrapped a string around their wiener and found they could bounce it like a yoyo. And they must holler, as if their stories were onstage performances for all those around to hear.

Loudmouths can be found in public places—restaurants, subways, libraries, grocery stores, just about anywhere where there are people. No subject is off limits. And they shout their words.

Once these yellers get in your space, you won't have a choice. They want you to know how much they hate Italian food while in an Italian restaurant. If you try to speak over them, they will get even louder.

CAUSE:

Speaking in a loud voice on any topic is a symptom of a bizarre and unexplainable phenomenon specific to loudmouths everywhere—these folks simply do not have a reflection. When loudmouths look into the mirror, they aren't there. No outline, no face, no semi-transparent flesh. Nothing. They don't exist in mirrors, or bodies of water, or glass.

It's a mystery that confounds even the greatest of minds among us. For this reason, loudmouths become uncertain about their existence. Are they real, do they count? As a compensatory measure, they try to assert their presence by letting all those around them know that yes, indeed, they do fucking exist, whether they have a reflection or not.

Loudmouths speak at high volume on attention grabbing subjects to negate their feelings of invisibility. When a voice booms across the room, a street, a hallway with obnoxious, or gross, or inappropriate statements, heads turn in the loudmouth's direction.

For this shouty type, attention serves as evidence of their being. When no heads turn their way anymore, this is cause for anxiety. When asked to lower their voice, they comply for a few seconds but automatically revert to their previous ear-splitting level.

It is only when the loudmouth is engaged in illegal or clandestine activities that they speak in softer tones. Fear of imprisonment can override their feelings of nonexistence. In fact, anything that may diminish their presence in society will influence their conversation style. They strive to be noticed, not to be locked away into obscurity.

RECOMMENDATIONS:

Although loudmouths cannot see themselves in a mirror, they are nonetheless real. If you are in the presence of a loudmouth, getting that person to quiet down will be as difficult as having sex in a tree.

Loudmouths need you to look in their direction, so oblige them by glancing their way but then leave. If enough people leave in their presence, they may get the hint. If you are a real looker, watching you run away might act as a deterrent for them, one that creates a fear greater than their current need for attention—becoming a babe repellent.

Remember, these folks want to matter. They need your eyeballs turned towards them to feel meaningful and alive, but they also need to be retrained to lower their voice after their presence has been acknowledged. Merely asking won't do. Habits are difficult to break and require diversion in order to change.

That is why a loudmouth, when in the midst of an embarrassing rant or statement, must be diverted to another task—dancing! Start things off by doing the whip/nae nae, or the bossa nova, or hip hop.

Dancing is a great segue way towards fulfilling a loudmouth's desire for attention. If it turns out that the loudmouth can really bust a move, they learn to spread joy instead of irritation, unless they dance at inappropriate times, like in a public bathroom, during a police stop, or while kissing.

The Manipulator

*aka: the conniver, the cunning,
the guilt tripper, the persuader, the schemer*

variation: the briber

Belinda wants a pair of big knockers and some extra fat snipped off her stomach, but she doesn't have the money for the procedures. If she could convince her in-laws to pay for it, then she could be on her way to a killer bikini bod. The trick is how to get those old farts to part with their cash when all they talk about is how expensive their meds are. She could badger her wimpy husband Willy into convincing his parents to sell their house and start renting instead. That way, they'd be cash rich and couldn't possibly refuse her when she hits them up. While she's at it, they could cough up some bucks for her son's braces too. They're ancient. Why should they have money sittin' around when it could be used to improve her life? She's got a half a century more of living to do. She gets to work right away on Willy, hounding him until he does what she wants.

The manipulator is a person who uses all sorts of tactics to get what they want, be that through crying or hiring a big guy with no neck to come "chat" with you in order to secure an outcome that would otherwise be different in the natural course of events.

Manipulators tend not to speak their mind in an open way, but nevertheless are experts at getting what they want. The cunning ones will make you believe you want what they want too, sort of like being told how calming it feels to get your head scalped.

Having a master strategist around is great if their job is to fool people into making you richer, but in everyday life, will eventually put you at a disadvantage when you find your nose pushed against the floor beneath a manipulator's foot.

Your life savings will somehow end up in the schemer's Porsche fund and you might end up stuck one evening with the earwax eating sister of the manipulator's hot date.

Not all forms of manipulation are for personal gain but the majority tends to be. Times when someone intervenes for the benefit of another include giving a good job reference for a friend known to disappear every hour for bong hits or arranging a blind date between two unsuspecting people who refuse to be set up.

There are different kinds of manipulation based on the schemer's special talent. The manipulator might be a master of guilt. Another might be great at implying things without committing to words, and yet another might be great at persuading some Hell's Angels to help you make a decision you're unsure about.

No matter the intention, the end result is something different than the natural outcome and that's not always a bad thing, except when it is bad thing.

CAUSE:

Can innocent playtime with little Shrek dolls and Lego mini-figures turn a sweet youngster into the conniving sort? Definitely! Defenseless dolls—imaginative personifications of real people—are at the complete mercy of a childish, immature mind that controls what the doll wears, eats, says, and how it interacts with other dolls. The practice of controlling a doll's entire life brings out the manipulative tendencies in a kid, coaching some children to unwittingly become future manipulators.

Excessive doll play shapes the way a developing child thinks, perceives, and approaches the world. When left alone, a child can make dolls do unnatural things that it would otherwise not do.

A Fiona doll might be forced to tell Barbie she's not invited to a birthday party unless Barbie punches Rebecca doll in the face. Optimus Prime may be forced to play footsies with Megatron. And Spiderman may be forced to do the most unspeakable thing a Marvel character would never do—marry Bitty Baby!

If real life stinks, if the child's parents scream at each other daily, then that kid may use their dolls as substitute parents and make them cooperate. This gives the child a sense of control over a shitty situation as a way to deal with an unpleasant home life.

Fast forward to the future when that child becomes an adult caught in a situation not to their liking, they revert back to their infantile state by mentally displacing real people with their childhood playthings, which gives them license to control and manipulate a situation into a more desirable outcome.

For example, in a manipulator's subconscious mind, their lousy boss becomes Lego Zombie Pirate, who can be influenced to change a negative performance review with the help of Lego Marge, who is really the friend at work with a penchant for wearing tight blouses and showing lots of cleavage.

RECOMMENDATIONS:

Doll play should be monitored and limited with frequent interruptions to the child's play time if the youngster is caught fabricating impossible scenarios that force the dolls to behave unnaturally.

It may serve the child and the parent better if the kid was given science lectures and language development games to help them earn better grades and have a possibly brighter future.

If the child insists on playing with dolls, then perhaps giving bars of soap carved as figurines would be a better way to go. Only allow them to play with these dolls while taking a bath, limiting how much time they get to play make believe with the figures.

The soap dolls will quickly disappear in a matter of days, helping the child release any emotional attachment or memory of them. This curbs any manipulative tendencies a child may have as they do not get to practice and develop any doll controlling behavior long term.

The Miser

aka: the bean counter, the cheapskate, the greedy, the penny-pincher, the skinflint, the tightwad

Furrank, your sweet little terrier of 10 years is going to die unless he gets emergency surgery for the removal of a tumor in his stomach. The veterinarian tells you the tumor is caught early enough to save little Furrank's life. He could live another four years with the surgery, but it must happen within the next two weeks or it will be too late. All you need is four grand to pay for the operation, which you do not have sitting around in your back pocket. You approach your rich Aunt Fanny. You hope she loves you enough to lend you the money. She knows how much your little friend means to you. You ask her for a loan. You promise to set up a payment plan, but she turns you down 30 seconds into your story, letting you know quite frankly that "money should not be spent frivolously and that you need to learn the value of every dollar." In other words, your dog will be going to doggie heaven, because Aunt Franny is a tightwad.

The miser is a person who hoards money—loath to spend a cent of it—and would rather eat a pair of stinky old loafers than to spend a cent on a good cheese hoagie.

    A miser may or may not be financially well off, but will dress in a shirt with tatters, holes, and grime, preferring to look like they've been sleeping on a dirt road all their life rather than the rich bastard they might be.

    Denial of pleasure, of comforts, even of sustenance to the point of self harm is not unusual. Alongside their penny-pinching ways, they can also possess an unpleasant personality and seem very grumpy.

    The most famous miser of all was Ebenezer Scrooge from the Charles Dickens novel, "A Christmas Carol." Rumor had it that Dickens based his main character on a real miser he read about who lived three or more decades before his time.

    Miserliness is not the same as poverty-based frugalness. To be a miser of the unflattering kind requires an unequal balance between saving money and maintaining a pulse. It also means refusing to help little Sally get that needed tonsil operation when there is enough to pay for a million Botox injections and some friendly escorts.

Misers have little or no compassion for others and are generally detested or ridiculed by others.

If there is a miser in your world and you get the rare invitation for dinner over at their house, make sure you eat a meal before you go or you may starve from their meager offerings.

CAUSE:

These penny-pinching souls purport to behave prudently with their piles of cash in order to support themselves in old age. For some of the milder cases of miserliness, that may be true. But for the hardcore misers, practical matters aren't the only motivating force. There may be a much greater underlying problem at play; misers may not want anyone to discover they were born with a monkey's butt.

There are strange medical conditions that have no known origin. Being born with a monkey's butt is one of them. A greater than expected number of people are born with an apelike back section and doctors do not know why. But what is certain is that people who are born with this unusual derriere exhibit aversion behavior, with miserliness being top among them.

When someone is a miser, their cheapness and frugality deters friendship, love, and sex.

People who are generous are loved by those who enjoy grand dinners, great presents, and jolly good moods generated by the giving soul. But the miser has few friends, because friendships can grow deep, increasing the possibility of clothes being removed at some point, as in the case of friends with benefits, or friends becoming comfortable enough to change their clothes in front of each other, or friends inviting each other to a nudist retreat or to an outdoor pool party where everyone expects you to bare some skin. In short, too much pressure to reveal personal anatomy.

Friends also introduce you to more people who may want to become friends in the future. When more people like you, the odds increase of meeting people who want to sex you up. That would be most humiliating for a person with an unsightly butt.

Misers are always on guard, must constantly self deny and wear cheap uncomfortable clothes. They must remain in a state of perpetual hunger so they can stay grouchy, lest they become intoxicated with happiness and spread joy to others.

When someone is joyful, they become more attractive. Being more attractive would put the miser in the uncomfortable position of fending off potential sex partners.

Misers must ensure they never become too wonderful in anyone's company, including family members, as family members have friends who may want to "do" the miser based on glowing remarks.

RECOMMENDATIONS:

If you are a miser, it is perfectly understandable why you would want to keep the persona of a miserable shit. As there are no cures for your condition, you are much too vulnerable to unkind individuals who may taunt, humiliate, or extort money from you.

Do not give up on love and sex. There are billions of people in this world. It is entirely possible to cast a net far and wide for someone who has a monkey butt fetish whom you can trust.

There is also the possibility of companionship through online dating. No need to be an island of isolation. Instead you can meet someone on an isolated island that you will never meet in person, someone that you can share good tales and a relationship with from a laptop or a small device. Virtual sex can be had without any nudity whatsoever.

If you know of a miser, don't judge them too harshly. If you were born with a monkey's butt, you too would act the part of a miser or possibly worse. You would do whatever is necessary to avoid nudity at any price.

Unless some medical breakthrough occurs whereby stem cells can be used to subvert chimp genes and allow for a new human butt to take hold, the miser will maintain their cheap ways in order to keep you away. Be thankful you don't suffer from the same problem and let them live in peace.

The Moody

aka: the erratic, the mercurial, the testy, the touchy, the unbalanced

You are in the cheeriest of moods this morning, but your girlfriend is not. In fact, she asked you not to speak to her, to look at her, or belch and fart this morning, because she's in one of those moods. You know to leave her alone when that happens. It was good enough that you had an evening out when she was happy, the side you call happy Hilary. But this morning it's mad Hilary and you know to keep your mouth shut and your head down. When mad Hilary is around, she might cut your balls right off.

A moody person is one whose emotions can change quite suddenly, sometimes without a triggering event, causing that person to behave inconsistently from day to day or hour to hour and sometimes from minute to minute. A person can go from "I love you so much I can't stand it" to "Did I say you had permission to breathe near me!" The mood swings can be quite severe and extreme, causing absolute befuddlement for those around.

If you should be so unlucky as to befriend or love one, hats off for your patience. I hope you have access to great drugs. If you enjoy the element of surprise, then this Jekyll and Hyde type might be the right basket case for you.

Even though a moody person's emotions change constantly the mood swings tend to be weighted on the glum, nasty side rather than the joyful or peppy one, making the company of a moody person as fun as a biopsy during a vacation.

People don't seem to complain about happiness, but they do whine about misery. Mood swings can happen to anybody, life is full of ebbs and flow. Shit happens and we react, but the moody person needs no real external trigger. They can switch moods on their very own, usually in the "I want to eat your face off" direction, making all those who must be in the presence of a moody person want to mow them down with a Go-Kart.

Moody people control the emotional atmosphere, whether they realize it or not. Some take medication for this condition and many more should be left in a dark forest. Psychiatrists blame these inconsistent moods on mental disorders, but the truth is much more straightforward.

CAUSE:

Moodiness is due to erratic internal thermoregulation influenced from eating hot, spicy foods and/or cold wet ones. Those prone to moodiness have an abnormal internal thermometer that swings wildly between hot and cold—friendliness and bitchiness—based on the temperature and spiciness of the grub they eat.

The temperature range of a normal adult is 97.8–99 degrees Fahrenheit (36.5–37.2 degrees Celsius). Not so with moody people. This person's emotions can change quickly based on what they had for lunch that day. Their temperatures can range between 85–110 degrees! Crazy.

If their menu included a Serrano pepper, you'll get an energized upbeat person full of zest and life, but if they had a cold pickled herring, you'll get the acidic person who is mean as an alligator on speed.

If you are a moody person, are involved with a moody person, or know of one, I feel your pain. Understand that this behavior is due to an anomaly in a person's physiological makeup.

Some in the psychological field attribute this behavior to certain chemicals in the brain needing modulation via pharmaceutical drugs. Drugs do help moody folks dial down their crazy side. But the real culprit, make no mistake, is that ice coffee they put in their mouth.

RECOMMENDATIONS:

A moody person may want to avoid bitter, cold, wet foods, such as beer or chilled bitter melon. Drinking and eating foods of this kind will create a highly caustic meany who will insult you at great length.

Sweets can make a moody person nicer, so keeping some ripe bananas and room temperature butterscotch pudding in a backpack can help save an afternoon.

For a big party, eating some spicy curry lentils can make for a festive personality.

Bland foods can tame the beast into a more cooperative spirit.

If you want to help the moody person, keep them in check by suggesting restaurants with healthy food that is moderate in temperature and flavor. If not, you may have a hard time keeping company with a moody's highs and lows.

The Nag

aka: the demanding, the fussy, the particular, the persnickety, the repetitious

Betty crawls on all fours on the bathroom floor trying to find every piece of hair that might have fallen off her head while she toweled off from her shower. After 10 minutes, she has examined each corner and underneath the sink in case a wayward strand got stuck there without her knowledge. If her roommate finds even one, she'll have a panic attack and nag her for the next 15 minutes to pick up after her disgusting mess. Betty has never lived with anyone so particular before and wonders if her housemate suffered through some type of hair torture in the past.

The nag is an individual who repeats a request, complaint, suggestion, or criticism over and over again until the person on the receiving end has turned into an impenetrable wall and wants desperately to silence the nagger with a taser.

Nagging is a behavior that can be witnessed in many homes and is considered a negative thing. However, the label of "nagger" is only applied when the requestor and the recipient have differing opinions on the value of the request.

For example, a mother directs her son to "clean up his room." If the son ignores her instruction, she will repeat her directive multiple times and will not stop until he does what she requests. However, cleaning his room is not a top priority for the son. He views her request as hounding and an infringement of his free will, a negative interaction he considers as nagging. As a result, he will ignore her or call her a four letter word starting with "c" or will clean up his room to shut her up.

The mother, on the other hand, has no interest in cleaning up after her son's lazy ass and his continued disobedience suggests to her that he is one or more of the following: disrespectful, hard of hearing, secretly sniffing glue, or born with a meatball for a brain. Her ongoing commands are attempts to penetrate the kid's thick skull until he finally does something to earn his keep.

This bad behavior has historically been associated with the female gender, some would say unfairly so. In mainstream media and pop culture, boys and men are often spoofed as harangued by their mothers, wives, girlfriends, and grandmothers.

Females are never seen as harassed by males to clean up their act, unless the females are drug addicts, runaways, or hookers, and the males plan to save them instead of pimping them out. Pimps don't ever save anyone.

In reality, nagging can come from anyone, though more likely to come from females due to men's simplicity; men are easily satisfied by sex and do not really care if you're a chainsmoker who eats fried Snickers wrapped in bacon with Jack Daniels for breakfast.

When males are nagged, they can become doltish in behavior and take on the persona of mud bricks. In turn, this increases the ire of the nagger, which increases the amount of nagging. It's a lose-lose proposition for all.

Females that are nagged tend to respond more positively and quickly, unless the female is young. Being young while nagged, regardless of gender, generally does not result in a positive ending.

CAUSE:

The cause of nagging is due to the childhood trauma of being raised in a household where dog and cat feces were strewn all over the place along with pet fur and dander, causing respiratory distress in young family members.

In a house where animal care is neglected, dogs and cats are left to relieve themselves wherever they can—in sofas, beds, pajamas, kitchen chairs, salad bowls, shoes, roasting pans, keyboards—all attempts to capture an owner's attention.

If an animal could speak in words, they would be screaming, "Hey asshole, get me outside! I have load to dump!" But as they can only communicate in their respective pet language, their barks, meows, howls become white noise to a busy, distracted master.

Adults may be able to handle the malodor, but not the poor children in the environs. Girls and boys, being closer to the ground, become fully saturated in the ammonia and fecal smell of their pets. It makes them sick. Their clothes reek and so does their hair and skin. Then they go to school.

Anyone who has ever attended a school knows children can be hellions whose purpose on Earth is to destroy a weaker child's self-esteem. They can taunt, torture, and terrorize. The shitty smelling kid becomes the target of fists, insults, kick me signs, and other horrors. This creates a cycle of fear and trauma.

As the foul-smelling child grows into adulthood the past is not far behind. Any evidence of filth triggers unresolved anger towards their parents. Seeing a dirty floor, for example, may generate memory of being kicked to the ground by a bunch of redneck ruffians. The nagger will not only become fearful, but will also become furious if the person who made a mess doesn't have the common sense to clean up after themselves.

RECOMMENDATIONS:

Cleanliness does wonders for the soul and spirit. Keeping a clean house will keep nagging at bay, unless the nagger's behavior becomes so ingrained they must nag about something to feel sane. In that case, more extreme solutions are necessary.

The nagging should be recorded and played back to the nagger as a way to help them become self-aware. With headphones on, have the nagger listen to themselves over and over again until they understand the full effects of their words.

After that time, the nagger is more apt to be in a suggestible frame of mind. That is when a strong dose of marijuana would help soothe the nagger into a more relaxed state.

Smoking a bowl of strong stuff, then listening to sedate music while looking at a picture of the offending item—a picture of overflowing garbage, a dirty litter box, or a pile of moldy dishes in a sink—will help the demanding person accept what they previously found horrifying.

The Name Dropper

aka: the fame-whore

variations: the status seeker, the social climber

Ken stops by your place unannounced one night as you get ready to stream in Orange is the New Black. He recently moved back from his summer job in Beverly Hills, and you aren't sure if you're up for his company; he always tries to impress you with something you usually aren't impressed by. You ask him the dreaded question of how his summer was. After five hours, you're ready to stuff a hand towel in his mouth, because he won't stop talking about the praise he got for his sideburns from a certain famous Twilight star who invited him to a party where he met some of the cast members from Big Bang Theory, and how it changed his life forever. He tells you about the jokes he shared, the drinks he had, the contacts he made, the toilet paper brands used. The more disinterested you are, the more he repeats himself with new details. You sigh.

A name dropper is a person who seems to believe their worth is elevated by insinuating a relationship between them and a famous person, in an effort to impress the pants off someone else.

Merely recounting an unusual or unexpected encounter with a famous person is not generally considered as name dropping, but falsely insinuating a chummy status with Paris Hilton would be.

Renowned folk tend to be immune from name dropping; their elevated status gives them access to people most ordinary folk don't have. Scarlett Johannson, for example, could probably score a lunch date with Google co-founder Sergey Brin in an hour. Your neighbor with the quail farm in her backyard probably can't.

When a listener is impressed, that makes the name dropper feel bigger and better. Sometimes, a listener is so impressed that they will drop their undergarments in front of the name dropper and give permission to access high security areas.

Name dropping can be more effective at bars and parties where no one knows who they really are, giving them the benefit of a gullible, unsuspecting, drunkenly receptive audience.

However, name dropping can also backfire, making the name dropper look as pitiful as a wet cat—the very opposite of their intentions.

CAUSE:

Name dropping, unlike the other bad behaviors discussed here, isn't so much caused by a triggering factor but more a desire to gain something. That something is perfectly understandable—a larger boner for men and bigger balloons for women.

For most people, when they feel confident and important, they stand taller and keep their head held high. But for the select few with unusual growth hormones, they not only stand taller but have a measurable physiological change in their body.

For dudes, their proud willies actually grow longer and for women, their breasts grow more voluminous as if bursting with milk.

For both, the change is approximately one-eighteenth of a centimeter for every hour of name dropping. Although it may not show, the person with the newly added bulk can sense a difference.

In popular culture, a man's junk and a woman's tits are presumed better when bigger. Or at least that's what it seems whenever you see a movie, print ad, or commercial. Big dicks and giant tits seem to get lots of attention from rich hunks and gorgeous babes. If a person doesn't currently have a big dick or ginormous tits—or think they don't have enough—they believe they are "less than" in some way.

But the idealized figure can be had for those with a special genetic gift allowing them to literally grow their flesh to a desired length or volume. All they have to do is to associate with famous people and then brag about it.

Doing so helps the phallus and mammary glands spontaneously spurt new growth based on the sudden burst of happiness and confidence that a name dropper gains from receiving attention and popularity. For this reason, name droppers tend to do so continuously and for many years until they have reached a satisfactory size.

In time, the changes become quite obvious and for the name dropper, quite rewarding.

RECOMMENDATIONS:

If you are on the receiving end of a name dropper's efforts, know you would be doing the name dropper a great favor by feigning admiration. The more you are willing to give the speaker attention, the more you are helping them on their way to a more sizable dick or tits.

If you are a name dropper, know that not everyone will enjoy your desperate desire to impress. However, your motivation is understandable. The best way to ensure decent growth of your protected parts is by name dropping to a number of people you won't ever see again. Do not continually name drop to the same person or boredom may result. Name dropping to strangers is preferable.

You may also try to name drop on people's pets, the ones who are responsive and give you assurance of your likeability with a lick on the face after you have given them a little name dropping story. This won't work on your own pet, because you know the admiration given by your pet is based on their need to get a good meal out of you and doesn't have the novelty factor. You will have a better chance of success on animals you don't know well.

Eventually, after your penis or breasts grow to a satisfactory size, you should stop name dropping, as there is no need to get greedy. You don't want to end up with such giant appendages that they end up dragging on the floor and stepped on. It ain't a pretty sight and will cause a whole lotta lower back pain.

The Napoleon

aka: the mini meanie, the short person syndrome

First day on the job. You meet your new co-workers. Everyone is really nice except for one person—that short guy Nicholas in payroll. He let you know right off the bat where you stand next to him. You may be taller, but you better not cross him or your paycheck will be all messed up. He didn't say this to you exactly. Instead he cracked loud insinuating jokes and insulted your shirt. Throughout the day, your concentration broke whenever Nicholas walked by. For a small man, he had an elephant's presence with his big stomps and booming voice throughout the office. Where does it all come from you wonder.

Like a Chihuahua who believes he is an alpha dog and has no problem protecting his territory from bigger beasts, the Napoleon is a person who suffers from the Napoleon Complex. This means a person of shorter than average height with a greater than average need to be rude, obnoxious, and mean.

The Napoleon complex is named after Emperor Napoléon Bonaparte of France. He was short, but he was a mean little fucker and led wars as a military leader.

The majority of short people tend to be similar to more elongated individuals, except for their keen awareness of being at a greater disadvantage whenever someone over six feet tall looms over them.

They tend not to provoke fights and generally behave like one of your good neighbors. They aren't stupid. They clearly have survival instincts to help preserve their own safety.

However, there are a minority of height-deprived individuals who behave as badly as twenty-foot ogres. You may have met them, the below eye level, overconfident, noisy jerk that is ruder than a chained Rottweiler taunted by a pan of roast turkey five feet away.

Surprisingly, this horrendous behavior has enabled some of these individuals to rise among the rank and file into higher positions of authority where they can exercise bad behavior at will. The Napoleon type can intimidate much larger individuals, able to whip fear into the hearts of giants with softer natures.

After a childhood of being overlooked, many petite people have learned to compensate for their height disadvantage. They learn to make strong impressions by being smarter or wittier than others. They excel in some topic or master some skill. They wear bolder patterns and develop a sense of humor—all in an effort to be noticed, to be admired, to be respected. This type of short person has learned to maximize their potential, because they realize they must do more to stand out if they want to be noticed.

However, there are a few who have taken it several notches above their peers and have ventured into the territory of rude and vicious. They want it known they are not afraid of you and your long torso. Instead, you should be afraid of them. They'll let you know within the first half hour of meeting you that they have a bite, so you better watch it. If you doubt their sincerity or ask for their help, you will be screamed at.

CAUSE:

Being closer to the ground makes a person of short stature more vulnerable to creatures roaming below knee level and has caused enough trauma for them to now behave fiendishly.

Fear of being mounted by a beagle? Absolutely! Fear of being sniffed at? You bet! As friendly as beagles may be, they can seem like hellhounds by virtue of the close proximity between their jaws and a short person's genitals.

Similar to children who can also be fearful of small animals and large insects, short people are quite vulnerable to attack, but unlike children, their fear is much more embarrassing to admit. A grown adult caught trembling before a four-legged fur ball or a feathery fowl is not a person's best moment.

Even worse, if the short person should come across a child bully they may not be able to defeat, they would be forever humiliated.

Somewhere in the Napoleonic's life, they had a frightening encounter with some small creature or insect—a large centipede or a vicious guinea pig. This has left the person permanently scarred and fearful of what may happen if they are not on their game.

Being openly mean, obnoxious, and pushy gives courage to the Napoleonic type and keeps their confidence up. It serves to give the false impression to all in their path, large and small, that a tough mofo is in the neighborhood and should be given a wide berth.

Acting like a meth head does make some short people feel more in control and does, in fact, scare away animals and child bullies. Unfortunately, this adopted behavior becomes standard practice after a number of years and a Napoleon is born.

RECOMMENDATIONS:

In order to deal with a Napoleon in your midst you may have to raise your voice louder than you are comfortable with, gesticulate with big hand motions, and laugh heartily. This will surprise the Napoleon for they are used to being the expressive loud one.

They may react in any of the following: reduce their volume as your actions may act as a mirror and reveal how loud you both are; feel threatened by your oversized motions and loud voice; or out shout you to regain their superiority.

In any case, whatever they do, they are sure to tucker out faster than you—having smaller lungs—unless you have an artificial lung or are smaller than the Napoleon.

Another way to deal with such a difficult personality is to wear platform shoes whenever you are in their company. Your added height will make the Napoleonic type avoid your company and your interactions should be briefer as they don't relish standing next to someone that makes them look shrimpy by comparison. It also reminds them that no matter how mean and nasty they are, they cannot scream their way into a taller body.

The Narcissist

aka: the conceited, the egotist, the self-lover, the vain

Mark couldn't stop staring at him. He was incredibly handsome. Anyone would be lucky to be in his presence. It never ceased to amaze him whenever he happened upon his own reflection, how gorgeous he was. Deep down, he knew he would never meet someone equal to his beauty, his physique, nor his talent. It seemed a shame to settle, but it was inevitable if he wanted companionship, for no one was as magnificent of a specimen as he. Mark had been called a narcissist by former lovers, but he knew they were merely envious. He dropped them as soon as they started to criticize him.

A narcissist is a person who is highly vain, has an inflated sense of self-worth, and is so physically attracted to mirrors that they need to seriously get a room so the rest of us aren't so embarrassed when they and the mirror start going at it.

The word narcissist comes from Greek mythology in which a good looking dude named Narcissus, who saw his reflection in a pond, fell madly in love with himself. He loved his own reflection so much he couldn't tear himself away to go grab some bread and cheese or some goat milk and a mutton chop. Instead, he was stuck there gawking at his own beauty until he died of starvation. The Greek myth serves as the symbolic gist of a narcissist's behavior.

These individuals are sometimes blessed with some supernormal trait, which has been positively identified and complimented on for years and years. This constant reinforcement elevates that person's self-assessment until Godzilla has been created.

The obvious supernormal trait of a narcissist is physical appeal; these individuals can be blessed with pretty faces. However, where they may have an underserved bounty of beauty, they may lack in other areas, specifically, in the intelligence department. They are also takers, seldom givers.

When a person possesses a multitude of talent and skill along with physical beauty, that person is more vulnerable to becoming a giant ass.

If you happen to be blessed with great genes, don't be that guy or girl everyone wants to hate. Remember, looks fade with age. Big pecs and perky breasts will eventually sag down to your knees.

CAUSE:

The origin of this self-loving behavior is rooted in childhood when a toddler has been left alone with a mirror facing its crib for long hours, serving as their sole companion.

Being left in solitude as the child develops can lead the child to see their own reflection as the nurturer/parental figure who is always available to them, regardless of their drools, tantrums, and fits. Whether the child is crying, hungry, or laughing, there is a trusted figure keeping them company crying and laughing with them.

As a result, the youngster's own reflection becomes the figure the child learns to love and care for above all others. Instead of recognizing the image in the mirror as a duplicate of themselves and not an external physical person, the child allows the reflection to become the surrogate parent. (If the child doesn't receive any mental stimulation, they tend to become kind of dim.)

The child suspends their disbelief that they are utterly dumped and forgotten, left to fend for him or herself. Self-delusion becomes a necessary survival skill for emotional preservation. If the child is extremely attractive, an additional behavior can form—narcissism.

With a physically appealing child, the image reflected back is a pleasant one for them to keep company with. As the child grows, he or she bears witness to the pleasing changes happening within the mirrored image's body and face—they can't believe that killer bod they see really belongs to them.

When the child comes into contact with the physical world and finds few faces or bodies that can match their own pretty appearance, that child naturally prefers to look in the mirror rather than all the ugly mugs around them.

First crushes are to be expected as a child integrates with their peers. For the narcissist the first love happens to be with their own face as oppose to the first student who gives them a valentine. You never forget your first love and so it goes for the narcissist.

Most people move onward from their first infatuation to the next as they meet more people, but the narcissist child remains hot for the reflection staring back at them.

Because these self-loving folks view themselves as the greatest gift on Earth, narcissists tend to be insensitive and say hurtful things like, "It's okay if you die. I can replace you."

RECOMMENDATIONS:

A narcissist won't see their self love as an issue. It's everyone else's problem.

If you are the parent of a narcissist, for shame, you should have been around during your child's formative years. You got the nightmare you deserve.

If you have a friend, a roommate, a co-worker, or a lover who has this condition, you are in a tricky situation. Sticking with these inflated egos means you are always second best. In their company, mirrors will become your enemy and so will any reflective material. In other words, stay far away from glass, water, ponds, lakes, and so on.

You might try painting a replica of Alf or Uncle Fester onto the narcissist's face some afternoon when he or she is napping. That might make you feel better and they might enjoy scaring kids for a day. Or it might get you smacked with a can of corn. If you do embark on face painting, make sure no painkillers or hallucinogenic drugs of any kind are taken. You don't want to have a bad trip once the scary face is completed.

You could also try discussing mortality and aging to the narcissist to remind him or her of the fleeting nature of beauty; tell them their pretty face and body will eventually rot and decompose, eaten up by several thousand maggots living in their dead flesh.

But a reality check may be useless if the puffed up baboon is too far gone. If so, you must leave if you wish to retain some modicum of self-respect.

Any and all problems that exist will be blamed on you, the inferior loser; narcissists view themselves incapable of any wrongdoing. Moving on is sometimes the only solution.

The Passive Aggressive

aka: the brooder, the resenter

variations: the spiteful, the vengeful

Darrell comes home from a long day at work to find his beloved Fifi in the front yard wagging her tail with a target painted on her butt and a dead rat glued to her back. Horrified, he looks around to see who could have done such an atrocious act. Across the way he sees the neighbor staring—the one who's yard Fifi crapped on last weekend all over the dude's prized daffodils. Could he have done this, wonders Darrell. When he apologized for his pet's bad bathroom habits, the guy seemed okay and was pleasant enough. Darrell hadn't known what his little Fifi had done; he only learned of the incident a few days after when his next door neighbor told him how ballistic the guy across the street became. The way he's staring at Darrell now, though, makes him realize that daffodil king is a passive aggressive and should not be taken at his word.

A passive aggressive is an individual who avoids confrontation and when asked directly, will not admit that they are boiling over with the desire to skin alive the person guilty of a transgression but will instead, show their displeasure by doing covert things like putting dead rodents in a mailbox and secretly transferring the transgressor's mail into the garbage disposal.

The transgressor mistakenly believes they have been forgiven until a stray kitty paws at the mailbox revealing the deceased rats and the passive aggressive's anger.

What makes this behavior so difficult is that the transgressor must be gifted with extra sensory perception (ESP) in order to know the passive aggressive's real feelings.

Persistence doesn't always get the truth out either. It's when you get the unwarranted and unsolicited comment about your low intelligence and your dumb looking shirt that you know it is payback time for that last slice of pepperoni pizza you took from the fridge.

If you're lucky, you'll get the silent treatment, but if you're unlucky, you'll wake up with mice in your sheets.

CAUSE:

If you don't trust a passive aggressive type, you're in good company. Even a passive aggressive can't trust themselves. That's because passive aggressive behavior results from three different brains within a skull.

Yes, you read that right! "But that's impossible," you say. Medical doctors tell us we can only have one brain per person. That would be true if alien science weren't involved. We are not alone. People in high places—not the stoner kind—know this.

We are surrounded by extraterrestrials hovering above us. We have been and continue to be observed and tinkered with by these higher beings for thousands of years. We have served as lab animals for these curious galactic travelers and if you don't believe it, you haven't spent enough time watching YouTube videos of extraordinary people.

Due to alien intervention, we now have people who can run naked in freezing cold weather; men able to leap over high buildings; toddlers able to lift 200 pounds with their bare hands; and women who can see through walls.

These are the success stories of experiments gone right. But with every success story, there are many more that go wrong. Passive aggressives are one of the more disappointing lab results. They are the tri-brained offspring of experiments involving newlywed couples.

From an alien craft's vantage point, weddings are easy to spot on Earth if held outdoors. After many centuries of observation, aliens know how to find subjects based on certain activities, namely birthday parties and wedding celebrations.

They know that after a wedding party, there is a lot of sexing up between the newlyweds going at it all night long. (It's easy enough to follow a newly married couple via an alien aircraft—they are way faster than our slowmobiles and planes.) They also know that the groom is useless after shooting his load. If he isn't snoring after a few minutes, the aliens make sure he does so by using a special beam of concentrated sleep chemicals on him.

With sperm newly inside the female, the aliens know it is a race with time to access the most tenacious sperm before one reaches the prized ova. It is at this point, right when the man falls asleep that the female is beamed up to the aircraft and messed with.

Pushing the boundaries of human potential, aliens have been playing around with our reproductive systems—without our knowledge—for a long time. They have tried to create a smarter human by enlarging our brain capacity with stem cells from multiple individuals, male and female, to see if this makes a difference in our way of thinking and behaving in an effort to make a less irritable and more intelligent being.

Through the alien's intervention, they are able to grow three miniature brains simultaneously within the confines of an average sized human skull. Without the alien's large, watchful fluorescent pink eyes carefully monitoring and affecting the situation, the developing child would have a gigantic head too big for childbirth. Any mama would scream bloody murder during delivery and probably wouldn't survive.

Space aliens don't want that. And the newborn would break its neck holding such a heavy head. What would be the point? However, creating three mini-brains that developed together offered real evolutionary change.

These experiments resulted in children with three different personalities, one who might be amicable, another who might be a prick, and a third who loved head cheese. Depending on which brain is in control at the time, you may meet the friendly one while at another time, Mr. Dick comes out instead.

If *you* think it's hard to get a straight answer, imagine what life is like for this person. Internal struggles are a daily ritual between the different brains, each fighting for dominance. This is the reason why the passive aggressive can't seem to admit their true feelings; the amicable one is probably in control at the time of questioning and the mean one may show up later that day.

RECOMMENDATIONS:

It doesn't take many clues to spot a passive aggressive. You only need to experience it a few times to know what type of person you have on your hands. Confronting them on their issue may be tricky if you get the unfriendly personality.

The person must somehow remove or subvert the extraneous brains that are causing trouble for the person, but this is extremely difficult as the topic cannot be introduced when the baddie is around. They may not be aware of their problem if the three brains occupying the tight space of a skull don't realize they are separate entities in conflict with one another.

Talk your friend into getting an MRI to get medical proof. Acknowledgement is the first step to resolution.

If you have been accused of being passive aggressive but don't believe it, you may want to seek answers. Ask your parents what happened on their wedding night.

If your mother has any missing or unaccounted time, or the parents don't remember what should have been the most memorable night of their marriage, they might have been subjected to an alien science experiment.

You may want to set up an audio recorder to track your daily conversations with others. If the words coming from your mouth don't seem to make much sense on playback, you should seek the guidance of a neurosurgeon who can offer possible options.

The Pollyanna

aka: the happy-go-lucky, the optimist, the positive thinker
variation: the idealist

It's a bird. It's a plane. It's a piece of debris from a cargo aircraft landing on top of your roof giving your home that demolished look, while you were out getting your chest waxed. Your peppy friend comes to help you, but ends up annoying you when she says, "Look on the bright side, you wanted a new paint job, now you'll have to get one." You know she's right, but her chipper remark still makes you want to want to tell her off.

The name of this bad behavior sounds as fun as polka or polyamory, but Pollyannas aren't nearly as enjoyable as the other two, unless it's a pollyannish polyamorous person doing the polka. A Pollyanna is a cheerful person who is optimistic about every thing imaginable and can find the bright spot in a nuclear meltdown.

When a person is down in the dumps, they don't necessarily appreciate a chirpy upbeat voice telling them to think positive. Getting lost in the Serengeti with no shade, water, food, phone, and a ravenous lion on your tail will end badly, but a Pollyanna would say, "At least you'll get a nice tan!"

Sometimes, people need to soak in a large pool of sorrow and don't want to hear the words "smile, tomorrow is a new day." For some, there is no new day. There is only today, in a hospital, with nurse Ratchet by your side.

The Pollyanna makes for a great guest at a children's party or a wedding celebration—assuming no one was left at the altar.

Pollyannas aren't bad people. In fact, they are generally good people, amicable, with plenty of friends. Having these types around is quite helpful when you feel that the human race is fucked.

Depending on the type of person you are, these happy peeps can either make you feel more sunny or have the polarizing effect of making you gravitate towards doom.

A Pollyanna who is fun, or possesses a great personality, or is smart and generous is easier to tolerate than one who wears only a stupid grin.

CAUSE:

The Pollyanna's bright outlook is due to the great fortune of being in the right place at the right time to hear humpback whales sing in the ocean.

In the vast sea, giant beauties roam freely singing their songs to attract mates and to communicate with other whales in the area for foraging coordination.

The sounds the whales emit from their whale lips are truly wondrous for human ears. Anyone within range of a whale's song cannot help but be mesmerized by the mystical sounds vibrating around them. Whale songs are hypnotic, bringing immense joy and optimism to those lucky enough to hear them.

The sequence of notes and the voice of a whale accentuated by the fluid sound of water activates the human brain's left prefrontal cortex, stimulating electrical impulses in that area. The more that left prefrontal cortex is activated, the happier a person becomes.

Usually, it takes lots of money and a lot of massage oil to make a person smile. Drugs help too. They help a lot, but their effects are temporary. So does a Fudgsicle—for about 10 minutes.

A whale song, however, has the power of a lifetime battery. A whale song will permanently activate the happy centers of the brain for as long as the person lives, unless the person does something stupid, like snorting flakka.

If the Pollyanna lives a primarily clean and conscious life, they will continue to be happy as pup with a large cow bone, while the rest of us will feel shitty by comparison.

RECOMMENDATIONS:

It would seem cruel to end a Pollyanna's bright outlook, but for peaceful co-existence with normal people and curmudgeons, sometimes it is necessary. To help the Pollyanna come back to reality, it might be helpful to remind them of the bitterness of life by giving them a couple of raw olives to eat.

Olives are an extremely beneficial fruit and are most delicious when cured and processed, but in its raw state, taste the way you expect scorpion venom to taste.

Having a raw olive inside a mouth, one cannot help but curse while the taste buds suffer through the astringent foul bitterness of the small little fruit.

A Pollyanna will recognize the futility of seeking positive words and will, after chewing an olive or three, break down and admit some things in life are plain nasty and will grimace in the process of telling you so.

The Pollyanna can be reminded of this unpalatable experience each time they try to look at the bright side of things. This will snap the Pollyanna into a moment of reality, wiping away their delusional optimism and stupid grin for a few minutes, making the Pollyanna more bearable to be around.

A better solution overall is for the rest of society to go on safe and nonpolluting sea expeditions to catch whale songs themselves. The human race could use a very large dose of happiness and optimism.

Audio recordings do no justice to these great mammals; it doesn't offer the full benefits of their vocalizations while at sea with them, marveling at their size and beauty. It's the difference between listening to a taped song through a landline versus a live concert. There is no comparison.

If everyone became a Pollyanna, 75 percent of the bad behaviors listed here might piss away forever.

The Power Tripper

aka: the megalomaniac, the power abuser

Kristine comes to work every day hoping that her boss will eventually show a more decent side than the rat he normally is. If he tells her to come into his office to sharpen his pencils with the electric pencil sharpener on his desk one more time, she might shove the pencil through his bulbous nose. Poor Kristine is stuck assisting a power tripping prick who deserves a few days alone with a heartless nun.

The Power tripper is a tool—not the type found on a construction site—of the worst kind. A power tripper is a person who abuses their power or position to feel important and, on occasion, to seize your catfish po' boy sandwich from your eager mouth.

Power trippers can be anyone at any level who makes you do things to remind you that you are shit in their presence, for example, the boss who throws reports on the floor so you are forced to bow down before him or her to pick it up.

Sometimes, the power tripper's position is tenuous, but while they have the upper hand, they will exercise it to make sure you know that you exist to be their personal slave.

You are especially prone to being a target for a power tripper if it is obvious you can do their job as well as they can while swinging upside down from monkey bars blindfolded.

Some seem immune to power tripping temptations and can treat people with courtesy and respect while others become real dirtbags.

Power tripping can happen instantaneously when a person is selected to head a group. When Angus becomes the new top dog, he can saunter around like he's the shit and doesn't have to eat his tuna sandwich with all the peons he used to work with.

Sometimes, the new power tripper becomes such a fathead that he or she takes the credit away from co-workers for a job well done. Sometimes, a power tripper can favor their stupid, lame buddy over someone who can do more than score points on 'Pokémon Go'.

Power pricks are generally despised by underlings who are victimized by them, collectively forming an energy surge of ill will that might cause the power tripper to break their teeth on some hard toffee.

CAUSE:

Power trippers can be found worldwide in every nation and every culture. Psychologists tend to believe power unleashes the uglier aspects of human nature hidden within all of us. That may be true, but in some cases, the worst of human nature can also be cultivated through secret power clubs, which have existed from the beginning of time.

In ancient history, the strongest male in a tribe or a kingdom always had some muscle power in his company to help rough up opponents. Only people who could help him stay top dog could belong. His enforcers would have been hulky henchmen who could quickly knock the head off a person and did so carte blanche. These were the early unofficial power clubs; very few could belong.

As time went on and the population grew, these clubs evolved into secret societies of modern day where powerful figures of some kind—a politician, a CEO, or other—can join. Like minds enjoy each other's company and it is no different with people who enjoy abusing their power.

In these clubs, people are encouraged to be real shits. Take for example, the Pol Pot Club, a fairly new power club that has emerged in the last few decades helping to spread power tripping behavior worldwide.

The Pol Pot Club is named after the ruthless Cambodian dictator who slaughtered almost a quarter of the Cambodian population—one of the biggest power trippers in history. This club has the largest membership with the most diverse group of any secret club and it encourages the very worst behavior from its club members.

When a certain CEO gets ecstatic over your fear of being skewered alive for attending your mother's funeral instead of working around the clock for three days, you can blame the Pol Pot Club (also see *The Blackmailer* as that may be a secondary cause).

After a person gains prominence, they are contacted by this secret society to join a local chapter. Those uninterested in joining are left alone, but those interested in membership are in it forever.

The club's founders swear they are in contact with Pol Pot's spirit. This spirit helps them attain riches and maintain power as long as his portrait is worshipped on a daily basis and as long as members honor his legacy by throwing up together naked once a month, contributing their bile in a cesspool of vileness.

Once upon a time, the Pol Pot Club was a relatively obscure group until they gained a big wad of money in a short amount of time. How they got their big influx was really through an extraordinary accident.

During the club's fledgling days a high number of potential recruits—a bunch of history flunkies—misheard the name Pol Pot as Pool Pot, believing the club's purpose was to smoke weed together at luxurious pools. Seeing opportunity within a malapropism, the core decision makers hatched a great business plan—why not deal pot to finance member's activities?

The Pol Pot Club enlisted small time street corner drug peddlers who wanted out from under drug lords and into their own operations.

The club helped these dealers start their own smuggling and dealing ring. In return, they had to share 70 percent of their gross sales but were guaranteed protection from all levels of legal enforcement (through membership connections) and had much of their operational costs covered.

Drug profits have helped the club soar, boosting its reputation through extravagant parties, luxurious trips with hired hookers, and outrageously expensive holiday gifts, making The Pol Pot Club one of the most famous club in the power tripping world.

The club guarantees its members great satisfaction, as long as they continue power tripping, pay homage to Pol Pot's ghost, pay high membership fees, and hit themselves with leather tassels.

Longstanding members are given cash rewards every year, creating incentives to stay. But should any one attempt to leave the club—that's another story altogether.

Because of the many illegal backroom deals among members and the criminal, drug, and illicit sexual activities involved, desertion from the club puts all members in jeopardy when the departing member no longer has any skin in the game.

Any dissension is met with fatal "accidents" delivered by the Punishers, the in-house assassins whose constant presence serves as both security guards and as deterrents to any potential defectors. Membership is for life.

RECOMMENDATIONS:

It is easy to hate a power tripper, a person whose face you wouldn't mind seeing on the side of a milk carton. But be careful. These putrid personalities have allies in areas you may not realize.

They can inflict harm through their member's intervention in ways you wouldn't expect, including making killer bees swarm your house, transplanting gophers into your yard, or leaving dead crows in your car.

Although power trippers are difficult opponents to take down, it doesn't mean you have no recourse; you can be an asshole right back. However, if you don't belong to gangs or biker clubs and don't have any trigger happy, criminally insane friends for protection, you are vulnerable to payback.

Power trippers tend to be high up in the food chain, so your options for inflicting harm are somewhat limited, but you can attempt some clandestine scheme to knock them out.

Enlist the help of a manipulator to get the power tripper in trouble, or at least out of commission for a few months. It's a dangerous road to undertake and not to be done lightly. Calling on a known sorcerer or a good witch might help. Don't do anything that can be traced back to you though.

If you are a power tripper but have a change of heart, you can play the part of a dick with a big stick to wield but no follow-through, thus being a faux power tripper.

You can also fake your own death to escape Pol Pot's fatal punishment and take on a new identity, but this is also risky with the amount of surveillance cameras around these days.

You may need to change your name and undergo major changes in appearance. You may need to switch genders and dye your hair, passing as the opposite sex until you are a forgotten face altogether.

The Prankster

aka: the joker, the jokester, the teaser, the trickster

Shauna opens a drawer to find a hairy black tarantula staring at her from her pile of designer underwear. With a bored sigh, she reaches in and grabs the fake arachnid by the leg. Suspecting her little punk brother to be responsible and probably listening behind her bedroom door, she tiptoes across the room with mischief in her eyes. She swings the door open quickly and tosses old eight legs right at his unsuspecting face. He screams like he's got a clamp on his dick, giving Shauna a satisfying conclusion to his lame prank.

The prankster is a person who has the common sense of a dust ball and will go to extremes to get a laugh. Sometimes that means making their victims scream, cry, and wet their pants.

A light innocent prank can be most entertaining. However, knowing the right prank to play, the right time to do it, and the difference between harmless and harmful separates the fun loving soul from the moron ripe for a lawsuit.

The prankster of the bad kind plays pranks that are dangerous, physically damaging, and scare the crap out of someone, enough to make them drop dead on the spot. Fake robberies and elevators with screaming ghost girls aren't recommended.

Knowing when to stop is vital to pranking etiquette. A person who doesn't know when to stop can be irritating on a daily basis.

With a little foresight, pranks that go terribly wrong and cause someone to chase after you with a cleaver, can be avoided.

CAUSE:

The prankster's constant shenanigans can't be helped, because these jokesters are genetically wired to perform mischief due to inherited leprechaun genes.

It is well known that leprechauns are mischievous little scoundrels; they will use a fart pillow in ways you cannot imagine. Anyone with this fairy's genes cannot help but prank and trip others.

At some point in a prankster's ancestral history, a leprechaun crossed paths with the prankster's foremother and "did" her. Using a glamour spell to hide his real appearance, a leprechaun was able to entrance the unsuspecting woman into a barn or onto a hay bale posing as a manly man. (Leprechauns are not the most handsome of fairies. They don't get laid much, but are just as horny as a teenager)

Leprechauns have exceedingly powerful sperm; they always end up impregnating every time they have sex. When the leprechaun is fully satiated and emptied of his magical load, he moves on until his horniness drives him to strike once again.

After the little fellow is long gone, the woman finds herself in a quandary. In a matter of months, she finds herself with a big belly, but no man in sight. Depending on the era when this seduction occurred, this could be extremely shameful for the duped female.

If the poor gal hasn't been shamed into exile, she heads off into the woods to deliver her babe with a girlfriend in hand.

The baby is then given up to a wealthy family who cannot have one of their own, but can give the kind of bright future that the biological mother cannot.

As the child matures, their natural instinct to play pranks and cause mischief is directly due to their father's biological contribution. The child cannot help it. His or her progeny will also share their ancestor's love of pranking people, no matter how far down the line and no matter the cultural influences.

RECOMMENDATIONS:

It is impossible to change one's DNA and more so if the genetic material comes from a fairy. The only way to really stop the prankster permanently is to prevent them from procreating, to stop the cycle once and for all. This is no easy feat, for people desire to see mini replicas of themselves. The prankster will want to have a child, as children are naturally mischievous, bringing joy to a prankster's life.

If you are involved with a prankster, you may want to dissuade them from having children. If you are a prankster or feel that you have a compulsion you cannot stop, it would be good to have yourself sterilized.

That or refrain from sexual relations of any kind except for the one with your hand or a suction hose.

The Prude

aka: the goody goody, the goody two-shoes, the puritanical, the uptight

Harold thought it scandalous. He couldn't take his eyes off the young mother breastfeeding her baby in the upscale French restaurant. Her carefree and indiscreet manner repulsed him. He never would have allowed his wife to display herself so wantonly. Didn't the young woman have any self respect or propriety? Disgusting! Harold, with his prudish ideas, managed to watch the young mother during his entire meal until she retired her large bosom back into her blouse.

The prude is an individual who is easily offended by nudity and sexual matters, preferring to talk in great detail about an ear infection, when you'd rather talk about your night with Big Betty and her bouncing balls.

An example of extreme prudish behavior can be seen in the 1976 hit horror "Carrie," in which a teenage girl with supernatural powers is stuck in a house with a religious mental case of a mother who is disgusted by men and their inherently evil (sexual) needs. Mere mention of a first menstrual cycle works Carrie's mother into a tizzy. Forget about boys, that makes her knife crazy. Most prudes are less zealous than Carrie's mother, but some get pretty close.

Behaviors that make a prude highly uncomfortable include public displays of affection, nude body parts, nude beaches, and interactions with sleazebags and potty mouths.

Sometimes, people feign prudish behavior; it is preferable to be viewed as a morally upstanding citizen than to admit a yen for cock rings and nipple clamps.

Some also choose to adopt a restrained lifestyle as an example to their children so their kids won't want to play doctor with the neighbor boys and girls.

There are those who choose to abstain from all matters sexual for the benefits it offers: a better night's sleep without: a) battling for blankets or b) strangling a snorer. There are also no messy body fluids to deal with and no constant changing of dirty sheets. In terms of housekeeping, being a prude saves time and work.

The definition of prudish behavior is also quite subjective. A streetwalker might consider you a prude if you are picky about your partners. A BDSM (Bondage, Domination, Sadism and Masochism) practitioner might consider the usual missionary position to be what prudes do when they get excited.

Luckily, prudish behavior is one that won't hurt you to be in the company of, unless you've a hankering for a bit of fun a prude stops you from getting.

CAUSE:

People tend to blame prudish behavior on propriety gone too far. They would be wrong. A little noxious spore called Aspergillus fumigatus is the culprit for this uptight behavior, specifically when the fungi is present in the bedroom.

People who are allergic to Aspergillus are susceptible to becoming prudes; they can't help but negatively associate bedroom activities as disgusting experiences worthy of biohazard cleanup crews.

All that bouncing on the bed and somersaulting (for the more active peeps out there) stirs the mold up into the air and into the lungs. This affects coitus, as lungs seize up and the person turns blue in the face gasping for air.

Aspergillus can also be found in couches, clothes, chairs, carpets, and many other surfaces. It can cause headaches, bronchial discomfort, nasal congestion, and stomach disturbances during intercourse or foreplay.

Aspergillus fungus is nearly impossible to eliminate and in fact, can easily migrate into sinus cavities and any other moist orifices and crevices.

When an individual gets Aspergillus fungi in their nose, which invariably happens when a face is deeply buried into mildewy sheets or body parts, the ensuing headache—along with the unpleasant odor—transforms an enjoyable frolic into a funnilingus/fellatio flop.

Repeated enough times and any sexual reference serves to remind the sufferer of the nasty, life threatening experience sex is. It's no wonder someone would associate sex with misery.

Parents would have greater success keeping their horny teenagers virginal if they used Aspergillus fumigatus as a sexual deterrent.

With this dangerous fungi around, the old saying, "Not tonight dear, I've got a headache" becomes "Not tonight dear, I don't want a headache" for the prude.

RECOMMENDATIONS:

To rid oneself of Aspergillus fungus, you must burn all sheets and clothing containing this dangerous spore. Aspergillus does not go away willingly. It will take an army of fungi combatants to rid these bad boys for good.

Slugs can help. Slugs—the kind you find on the sidewalk and accidentally squish with your foot after a good downpour—eat fungi. Having plenty of slugs placed around the room, in the bed, in dark dank places will help get a start on all those unwelcome nasty spores.

In the body, this fungi is much more difficult to eliminate and requires some heavy artillery in the form of antibiotics and some really sterile discussions. All hard surfaces as well as skin should be wiped down with borax.

Once the fungus is removed, it will take some effort to reintroduce sex in a positive light. This will require something tasty. Try strawberry sorbet or banana cream pie smeared all over the sexual partner of the prude.

All bedroom sheets and covers should be new, along with room deodorizers carefully placed in every corner. Remove all slugs and slug corpses you may have stepped on.

Hire a mariachi band to play in your bedroom while doing the deed. It will make everyone in the room feel more alive and energetic.

In time and with repeat performances, the prude will enjoy talking freely and explicitly about all the wonderful things they can do with their bodies.

The Psychic Vampire

aka: the energy zapper, the soulsucker

You're about to head out the door when in the distance you see Fred coming towards your house. You feel a sense of dread. Fred is a nice guy for the most part but can drain any excitement you have for living. That's because Fred dumps all his problems on you, expecting you to sacrifice your free time to help him fix up his messed up life. You would be more than happy to help a friend in need, but Fred is always in need and he never follows your suggestions anyways. You told him it was a bad idea to pick up girls at a high school. You told him not to tweet for medical advice using pictures of his bloody, mysterious genital infection. You suggested he adopt a dog from the Humane Society instead of swiping a bear cub from a national forest. But he did what he did and his life is a revolving disaster. He always wants to drag you into his mess and has no consideration for your needs. You do feel some sympathy for him, his life really is the pits, but you're sucked dry and you know it will never end. At one time, he was your wingman but no more.

The psychic vampire is a person who needs your help constantly, any time of the week, day or night. If you don't offer your services on the spot to the psychic vampire, you are considered a heartless squid.

Having a relationship with a psychic vampire is a one way deal. If you ever need anything, they aren't available, because their dick is caught in a zipper, their dog has eaten a bottle cap, they're in the middle of whitening their teeth and can't possibly help you get to the emergency room for that bleeding eyeball, but if you are free on Thursday at midnight next week, they're available.

The psychic vampire always has a crisis, and if they don't, will be sure to create one.

Psychic vampires expect you to listen to their problems for hours on end and then solve it for them. After that, you are expected to sauté your arm in a butter sauce to feed them too.

Like the vampires popularized by tween movies, psychic vampires have appeal of some sort—good looks, charisma, flair, charm—all to ensnare you into their world. Once you are drawn into a psychic vampire's inner field (approximately one foot), that person will court you until you are seduced into a relationship.

Psychic vampires are brilliant in deconstructing a person's innermost psyche and will initially ply you with all sorts of feel good observances and compliments until you are trapped.

Once that unspoken friendship is established, the true workings of that soul sucker will be revealed. You will become their personal chauffeur; their dog, cat, hamster, pot-bellied pig, and lizard sitter; and their personal housekeeper, banker, and cook. In short, you will be sucked of any life you had whenever they have an emergency, which is quite often.

Psychic vampires can also exist in the workplace or with acquaintances you know. In more distant relationships, it is easier to escape their clutches.

CAUSE:

Psychic vampires can be created when a soul departs from a body during sleep and fails to return to its owner, causing a sense of soullessness in the abandoned body.

Astral travel is the phenomenon by which a dreamer's soul leaves a body to travel far off and away. This type of psychic travel happens during the dream state when the mind is knocked out at rest. It is during this serene time when the spirit feels unfettered, free to run off to other lands, to other planets with great ease and unimaginable speed—think Superman in jump drive.

Not everyone has the ability to fly away during sleep. Only a person with a curious mind and a love of travel can boldly seek new vacation spots where they couldn't afford to go before. Travel to Venus? Hell yeah. Fly to the moon. Sign me up!

Most people who are able to astro travel are also able to return to their bodies easily, but for some—those with a lousy sense of direction—finding their way back from Saturn may be difficult if their soul is lost in space somewhere. It is with these folks, failing to reconnect their soul with their body, that psychic vampires get created.

Having a soul is what helps anyone meet life's challenges, but when the soul has gone missing, losing a toothpick can become extremely overwhelming. The psychic vampire feels very hollow inside and cannot help but fill it with melodrama based on all sorts of stupid decisions.

For the self-disparager (see *The Self-Disparager*), having a fragmented soul makes a person despise themselves, but having no soul makes a psychic vampire want another's.

When a psychic vampire meets a generous, patient, and kind-spirited person, they sense a potential soul they can capture for their own. It is not something that the soul sucker is necessarily conscious of. They know something is missing, and they feel the other person can help them somehow.

RECOMMENDATIONS:

A psychic vampire depends on another person's kindness to stick around. Being mean, mocking them, and sometimes telling insensitive raunchy jokes is what will keep them away (except in cases where a psychic vampire happens to be a cusser too). Generally speaking, they do not deal well with inconsiderate, hurtful people; they have enough problems so they tend to stay clear of nasty types.

If you are a psychic vampire but didn't realize it until now, you need to stop draining other people's energy. If someone doesn't return your calls, if they avoid you, if they change the subject constantly, get a clue. These are all signs of displeasure. Stop pestering them and start sending out an astral SOS to your lost buddy.

Light a candle by the window and call out to the skies. See if you can get your soul's attention. Help them find their way home by leaving your favorite food on the windowsill.

When you become conscious of your soul's disappearance, you become a homing beacon. Sing to them and they will zoom their way back into your body.

Eventually, once you feel complete again, you will be able to handle the worst of problems with the greatest of ease.

The Psychopath

aka: the cold-blooded, the psycho
variation: the sociopath

Johnny was always a little different. From an early age, he could be found at recess thwacking, smacking, and striking other kids with his thin stick of pain. They always gave him what he wanted when he demanded it, their lunch money or a coat he needed. They would cry and their face would make all sorts of strange expressions that were foreign to him. He never cried. He didn't know how.

You can never have too many friends, except when one of those happens to be a psychopath. A psychopath is an individual who cannot feel empathy, guilt, remorse, and cannot create an emotional bond with other people, but instead uses them as a means to a creepy end, which might mean ending up in a pickling jar.

Psychopaths operate well mentally without involving emotions; their existence is to feed their instincts, such as hunger and physical gratification. To this end, they will stop at nothing to get what they want, which is why these folks are seldom seen in support groups and ice cream socials.

Psychopaths are not to be confused with sociopaths—which is confusing—because they display some of the same atrocious manners, but some experts will tell you they aren't. Psychopaths appear to be born that way the moment they are hatched out of the egg. Sociopaths may not be. For this reason, experts don't know how to handle this problem, except for maybe utilizing the nasty treatment seen in a certain famous Stanley Kubrick film or through prescription of some heavy drugs—not something a psychopath would accept when they think they are smarter than everyone else in the room.

Some psychos exhibit bad behavior that can lead to the very worst behavior—killing. But not all psychos kill and some do perfectly well in business, finance, and politics. Having mentally challenging goals helps preoccupy the psycho from going for an afternoon of stabbing.

When dealing with the murderous type, however, there is no good outcome unless they are caught before they succeed in their objective, but that's hard to do considering psychopaths know how to say "please" and "thank you" when necessary.

CAUSE:

If you think psychopaths are inhuman, you wouldn't be far off from the truth. To comprehend the inner workings of this seemingly cold, unfeeling type, you must think outside the box or even outside the planet. We are not alone. In fact, we are populated by intermixed species of all kinds and some that would shock you.

Astronomers have discovered a small planet, identified as KLL222 in Canis Major Overdensity—a galaxy not far from the Milky Way—inhabited by a large population of alien beings who have been possessing homo sapien bodies for some time.

Based on the revelations of a scientist (identified here as SCB1 for security reasons) formerly employed at Area 51, a top secret facility that is off limits to all but the very top levels of government, natives of KLL222 were first discovered in 1945 in prisoners of war.

During interrogations, some of the prisoners went into a seizure of sorts. During these seizures—to the surprise of the interrogators—luminescent extraterrestrials came forth from the prisoners' bodies whenever torture was used. This discovery was a shocking revelation for military officials, one they are still trying to understand.

Eventually, a number of these beings, labeled AB-AA6, were extricated from the prisoners and kept indefinitely for scientific research. Unfortunately, the human prisoners died once these beings departed from their bodies. Reasons remain unknown as to why that happened.

With time, scientists were able to deduce some basic information even though they could not easily communicate with these aliens.

It was discovered that AB-AA6 was responsible for psychopathic behavior on Earth. AB-AA6 belonged to a class of workers on KLL222 responsible for eating decaying and dying aliens for the sole purpose of reconstituting them into nutrients for the planet's surface. In order to do their job effectively, they were bred to have no emotions and no attachments.

There are no genders on KLL222 of the kind we are familiar with on Earth. Instead, their planet's inhabitants are differentiated through their function and what they can do for their community. AB-AA6 would be considered the worker bees on their planet.

The aliens' presence here was an unfortunate mistake, having crashed into our planet while headed to another destination. Unable to signal for rescue due to lack of materials on Earth, they adapted as best they could.

In order for these stranded aliens to survive our atmosphere long term, they started inhabiting human bodies, regenerating and reproducing with humans for a very long time. When they did so, they negated any innate emotions or feelings that the host carried, creating a psychopath in the process. A person inhabited by a KLL222 alien becomes driven by instincts and primitive needs without the attendant emotional baggage.

Area 51 was built to contain the growing number of captured E.T.'s emerging from host bodies, but the building's true purpose was never revealed. Instead, the Department of Defense uses the cover of building military super planes as a way to legitimately keep out curious minds.

RECOMMENDATIONS:

Must write in a journal.
Five million times, "I will not hurt people."
From behind a heavily secured area.
With a very large, hairy, unfriendly guard posted outside.
Until a safe way of extracting these aliens from human bodies can be found without damaging the host, we can only keep them stowed away when they insist on doing bad things.

The Sadist

aka: the cruel, the inhumane, the tormentor, the troll

variation: the unmerciful

Theodore typed his response quickly. "He'll bleed to death from the inside and his organs will explode in your face," in response to a young woman's frantic posting about her sick cat. It was 3:00 am and he was wide awake in his dark basement. It excited him to think how broken up the cat owner would be after reading his words. The whole world was full of easy targets and he had so much time to torment others, as long as he didn't wake his mom sleeping in the next bed.

The sadist is a person who gets their feel goods and jollies from causing others emotional or physical pain.

Sadism comes in many forms: trolls, sexual dominators, and torturers. Sometimes, sadists are also psychopaths (see *The Psychopath*), which makes them a holy fuckin' mess in the character department.

Unless you're a masochist—a person who gets excited by a kick to the knee—sadists aren't the people you want to be stuck on a deserted island with. It would be the same as having your worst nightmare from grade school beat you up on an hourly basis.

Sadists are great at making a person feel really really shitty and can be hired to torment the jerk who used to torture you after school, because you parted your hair in the middle. This gives the sadist a chance to contribute something useful to society in the only way they know how to.

The sadist that prefers the sexual role playing game of dominating over a so-called "submissive" in the bedroom is generally harmless; they tend to restrict their whipping to bare bottoms. For this type of sadist, a stiletto heel in the butt and a dick whipping is a great start to a waffle breakfast and is quite different from the sadist who wants to hurt others on a deep level.

For the sadist who delights in reducing someone to terror and tears, they would make the world a better place by going for a swim in the Atlantic during a thunderstorm.

CAUSE:

Unlike the bully (see *The Bully*) who is driven by a reptilian brain and only appears to be cruel due to their primitive and aggressive behavior, the sadist is truly cruel and enjoys every damn minute of it.

The sadist's malevolent soul is the direct result of the circumstances around their conception; the parents of a sadist are entirely to blame for the creation of a bad seed by the disrespectful act of doin' the nasty on top of a freshly laid grave.

When someone is laid to rest in the ground, their spirit can linger near the body, unprepared to leave the form they spent so much time inside.

After a proper burial ceremony where friends and family say really nice things about the deceased that they never bothered to say when that dead person was alive, the spirit feels sad about dying and hangs around for a bit.

If a couple of horny toads decide the peaceful setting of a cemetery is the perfect place to bang each other, then the two have entered into dangerous supernatural territory.

Sometimes, a vigorous romp in the grass can span a large area, inadvertently landing the randy pair onto a new grave. In the heat of the moment, the carnal horndogs may not realize they've crashed onto someone's new home, annoying the spirit of the deceased in the process.

If the deceased happened to be a person who never got their due or was pushed around a bit in life, they get payback as a spirit by cursing the horny pair with the conception of Damien.

After the thrill of passion is fully satiated, the poor unsuspecting pair has unknowingly conceived a monster child who will torment them and others for life, unless they terminate the pregnancy early on. But a cursed embryo does not go willingly and will bring the mother down if possible.

RECOMMENDATIONS:

If you have recently had sexual relations in a cemetery on top of a freshly laid grave and are concerned about birthing evil spawn, you may wish to go back to the site and speak to the spirit there.

Apologize for your appalling behavior and promise to sweep their grave of falling leaves once a month. Bring fragrant white flowers and a fruity mango libation to sweeten the deal.

If you're lucky, the spirit will reverse the spell on the embryo and you get either an average kid or a toned down version of a monster.

If the sadist also happens to be inhabited by the alien being (Specimen AB-AA6) mentioned in the psychopath section, forget rehabilitation. They are a goner for sure.

The Sarcastic

aka: the acerbic, the contemptuous, the derisive, the ironic, the smartass

variation: the cynical

"Great job," says Donte with a sneer as he looks over the chicken coop Leticia built in her spare time. She grins, proud of the effort she made for her colorful chickens so the hens could freely turn and hop. Donte was being sarcastic, but she doesn't realize it. If she knew what he really meant, she'd wipe his face clean with a few of the chicken offerings from around the yard.

The sarcastic is a person who speaks, remarks, or answers in an ironic or mocking way in order to convey what a doofus you are without explicitly saying so.

These people have an inner snarkiness, seemingly driven by a strong belief in their mental superiority. That's because a sarcastic has trouble saying something plainly or directly. Their little jibe is a personal joke with themselves, which you are the subject of.

The sarcastic will sometimes make wry comments that fly above your head to avoid engaging in a topic. In doing so, they believe you to be incapable of intelligent conversation but defensive enough to be combative if told so. This way, you are left puzzled and they are spared the effort.

For the speaker who is more direct, a conversation with a sarcastic type can be frustrating. Few people find much enjoyment trying to glean the real meaning behind veiled words, kind of like trying to pick the gold band out of your dog's poop after it dropped off the table and into their jowls.

Two sarcastic people out snarking one another is not a pretty sight and not good company for the sincere and naive. Mocking quips get old real fast and if you're in a rush for an answer, you'll come to resent this type of person, wishing you could wipe that smartass grin off with a belt sander, but perhaps this is a bit too harsh. After all, a sarcastic person's ironic comments require great wit and a keen intellect.

Yeah...right.

CAUSE:

A sarcastic gets created when he or she is punished at a young age for speaking openly and frankly. As a result, they have learned to develop a style of speech that masks their true meaning, avoiding any possibility of getting their ass whipped or their arm punched.

As children start forming sentences, they say directly what's on their mind without any filters. For example, a boy may say to his father, "Daddy, you're a dumb fuck," or "Mommy, you look like the Rancor monster." These words, innocently spoken, can end up with a punishment of some form—a hard spanking or a favorite toy being given away to some other kid who never talks.

In time, the child comes to understand the dangers of explicitly saying what they think. However, the need to speak is unavoidable as children must blab incessantly.

As a way of coping with this conflict, some kids learn to circumnavigate saying what they really mean by using words or phrases that mean the opposite of how they really feel, turning language into a game of irony that only they know is being played.

Other times, the child may obligingly say what they think the other wishes to hear, but does so in an insincere tone. They can't help but convey contempt—out of resentment—because they deeply wish to tell the other person he or she actually sucks rotten eggs and is dumber than a shoe umbrella, but are prevented from doing so for fear of being smacked in the face.

If the person on the receiving end of a sarcastic's remark becomes confused or puzzled, this can make the sarcastic feel superior, because the other is clueless to the game that is being played.

After many years of talking this way, speaking plainly and directly becomes difficult and unnatural.

RECOMMENDATIONS:

If you have difficulty dealing with someone who continually speaks in a sarcastic or ironic manner, have a book of poetry at hand to share.

Open the poetry book at random and toss it at the sarcastic's feet. With luck, the book will land open to a worthwhile poem for the sarcastic to read.

The unanticipated action of getting a book thrown at their feet will surprise the sarcastic, stopping them in their course. Ask them to read aloud the poem that appears in front of them.

If they are unwilling to move their lips, read the poem to them. Show them what kindness, anger, creativity, sorrow, joy, and despair can sound like in the hands of a master poet.

Exposure to poetry will offer the sarcastic another avenue of possibilities, a language game of sorts to employ other than irony or sarcasm.

Poetic verse is a step in the right direction to helping the sarcastic become more direct in their speech and is also pleasant to hear. In time, the sarcastic will become more straightforward when they discover no one will take their toys away or slap them silly for it.

If this remedy fails, stop hanging out with them. No need to waste your time with someone who can't talk to you like a regular human being.

The Scene Stealer

aka: the attention grabber, the attention whore

You tell a story about the time you climbed the Teton Range to a group of friends when Kareem interrupts with a tale of his own, about the time he reached Mt. Everest's peak with a broken toe after being trapped in an avalanche for several hours, by which he escaped by clawing his way out, surviving on crushed rocks and dirt when his local guide abandoned him to go protest for better work conditions. Kareem always steals the show. No matter what story you tell, his will always top yours.

A scene stealer is a person who must outshine you on any subject, be it snorkeling, tree climbing, or nose picking. Whatever the subject, you will look as exciting as a drainpipe.

The scene stealer should never be invited to a gathering or event where you are the main attraction, for this individual will usurp that spotlight away from your beaming face faster than you can say "Where's my beer?"

Scene stealers love an audience so they are usually found in groups—the bigger the group, the more incentive to steal the show.

When it is just you and the scene stealer, they are less apt to steal the whole show, especially if they are a friend or a relative, but once the numbers are up, you become a bar stool. This social usurper can't wait for that chance to say, "Hey look at me! I am awesome and I shit gold too."

Scene stealers can also be know-it-alls but not necessarily. For this type of person to really succeed, they must possess an air of confidence, a strong voice, and a conehead. If they lack in any one of these three qualities, you can steer the attention back to you.

CAUSE:

The scene stealer may seem as if they live to steal your thunder, but in reality, they are manifesting symptoms from a childhood of being mistaken for a shrub.

Some people are naturally more charming and popular while others are not. Sometime in a scene stealer's past, they wanted acknowledgement from their peers and teachers but didn't receive the much needed validation. In fact, they weren't seen for who they were at all.

Instead, they were seen as a small immobile green plant rooted in the background somewhere. Insignificant, not particularly fragrant and not very useful, they were passed over for compliments, accidentally bumped into by more dynamic personalities, and sometimes urinated on by a passing dog. This neglect can have dire consequences.

As the shrub-like child grows older, their need to be noticed becomes great, to the point of usurping someone else's moment in the sun. Unless a person has been ignored to the degree that a scene stealer has, people may not understand how a young person can be affected so deeply by a simple misperception.

For most kids, show and tell is something to look forward to, but for the scene stealer, show and tell became show and ignore. Parents didn't help, nor did siblings and teachers.

For a child that happens to resemble a shrub, it can mean years of being overlooked, picked last for volleyball, pissed on, and constantly having cow manure thrown at their feet by the school's groundskeeper.

As adults, these neglected souls have become attention whores, dressing in clothes with wild patterns, telling stories with exaggerated details, and doing things that garner admiration. In short, they are demanding to be noticed, to be given some adulation in order to feel they are a meaningful part of society. They have no interest in blending in the background. It's their turn to shine, something they didn't get to do in their youth.

RECOMMENDATIONS:

No one likes to be ignored, unless they are in a criminal lineup. A scene stealer may not be easily squelched, for they are working out years and years of baggage, trying to elevate themselves to feel better.

You may try—though it may not work—to tell the scene stealer they remind you of a tree with big branches and pretty blooms. Feed their ego for awhile and let them know they are noticed, enough to fulfill their deep inner need, so they don't have to spoil your moment.

If you bond with such a person, their affection for you might override their scene stealing tendencies, but it requires some effort. This tactic may or may not work. The scene stealer might become addicted to your attention and may not let you get a word in edgewise.

If that is the case, you may have to do something drastic along the lines of humiliation. You may need to insult the scene stealer, tell them that their hair is a haven for inchworms, their face could use a little trimming, and they have a bad case of powdery mildew. Let them know they are capable of receiving bad attention if they don't stop hogging the stage.

You could also carry a battery-powered cordless mike with a mini amp and speak over them whenever they start up.

The Seducer / Seductress

aka: the Casanova, the charmer, the heartbreaker, the home wrecker, the lothario, the lover, the man eater, the playboy, the player, the smooth operator

At her friend's housewarming dinner, Trisha and her husband sit down with 16 new people at a table. A charming guy with captivating eyes takes a seat across from her. Her husband leaves the table to go wash his hands. While he's gone, the man in front of her smiles in her direction. Aware of his intense gaze, she says "hello" to break the awkwardness of his stare. "The goddess speaks," he answers seductively. Before she knows it, she finds herself in her friend's bathroom with ole pretty eye's hand inside her blouse fondling her cupcakes, and her husband has no idea what is happening. She doesn't quite believe it herself. She's never done this type of thing before, but then again, she's never met such a smooth operator before.

The seducer is a person motivated by the challenge of seducing unattainable or otherwise committed individuals and has no interest in the easy mark standing in the corner of the room with the words *Ride My Face* printed on their t-shirt.

Seduction is a slippery sort of behavior that goes beyond harmless flirtation into home wrecker and/or conquest territory. This is not the garden variety player who is looking to get laid. No, the quintessential seducer loves a good chase.

This is true for both men and women, gay and straight. At a party, there could be a hundred singles available for sleazing around with, but to a seducer, the only game worth hunting is the extremely difficult target—the one with the wedding ring around their finger, or someone famous, or someone out of their league, or someone heavily loaded in currency.

Similar to a lion thrown into a cage of plump, juicy chickens, the seducer sees all those attracted to him or her as easy prey. Unlike a lion who just wants a good meal, the seducer isn't satisfied with an easy catch; this hunter wants a challenge that involves tracking, trapping, pursuing, and then the killing of a committed relationship or cashing in on some ultimate prize.

Seducers have a long rap sheet of broken hearts. The more resistant a target is, the more the seducer tries their wily moves on them.

Either the prey takes the bait or it doesn't. If it doesn't after repeated attempts, then the seducer goes home to cry in a face towel, but if there is even a hint of interest from the prey, then watch out! The seducer will do whatever it takes to get what they want.

In any case, the seducer is not interested in a long-term relationship with their prey. After the target is seduced, the seducer moves on to the next game.

The seducer feels no guilt for any damage they incur. To them, it's just part of the sport.

CAUSE:

Seducing behavior is driven by a little known disease called Llamydia, a relative of the sexually transmitted disease (STD) Chlamydia.

Different from its well-known counterpart, Llamydia is of unknown origin, though there is some consensus that this disease probably resulted from sex with a llama.

The disease causes irritation of the genitals as well as swollen lymph glands around the groin, although not as severe as some other sexually transmitted diseases. Sometimes, the irritation is so minor it could be mistaken for chafing from jeans or ants in the pants, and the carrier may not even know they have an infection.

Unlike Chlamydia, this disease also presents with the odd psychological need to conquer one or more of these types of individuals: the uber hot, the big spender, the happily married fool, or the very famous and popular.

Also unlike other STDs, this bacteria-caused disease seems to desire human hosts that can ensure it gets spread around easily. It can enter the blood brain barrier and once there, these small microscopic pathogens incite its human host to sexually co-mingle with as many healthy, well fed individuals as possible.

A person with a significant other is more appealing, because there are two people instead of one who can be infected by a seducer's successful seduction.

What better way to spread the bacteria than through famous hotties, such as Kim Kardashian or Shemar Moore or Bradley Cooper or Rihanna, all with the potential to attract mile long queues of eager fans happy to wrestle naked with them, ensuring the bacterium's future survival. For this reason, hot celebrities should be especially wary of seductive people.

RECOMMENDATIONS:

If someone you know seems to be suffering from seducing behavior, tell them to mix up a bottle of tiger urine, oregano oil, garlic juice, peppermint, eucalyptus oil, and chili oil to use as an inhalant and also as a spray for their genital area.

This will help combat the Llamydia bacterium that is obviously affecting the will-power and consciousness of a seducer.

This potent cocktail helps thwart any sexual desire, replacing it with a burning sensation that will kill the bacterium and the libido. Ice cubes rather than a warm body will be desired, keeping the seducer in check from breaking marriages and spreading their disease.

If tiger urine is too difficult to procure, cat pee might work but is not as effective as a larger cat's output.

The Self-Absorbed

aka: the egocentric,
the self-centered, the self-obsessed

Your eyes tear up when you start telling your new friend Malika about the night your loving grandpa died after choking on a Twizzler. It was one of the most tragic events of your life and you haven't gotten over it after a year. You think about him all the time and miss him like crazy. The week before Christmas is the worse—that's when you and grandpa used to throw snowballs at the local pervert's house together. Malika seems to be listening attentively, nodding her head as if she sympathizes. But then she says something that takes you by surprise. "This pastrami sucks. It's too salty and it's got too much gristle. I'm not paying for this crap," she complains. You blink, floored by Malika's comment. You realize in that instant Malika hasn't heard a word you said and probably never will.

The self-absorbed are self-centered people who take zero interest in other people's lives unless it relates back to them in some way. They can be counted on to give you a vapid stare when you ask them to repeat the story you just told about the time you were robbed by a dude in a Big Bird costume.

This bad behavior differs from the narcissist who is in love with themselves (see *The Narcissist*). Self-absorbed people aren't quite that far gone, but they are consumed with the importance of their own lives and problems. They are somewhere a million miles away when you talk about anything but them. Unless they benefit in some way from listening to you, they couldn't care less about that black, fist-sized mole on your back.

Everyone can be accused of being self-absorbed to some degree—no one takes greater interest in us than ourselves, minus the stalkers. As children, we are naturally egocentric—every gold star we get is more important than the girl next to us who won the national spelling bee.

As we grow up and interact with others, however, we discover a wide world of vastly interesting people; people who can ride a bicycle backwards, who can touch their ears with their tongues, who can sing the national anthem with a mouth full of marbles.

Eventually a friendship develops, and you too can learn how to sing with your mouth full of hard objects, in exchange for giving a ping pong lesson. It's a give and take sort of thing with the expectation that both parties have something worthwhile to share with each other.

Not the self-absorbed though. Meeting other people creates new opportunities to get free therapy on their complex life for the next eight hours.

There are telltale signs that reveal whether you're in the company of a self-absorbed person. Does that person wear the same expression on their face when the subject changes from repairing car engines to finding a rattlesnake in a gym bag? Do they ask you how your sister is doing after she fell out of a burning building? Do their pupils seem to have a random orbit instead of focused on you?

If these descriptions sound like a friend of yours, you might want to program your phone to auto-reject their number. If these descriptions fit you to a tee, then you kind of suck.

CAUSE:

Like the narcissist, this bad behavior is about self-obsession. Unlike the narcissist who becomes this way based on how they see themselves in the mirror, the self-absorbed gets created based on the way they perceive a projection of themselves in the world.

Most people recognize the "I" as the self, while the "other" as another person. For the self-absorbed, however, the "other" is really them, seen as split from themselves—in short—I and I.

That other I is situated on their lap in the form of a transparent person (identical to them) that they can see, but others cannot. There is no "you" while the other I is around, because that other I blocks their view of you.

The self-absorbed will sometimes refer to this other I in the third person, speaking about themselves as if they were really another person.

If this sounds confusing, it is, because you are dealing with one person who identifies themselves as two different beings, both number one to them.

They are interested in all matters related to their I self and only perk up when others take interest in their other I too. The self-absorbed is quite concerned with the other I's future prospects, especially when they are short on cash, love, and work.

This other I is their best friend, someone they will probably marry in the future to the tune of "Me, Myself, and I." They will also have a grand honeymoon with this other I, with sweet backrubs, loving words, and hot sex.

RECOMMENDATIONS:

To cure a self-absorbed person requires shattering the other I with an imaginary death ray.

When in the company of a self-absorbed person, tell them you must destroy their other I, so that their vision of you can be restored. The other I is getting in the way of you having a real conversation. If they say they don't know what you're talking about, don't believe it. They are trying to protect that other identity on their lap.

Invoke the mantra for the imaginary death ray with the words "eximo amicus meus." Flip your middle finger towards the forehead of the self-obsessed person, allowing the imaginary death ray to flow from your hand into the other I seated on the self-obsessed person's lap.

This may initially be awkward, but it will call attention to the situation at hand and will also help the self-absorb snap to. They should be sufficiently embarrassed, forced to focus on you instead of themselves.

The Self-Disparager

aka: the self-denigrator, the self-hater, the self loather

Your roommate Tim plays Rachmaninoff Piano Concerto No. 3 flawlessly during an afternoon when you were supposed to be at work, but were actually laying on your bed feverish with the flu. When he's finished, you float out to the living room and applaud, startling him. "That was great," you gasp." But his response isn't "thanks." Tim hangs his head low and replies, "That was shit. I can't play worth shit." You protest but to no avail. He insists he's an untalented loser, and you are way too weak to argue. You know from past experience it's no use. Tim has so much self-loathing that any compliments you give are no match for his self-disparaging words.

The self-disparager is an individual who berates, belittles, or disparages themselves so vehemently that one can't help but want to plaster duct tape over the poor sucker's mouth to shut them up.

Sometimes, the self-disparaging remarks are brief and other times, they can last a whole afternoon. This type of person might insist that they are stupid, brainless, and worthy of a weed wacker for a mate.

If you pay a self-loather a compliment, they are sure to shoot it down. Attempts to contradict them will only get you into an argument.

This behavior can sometimes arouse you to do aggressive things you wouldn't normally do, like twist someone's nipple hard until that person can pay themselves at least one compliment.

If the self-disparager wins a Nobel Prize or discovers a cure for receding gums, they will still, in their own eyes, be the same as foot rot.

Self-disparagers don't usually trash other people, unless the self-disparager has some other bothersome personality trait.

Sometimes, this type of person might inspire you to understate your own abilities, making you more modest than you would normally be. In a conceited society, this is not such a bad thing.

CAUSE:

The self-disparager had a sad start early in life. At the moment of birth, fresh out of the safety of their mother's womb, the future self-disparager experienced an initial traumatic episode; they were likely slapped across the face by a sleep-deprived hallucinating obstetrician.

Covered in blood and barely human looking, the newborn can resemble Satan's child to an exhausted doctor.

A tired mind's cognitive processing ability is much more delayed than in a person with adequate rest. In a moment of fear the doctor may reflexively slap a newborn's face instead of its bottom. A doctor smacks a baby's body in order to force a cry from the newborn, thus forcing the little lambkin to take their first breath. Because a newborn is lousy at following simple instruction, you can't really order them to breathe.

A baby fresh out of the womb isn't a pretty picture and a doctor can hardly be blamed for their momentary lapse, but unfortunately, the reflexive slap does set the course for the baby's life.

A blow across the face upon entry into the outer world is a harsh first lesson for the fragile newborn, enough to fragment their soul, with little pieces of the baby's spirit flying away to better places like Six Flags Magic Mountain and Disneyland, leaving the tiny body somewhat incomplete. When a soul is fragmented, this makes a person feel that a part of them is missing, that they are never whole, because a complete person would never berate themselves so harshly.

The act of self-denigration in the face of compliments is the self-disparager's way of trying to re-establish how they naturally feel inside from the very first moment they were slapped in the world. Compliments disturb the familiar feeling of self-loathing; insults and punishment feel more normal.

Luckily, the practice of smacking newborns is no longer common practice in the last decade and a half. Other more delicate and careful methods have replaced this unkind procedure. However, if a parent hits the baby's face soon after birth, it has the same traumatic affect.

RECOMMENDATIONS:

As in the case of so many bad behaviors listed here, what is done early in life affects behavior in adulthood. It takes drastic measures to remedy such early shock and a very gifted person with the right skills to do the job.

A psychic healer with the ability to clean auras, clear karmas, and wash the floor would help the wounded person tremendously. This healer must understand how to retrieve the lost essence of the self-disparager, seeking all the pieces of the soul that departed after the baby's face was struck.

This grand effort requires mental time travel and soul searching. The psychic could try the hospital where the self-disparager was born. A piece of the the fragmented soul may have staked a place in the hospital cafeteria where it can access buttered mashed potatoes all day long. Or it may have joined with another fractured soul that had better looking, richer parents, or the soul may have left on a plane with first class service to Cancun.

Wherever the fragmented soul has gone, a talented healer will be able to locate it and cajole it back to its rightful owner. Once the soul has become complete again, the desire to berate one's self disappears.

The Skeptic

aka: the doubter, the disbeliever, the doubting Thomas, the rationalist

When you were 15 years old, you overdosed on laughing gas, enough for you to end up in a hospital unconscious. You remember the sensation of flying out of your body into another room where you saw your parents pacing up and down in the waiting room while your little sister was having a meltdown with the vending machine. You also saw your aunt and uncle in another state cross dressed in each other's clothes. Then Saint Michael floated to your room with a big bag of Cheetos—your favorite. When you were conscious again, you remembered everything. You're convinced you had an out of body experience and later verified with family members everything you saw, which they confirmed (except for the aunt and uncle). The experience changed your perspective on death, and you were never the same. You tried to share the story with your current doctor, but she shook her head and told you it was all a delusion caused by oxygen deprivation to the brain. No matter what you say, your skeptical doctor will rationalize your spiritual experience as a physiological event and nothing more.

A skeptic is one who questions the validity of something that cannot be replicated or scientifically proven. That something can include paranormal activities, such as ghost sightings and psychic phenomenon or the existence of unusual animals, such as Big Foot and unicorns. It can also include reincarnation or an afterlife, and other things you can't prove easily in a lab.

Many would consider skepticism a laudable quality rather than a lousy one. Skepticism is highly regarded in the scientific world and is utilized as a valuable asset for research and objective reasoning. It is most useful when someone tries to sell you a flying car.

However, trying to convince a skeptic that you saw your own liver in the spindly hands of an extra terrestrial is damn near impossible, and no way will they believe that the thin new scar on your abdomen was caused by any alien scalpel. This can be quite frustrating.

For those who believe in the supernatural and have spiritual leanings, a skeptic elicits the same response as a nose hair found on a banana pancake.

In situations where bizarre things happen, namely dishes levitating out of cupboards, glowing shapes wandering the hallways, the words "you will die tonight" seeping from walls, skeptics are apt to find rational explanations for what the average person calls a "haunting." Skeptics always seem to have a logical explanation for everything, but when their reasoning sounds no better than a magical one, being around a skeptic is similar to having blue balls—not enjoyable.

When a glowing figure orders someone to swear an allegiance to Satan or be punished with an exploding kidney, the skeptic would have a pretty tough time convincing that person to ignore the "figment of their imagination."

CAUSE:

Skepticism starts early in a young person's life when their bubble got burst by revelations that old St. Nick is a fat man paid to act like he gives a shit about kids and that Narnia is a place created from some middle-aged dude's imagination.

These truths may not be earth shattering news, but to a child who believes in magical worlds, such a startling dose of reality can cause terrible disappointment, humiliation, and a sense of betrayal.

When the kid learns the truth the harsh way—at school from older kids who taunt them for their naïve and childish beliefs—the kid can become disappointed for life, enough to become a hardcore skeptic to arm themselves from any future tauntings and let downs.

Captain America, Aslan, the fairy godmother—all lies. Let's admit it. Life sucks. Which would you prefer? Getting a tooth yanked from a grumpy dentist with a head full of dandruff flaking into your open mouth or riding a dragon to a whimsical place where wizards can turn your enemies into sea slugs.

When you believe there is a fairy godmother who can rescue you from the shitshow you're in, things don't seem so bad, but when it turns out only the crappy stuff is real, why would anyone want to get up in the morning? The greater the disappointment, the more skeptical that disillusioned youth becomes.

You can never hope to change a skeptic's mind. There's always an explanation for everything. If someone accurately predicts a telephone pole landing on your car at 6:08 a.m. tomorrow, it's merely a lucky guess; if an Italian sub sandwich magically appears on your lap, it's only atomic particles realigning themselves.

Not one to believe in mystical ways—it got them in trouble once and disappointed them greatly—the skeptic will turn blue in the face before they admit something is supernatural. They remember all too well the faces of their childhood tormentors laughing over their love of Santa.

RECOMMENDATIONS:

A skeptic will never admit, deep down in the recesses of their heart, they really want that water-stained image on their bathroom wall—the one that looks an awful lot like the Virgin Mary—to truly be a visit from her. They want that image to spontaneously come to life and slap them on the face, to tell them to stop doing bad shit like sniffing gas, scamming kids for their lunch money, shooting birds, and stealing tip jars.

They want to know that ghosts are real and that Aunt Buffy will be waiting with an apple pie in heaven for them. Unfortunately, the more skeptical a person becomes, the less of a chance something magical will happen to them.

One way to help them tear down their armored wall is to get some good psychedelics. Magic mushrooms can synthetically help them restore some of the awe(someness) they lost at a young age.

The Slanderer

aka: the defamer, the disparager, the libeler, the maligner, the muckraker, the mud slinger

Daniela can't believe her ears. Someone has spread a wicked rumor about her. Through her lunch friend, she discovers her co-workers believe she has a kinky relationship with a corgi. She doesn't understand why anybody would spread such a vicious rumor. Daniela has fallen victim to a slanderer.

A slanderer is a person who has a nasty mouth and uses it quite liberally to spread untruths, malicious gossip, and absolutely embarrassing crap about another person who may or may not deserve it.

Saying something untrue is not necessarily slander if the false report is harmless. For example, let's say, "Tom loves to eat chocolate." We know Tom actually detests chocolate, but it's no big deal, because no harm is done. Eating chocolate is not considered a vice and has no bad repercussions one way or another.

However, if the statement were to include a few extra words added to the end of the sentence, it can change everything. See how this sounds. "Tom loves to eat chocolate while choking the chicken in the front yard as little old ladies walk by." This second sentence probably won't fly too well with Tom. The inclusion of Tom's personal sexual habit paints him in an embarrassing light; choking his chicken in public view is considered a big fat taboo, turning this sentence into slanderous material.

Slandering can happen as a result of a feud between two people or as a way of undermining a competitor.

When a person has been defamed and loses their good name, they usually get very angry about it. They may take the slanderer's ass to court, or take revenge by putting a slanderer's home address on a bathroom wall, or may tell everyone that the slanderer has a two-inch corkscrew penis.

CAUSE:

People who say crappy things about others may seem to be responsible for the bad things coming out of their mouth, but really, those words belong to their invisible childhood friend, a little ghost.

As many parents know, children sometimes have so-called "imaginary friends," supposedly created from the safety of a child's active imagination, but these unseen pals are neither imagined nor harmless.

Many homes contain the spirit of a deceased child who has lingered on for some reason, usually due to some tragic death.

Children, being much more open and accepting of the unseen world than their closed off parents, may befriend a lonely lingering disembodied boy or girl ghost hanging around the home. If the real child does not have many friends, this spirit child becomes their BFF.

As the child grows up, the disembodied spirit stays close to them, becoming their lifelong companion. They can become so close that the child may permit the spirit to borrow its body, on occasion, to re-experience the joys of drinking a root beer float and riding on a merry go round.

The disembodied child never really grows up, frozen at the maturity level of their death age. But living children do grow and change, unlike their BFF. Still, the two remain best of pals.

Sometimes, a person has a rotten time of it with another person. A person's disdain and disgust towards another, if they aren't a looney bird, is not something they scream out to every person they know, but they will bitch about them to their close invisible ally. (Many adults know enough to keep their mouth shut when it comes to bad mouthing others publicly if there is the remote possibility of those words coming back to haunt them, but an infantile spirit would not.)

When the disembodied spirit is inside the flesh of their living friend, any reservoir of ill will the living has towards another gets exposed by the child ghost (the child spirit, who is still very immature, is naturally quite protective of their best friend). This happens when the live person is so tired they can't think straight, unconsciously allowing the ghost friend free reign of their body and mind.

Unfortunately, the child spirit gets full access to the live person's speech, with disastrous results. For example, if the living body was mad at co-worker Ramona for always leaving a mess in the break room sink, the immature ghost can feel her friend's frustration and due to their protective anger, will tell everyone Ramona vomits on the counter when no one's around and masturbates with binder clips in the supply closet.

Before a person knows it, that infantile spirit says all sorts of shit that can land their best friend into legal troubles.

RECOMMENDATIONS:

If you have been slandered or defamed by someone, know that it is really a childish spirit that has spoken poorly of you. You may need to take legal action if the slanderer has caused you financial loss or ruined your somewhat clean name. If you come face to face with a slanderer, you might want to scold the immature being inside your enemy.

If you have been accused of being a slanderer or defamer, have you unwittingly allowed the spirit of an immature child take over you? It is time to help the child ghost go on its merry way. Tell the little spirit to head for the light, and don't come back until they have reincarnated as a real sexy thang who can visit you once they reach the sweet age of 21. At that time, they can possess you all they want. Right now, it's time for you to make friends closer to your own age.

The Sleaze / The Slut

aka: the horndog, the lech, the loose, the sex maniac, the sleazeball

Whenever Candy waters her tulips in the morning, she can expect to see a different woman leave her neighbor Leon's house. Leon doesn't seem very picky. The women that come out seem as different as the people she passes on a street corner each day. Leon seems to sleep around with anything that walks. Candy tries to finish her watering before he wakes up to get his morning paper; he always wears whitey tightys and nothing else when he picks it up. His "come hither" stare makes her feel gross, as if he had already slept with her in his mind. There is no way she wants any part of that horndog's overused penis near her healthy clean female parts.

A sleaze/slut is used to describe a man (sleaze) or a woman (slut) who has no common sense or judgment when it comes to sex, getting a bit too excitable the minute something with two legs comes into view.

Having an active sex life with numerous partners is not necessarily considered sleazy/slutty behavior. In fact, an active libido makes one look like a real sex kitten or a stud muffin, but sexualizing every interaction during inappropriate times and with inappropriate people does makes one look kind of pathetic and sad. No, the mail carrier does not want to blow you on top of the mailbox.

Because everyone has a different opinion on what is considered as excessive, defining this behavior can be quite subjective. What a prude considers sleazy, a regular person might consider ho hum.

Sometimes, a person can be intermittently sleazy or slutty, depending on how much fish and whiskey are involved. A person usually knows by the next morning if they wake up with some stranger's underwear caught in their teeth and their friends won't ever let their BF or GF spend time alone in the room with them.

CAUSE:

Extremely sleazy or slutty behavior that goes beyond alcohol-induced one night stands is caused by a common fungal pathogen known to humans everywhere as candida albicans.

Candida albicans naturally lives within our bodies, kept under control by our immune system, but when our immune system is down and we eat foods that feed candida's uncontrolled growth, strange things are known to happen, specifically, itching. Uncontrollable itching. Everywhere. In those dark private areas you don't show your mama after a certain age.

If a person has unfulfilled sexual desires and is woefully unhappy, they may indulge in comfort foods without restraint, such as downing a bucket of mango sorbet, 20 packages of Ding Dongs, 10 Hershey bars, or an entire loaf of marbled pound cake. This feeds the candida into frenzied growth.

To kill multiple birds with one stone, the sleaze or slut seeks relief from other humans that he or she cannot give to themselves. Sexual activity provides pleasure and itching relief on a deep level.

Unfortunately, when candida gets out of control, the candida-ridden person can become too pushy for sex. This desperation can backfire on them, making it seem as if they might be a serial killer or a satyr.

After awhile, if the yeasty person doesn't succeed in getting sex with a preferred lover, they will sleep with anything that walks, making them look pitiful and a magnet for sexually transmitted diseases.

RECOMMENDATIONS:

Dieting, a good yeast killer, lots of onions and garlic, and a good vibrator can provide relief on many levels, eliminating the need for another human's companionship.

Onions and garlic both have anti-fungal properties and can destroy yeast. It also gives you stinky breath to keep others away.

A good vibrator with a dollop of yogurt can relieve itching when applied to the urethra, vagina, or anus. But beware! Yogurt may splatter on the walls, on your face, and on the carpet depending on the vibrator's speed setting.

Avoid scratching and stop eating sweets. Soak your bottom in a pan of apple cider vinegar, or if male, wrap a vinegar cloth around your junk.

Repeat the words, "I will not try to hook up with every person I see in the next hour."

You can also contact a physician who may or may not have sexual interest in sexing you up but can provide killer antibiotics.

The Slob

aka: the messy, the pig, the slovenly
variation: the litterer

You've got a beer and burrito in hand. You turn on your fave sitcom. You park your butt down on the couch. There's a strange sensation on your ass, a feeling of something wet, slimy, and hard. You get up to see what it is—thick moldy spaghetti sauce on a plate and now on your jeans. Your slob roommate strikes again.

The slob is a person who is filthy in appearance, has no regard for cleanliness, leaves their possessions all over the place, hasn't heard of laundry detergent, and pees on the sofa.

Slobs seem to have all sorts of issues that make them difficult to live with: noses that aren't bothered by stench; disregard for house chores; a problem hearing the words "clean," "sanitation," and "wash"; and a morbid fear of sponges, detergent, and bleach.

Staying at a slob's house overnight may gain you some new friends—fleas, bed bugs, nasty bacteria.

Never consent to having dinner at slob's house. Dinner might include maggot-infested beef peppered with a garnish of roasted cockroach—not intentionally of course. Being slobs, they don't seem to notice when food goes bad.

Slobs are also the worst litterers; they will toss their takeout containers out the window in a national wildlife sanctuary and chuck their beer bottles on a beach. The flip side of having slob friends is that you can trash their homes, and they don't seem bothered—probably the only benefit to having slobs in your life.

If you know a slob, you might be tempted to take a mop to their kitchen, but you may discover things that scare you, that haunt your dreams at night. The slob not only trashes their own house but will trash yours as well, so think twice about letting them crash in your sacred palace.

CAUSE:

Metal. We need it. Some of us love it. It's quite useful for making household things. But what happens when metal ends up in our bodies? We get heavy, real heavy, making it very difficult to take a shower and pick up old beer cans lying around and lift the lid of a trash can.

Copper, mercury, iron, lead, nickel, aluminum, steel—you can't escape them. They're in pots, pans, dental fillings, toys, candy, paint, and much more. The average person ends up eating a tiny, harmless amount while others chow down a whole lot more. They do so not because these metal objects taste so delish, but in childhood (when humans are at their very dimmest), tots swallow anything that isn't bolted to the ground.

A kid could swallow metal marbles mistaking them for malt balls. They could eat a handful of dimes believing them to be chocolate coins. Maybe they liked the way button batteries felt against their tongue. Shiny bullets left on the floor? Kittens? Sure! It wouldn't be so bad if they spit the objects out, but they don't. They swallow. Children are foolish little things.

Whatever the metal objects may be, the slob has eaten a whole bunch of them that have somehow lodged in the soft tissue of the stomach instead of being pooped out, weighing down their center of gravity as a result.

With this much heavy metal in their body, a person has to deal with the stronger gravitational pull from the earth's core, making them move as if they were trapped in a slow mo shot from The Matrix; they must constantly fight against the magnetic attraction towards the ground.

If the person doesn't die from a ripped intestine, they definitely get other side effects, such as lethargy, pain, and a tolerance for dirt.

Throughout their life, the slob feels as if their whole body is encased in cement. Forget chores. Imagine trying to vacuum with barbells attached to the center of your belly. No wonder slobs don't bother; they are way too tired.

Pissing on the floor or in a recliner is a whole lot easier than dragging a weighty ass to a bathroom where you must open a heavy door and lift a thick plastic toilet seat cover.

RECOMMENDATIONS:

To rid a slob of all that metal inside their gut, they need to get x-rays to see what is hiding inside them. Once the objects are identified, they need to be removed as soon as possible. Rust and corrosion can develop from stomach acid.

If mercury is one of the culprits, eating several pounds of organic cilantro pesto will help eliminate it from the blood and can be done at home. In order to make the cilantro work more effectively, a person must play air drums (to improve circulation and blood flow) no matter how difficult it may be to do. Channeling John Bonham from a seated position is a whole lot easier than going out for a jog in the elements.

Drink a gallon of lemon water on a daily basis and avoid any beverages or foods contained in metal of any kind. Forego the iron pots, use glass and ceramic. Don't use metal flasks to drink booze. Also, do not lick the exterior of houses painted before 1978 no matter how tasty it looks.

Help the slob by secretly tossing away gross items from floors, tables, and chairs. You may need to help research options for your slob friend; typing on keyboards and smartphones might be too strenuous for them.

If all these symptoms resonate with you as a slob, go get some x-rays as soon as possible.

The Snob

aka: the arrogant, the cocky, the elitist, the hoity-toity, the self-important, the snooty, the snotty, the too cool

You haven't seen Rene in two years. Last you heard, she got a fancy job and is doing well. So it was a pleasant surprise when you run into her at a new restaurant you were trying for lunch with your boyfriend yesterday. Except it turned out to be not so nice when Rene seemed embarrassed to talk to you in front of her friends in their power suits. So what if you had a Phish t-shirt on with a hippie skirt and sandals? It's not like you were dining with the Pope. She acted as if you were some distant acquaintance instead of the friend who held her hair back while she puked into a plastic bag at a Lady Gaga show once upon a time. Rene thinks she is too good for you now.

There are those who believe they are a cut above the rest, a beacon of light among unenlightened souls; these individuals are called snobs.

Snobs are people who act like they believe they are superior to you, because they know more long words or have denser arm hair or possess longer earlobes or own a "yes" man to agree with every precious word out of their snooty mouth.

Encounters with snobs can start early in life, usually in schools where children with differences of some kind—usually economic ones—get lumped together, resulting in a hodgepodge of richer kids with poorer ones. Economic differences are easy to spot among children; rich kids get whatever they want by pissing and whining, poor kids get a muzzle when they do the same.

Young girls can excel at snobbery, being sharper and more able to detect subtleties and distinctions between people whereas boys seem to be slower at this game, being easily distracted by moving lights, insects with too many legs, and explosions. However, boys can learn to become snooty too as they grow up.

Snobbery can run in families but not always. Snobbery can arise without parental influence through social groups. There are art snobs, book snobs, clothing snobs, film snobs, religious snobs, food snobs, car snobs—the list is endless.

Being in the presence of a person who regards you as inferior is about as enjoyable as getting your hair combed with a garden rake. No one should look down on you—except taller people who must look down on you.

CAUSE:

It may come as a surprise that eating high quantities of potato chips, fried chicken, and french fries can lead a person to stick their nose up in the air, but it can due to the high amount of mucus that gets formed in the gut when too much fried oil is eaten, creating a snotty person in the process.

In many Eastern medical traditions, good physical and mental health depends on the proper balance of heat and dampness in the body. If one or the other is out of balance, then illness and mental functions will be out of whack. Excessive dampness inside the gut in the form of mucus—too much of it—causes great discomfort to the body and mind, resulting in behavior that appears to be snobbishness.

Excessive mucus in the gut leads to severe congestion in the sinuses, which is one reason snobs hold their noses high; snobs are attempting to prevent their noses from dripping mucus when a tissue isn't available. This is primarily the reason that snobs sniff their noses at others—they need to force the mucus back up the nose or face an embarrassing mess of themselves in mixed company.

A person who eats excessive amounts of fried foods can't stop their love of the greasy stuff. They will continue to eat way past the point that they should, not understanding the connection between mucus and fried oil.

Onion rings are dangerous for such a person if they cannot control themselves, and you want to be far away if they indulged in a whole plate of it. They'll want you to be far away as well. Their rude behavior is a fervent attempt to force your departure in the event that a snob has an explosive sneeze, sending their snotty salty spray into your minty Mojito.

If you meet a snob at a dinner party or social function who offends you by their condescending attitude, they most certainly have a severe sinus problem. They will make all sorts of snobbish remarks to separate themselves from you, because they don't want you near them if they start having uncontrollable post-nasal drip or uncontrolled sneezing, bound to be quite disgusting.

RECOMMENDATIONS:

If you meet a snob, you might want to mention a good nutritionist who can give dietary advice. If that seems too forward, hand the snob various mucus reducing snacks. Offer them whole grain crackers, wood chips, or activated charcoal. Never offer them anything that might increase their mucus load such as bacon wrapped figs with fried mozzarella sticks.

Never, of course, offer lemonade or orange juice after you've seen the snob down a bowl of fried calamari, for the fruits will break down immediately on top of their fried proteins, causing heavy fermentation in their gut that could cause a nasal explosion of horrific proportions. Only a cruel person with a conniving mind would do such an unkind thing.

The Snooper

aka: the busybody, the eavesdropper, the nosy, the spy

Whenever George visits anyone's home, he opens cabinet doors, drawers, and looks in people's closets. He knows his host would be pissed if they knew he was snooping around. He wouldn't want the same done to him, but he does it anyway. He hopes to never get caught because he doesn't want to get yelled at.

The snooper is an individual who has no business being in yours, but there they are, sneaking peeks in your checkbook, thumbing through your bills, reading your old love letters, and sampling your cheese collection.

Like a fruit fly you can't seem to shoo away, these little pests sneak up on you and before you know it, are all over the stuff in your home.

These busybodies want to know these personal details not to enrich their friendship with you in any way, but because they have an ulterior motive that may not be obvious.

Snoopers don't have a sense of boundaries, don't respect privacy, and have the maturity level of a six year old. Snoopers can be found in the workplace as well—someone wants to know what interesting snacks you keep in your locked shelf and how many pens you keep in a drawer.

If you happen to have a secret identity or own a collection of kinky sex toys, you probably don't want a snooper in your home. If a once chatty friend can no longer look you in the eye, you can bet they've been digging around and found something very embarrassing about you.

CAUSE:

What would cause a person to take such a strong interest in your personal business? Could it be your fascinating life or your charismatic personality? Probably not. Perhaps curiosity drives them to behave the way they do? Maybe, but something much more sinister is possibly at play.

A snooper may be accessing your personal life, gathering information on you so they can successfully plot your demise in order to snatch your body to feed a pet anaconda, a lion, or some other large exotic animal they own.

The exotic animal trade is unfortunately going strong, displacing rare species from their natural habitats into some clueless jerk's living room or apartment. Sometimes, an animal might land on someone's ranch or mansion, but in many cases, it's just a small backyard.

When an animal gets smuggled in, they are almost always baby sized, small enough to stow away in someone's luggage. This causes the animal excessive trauma as they are torn from their mother so ruthlessly. Sometimes, they die in transit. If they survive, they grow.

Unfortunately, the fool buying the lion cub fails to think long term, forgetting their cute little plaything will eventually turn into a giant creature with a gargantuan appetite.

If the owner doesn't have the money to buy a whole cow every other week to feed their hungry friend, they will start looking for cheaper ways to feed their companion. That's where you come in.

A snooper rummages through your stuff to see if you are a potential candidate for pet food. They need to gather as many details about you in order to concoct the most plausible way to end your life without raising suspicion. They need to know how many friends and relatives you have to determine whether you will be missed in the event of a disappearance.

This means that pissy, mean, shitty people stand a stronger chance of ending up as pet food as they are less likely to be missed. Popular people, on the other hand, will have close friends who won't give up until they get satisfying answers to their friend's strange disappearance.

The snooper also wants to know what they can keep for themselves when you are gone. If you've got a couple of cases of Lagunitas in the garage, guess who will help themselves to your stash right after you're taken out.

Sometimes, in the course of snooping, a snooper will find out you're a rich mofo and instead of doing you in, will divert some of your funds into their account, sparing your life in the process to feed Whiskers.

So if someone recently visited your home and soon after, your bank statement shows a large sum missing, count your blessings you are still alive and not in the belly of a hungry beast.

Snooping behavior can be more pervasive in states that allow pet ownership of large endangered animals. However, in states that have bans on large cats, you should still be concerned if alligators, mountain lions, wolves, bears, and coyotes are allowed as pets. These native creatures are easier to hide than non-North American animals that get smuggled in.

RECOMMENDATIONS:

Anyone who has a large, carnivorous animal in their possession, but not the income to feed such a grand creature, is a potential snooper. Watch your back.

Never visit their home and do not let them into your house for any reason—ever, especially when their pet is with them. In fact, you may want to report them to local authorities if they have any type of large wildlife and they are not a close friend.

If you suspect a friend has been snooping around your home, never invite them back. Plan your meetings in public places or drop them altogether. Anyone who can't respect boundaries is not a good person to have in your life and is probably planning to do you in anyways. ·

If you want to find out if someone is indeed snooping, you will need to set traps that will snare, hurt, or embarrass them.

If you catch the snooper before they can amass a huge file on you, you can end the relationship before they can do any harm. Keep a weapon on your body at all times.

As a safety measure, become a nicer person. Do things for others, grow your popularity and don't be a nasty shit that won't be missed if you end up as alligator food.

The Stalker

aka: the chaser, the obsessor, the pursuer

You come home from happy hour with friends to find a bouquet of roses waiting for you at your doorstep. Your heart nearly stops. The flowers are from a man you have no romantic feelings for who keeps calling, texting, sending you gifts, and driving past your home throughout the day. You glance around quickly. He's probably watching you from somewhere now. In the beginning, you were flattered but by the fourth month, you became scared. You made it clear you wanted him to stop, but that hasn't deterred him. Now you have nightmares of him lurking around every corner.

It's an ego booster to have admirers lust for you from afar, but what about the dude in the green fatigues camped out with binoculars in his Chevy across the street? A stalker is an individual who has an obsessive interest in another person, so much so that they spend most of their waking moments thinking about their subject in every icky way imaginable, acting on their obsession by contacting, spying, harassing, or hunting that person down.

Stalkers are consumed with their target person, feeling either immense love or hate. Men predominately outnumber female stalkers four to one, but when women get in the game, they are equally wackadoodle.

Celebrities, attractive people, and the very rich and famous all tend to attract stalkers. Anyone in the public eye can be a target for stalking. People who stalk the famous covet their victim's imagined existence and/or suffer the delusion that their love will be reciprocated by the object of their affection.

The very famous don't spend time stalking anybody; they're too busy enjoying their money, fame, adoration, and freebies wherever they go. However, stalking isn't only reserved for those in the spotlight.

When love goes sour between two people, love can turn into hate. A bad breakup can precipitate the nastiest type of attention—a need to inflict pain, to get even. Hence, a stalker is born. The dumped person's fixation on the former love's coming and goings may be due to some evil plot in the making: a desire to get revenge by starting a fire, smashing a car window, setting off grenades, painting naughty pictures on a garage, and worse.

Stalking can also be more subtle in situations when a person is in love with another they cannot have—a neighbor, a married co-worker, their best friend's wife. In these scenarios, the stalker pines quietly and stalks privately. This can mean an overabundant interest in the hobbies and social life of their just-out-of-reach love interest.

Stalking is an indication of a sad, unsatisfying, or lonely existence, one that could be helped tremendously by parlor games, dog shows, book clubs, and magic mushrooms.

CAUSE:

Not all who love or hate their exes are stalkers. Not all fans of the famous are stalkers either. Those who are more predisposed to stalking behavior may be the result of unethical experiments involving alien science.

For as long as science has existed, there have been curious minds responsible for unusual creations in hopes of discovering something incredible. Sometimes, scientists and researchers actually do come up with great things. In vitro burgers, anyone?

Where they get into questionable stuff is when they mix the DNA of different life forms to produce weird offspring that shouldn't exist. Ever heard of ligers, tigons, and hu-gers?

You may have heard of the first two but have probably not heard of hu-gers. Hu-gers are humans with a mixture of homo sapien and tiger DNA.

Thanks to a joint effort between the governments of the United Kingdom and the United States, researchers have been working with alien scientists for over a hundred years, unbeknownst to the rest of the population.

In contrast to some of the more sinister type of aliens frequenting our planet, these aliens that are allied with our human governments are from subterranean Mars. Yes, there is life on that cold planet—way beneath the surface—and we are on friendly terms with them. However, this is all kept secret as these aliens are difficult to look at. The average person would scream in the presence of these highly intelligent, but strangely textured Martians. The majority of us are not mature or smart enough to be in their company.

This cooperative effort came about as a way to learn from each other; alien knowledge in exchange for Earth's resources. Earth scientists learned all sorts of swell techniques while our government supplied prison inmates, transients, and animals as research subjects. Aliens conducted wild experiments on these poor lab rats, pushing the boundaries of science to their crazy limits.

Not too different from a kid who wonders how mayo in root beer might taste, human scientists wondered what would happen if a human ovum was fertilized with human sperm that had tiger DNA attached to it.

Normally, cross fertilization between wildly differently species will not produce a viable embryo. Human scientists tried and failed, but alien science succeeded where humans couldn't.

These alien scientists knew how to piggyback tiger DNA onto the tails of human sperm to help penetrate the barrier of the human ovum.

Once the egg started cell division, the aliens help the zygote grow into an embryo inside of an artificial uterine chamber, with nutrients provided by female "feeders" who were hooked up to these chambers.

Instead of spending their time creating something truly useful such as the one-hour orgasm, these aliens birthed several hundred hu-ger babies in the laboratory by around 1911.

Unlike ligers and tigons, a hu-ger did not necessarily resemble a tiger or have any physically identifiable traits of the big cat; hu-gers possessed mostly human DNA. But they did and do carry some of the tiger's genetic coding along with some of the tiger's instinctual behavior, one of which is stalking.

Hu-gers that developed into full grown adults acted the way tigers would, becoming unruly and wild when their hair was combed the wrong way and mesmerized by long pieces of string. Other than sharing some of the big cat's natural instincts, hu-gers were not faster runners and did not exhibit superior strength as many military leaders had hoped. However, their need to be loved, petted, scratched on the ear, share a bed, and get cat treats is what consumed them.

When hu-gers found people who they sensed might be great pet masters, they became attached, developed obsessive feelings and waited in the shadows watching their desired person's every move, similar to how cats camp out all day in wait for the return of rats and mice.

The novelty of creating hu-gers eventually wore off and the aliens went on to conduct more interspecies blends, not all of which are known. These early hu-gers had short lives but were still able to produce children before dying in their early 30's.

The progeny of hu-gers, after a century, continue to carry their foreparent's tiger DNA as well as the desire to obsess and stalk a desired person or thing.

After six generations of hu-ger progeny, the numbers of stalkers have increased and will continue to do so ensuring the harassment of future celebrities, love interests, and ex-lovers.

As a side note, this research program was halted when the internet became widely available to the general public. No longer able to control how information was disseminated, government officials realized they needed to end this creepy research before anyone on the outside found out. Regardless, aliens have and continue to experiment on Earth subjects with or without the assistance of governments.

RECOMMENDATIONS:

Hu-gers, like tigers and cats, are easily distracted if something else crosses their path during a stalking episode.

If you sense someone lurking in the shadows, first, barricade yourself behind a thick door. Call a friend for help. You could try calling law enforcement, but there is not much they can do unless the stalker lays a hand on you.

Have a friend come over with raw meat and a laser pointer. When the friend is about a hundred yards away from your doorstep, tell the friend to fling the meat in the opposite direction from where you are and see if the stalker comes out. If nothing happens, give it time. A warm sunny day should heighten the smell of raw flesh after a half hour.

Invariably, the stalker's nose will distract them from you as they go for the meat. Their desire to feed will override their need to get affection and petting from you. The same goes for the stalker with vengeance in their heart. The stomach always wins.

Once fully satiated, the stalker will become less interested in you and will start licking their fingers. At this point your friend should aim the laser pointer at the ground near the stalker and run with it. This will naturally bring out the chasing instinct in a stalker. Have your friend lead them far away from you so you can escape from your location.

If no friend or help is available anytime soon, get a bottle of vinegar and slather the pungent liquid in front of your doorstep to keep the stalker away. Tigers hate sour smells.

If someone is stalking you, you may feel scared but should feel flattered, for the stalker sees you as an appealing person, able to provide a comfy home for them to lounge around in.

In the case of ex-lovers, deliberate cessation of caressing and petting makes them desperate for the old days. If that is no longer available to them, their anger and hurt triggers their animal instincts to take over, and they watch your every move. In doing so, if they catch you romantically involved with someone new, they may try to destroy your life.

The male progeny of hu-gers is much more dangerous than the female. As a last resort, you may need to keep a big dog—the natural enemy of a hu-ger—in your yard.

The Stoner

aka: the pothead, the red-eyed, the wasted

One of the first things Sandeep does when he wakes up in the morning is to light up a spliff. One of the last things he does before he goes to sleep is to light up a spliff. In the afternoon for lunch, he sucks in bong hits and for daily snacks, he takes small tokes on a pipe loaded with Purple Kush. He can often be found sitting quietly staring off into space. Twelve hours later, he can be found sitting quietly staring off into space. Twenty-four hours later, he is still sitting quietly staring off into space. Life moves kind of slow when you are a full-time stoner.

A stoner is a person who uses marijuana excessively on a daily, sometimes hourly basis and will hog all the pot in a smoking circle.

Getting high from smoking or eating marijuana makes many users slow down to almost an inert state, becoming like an immovable rock or stone, hence the label "stoner." This makes them quite handy as a cat companion with an available lap for a whole day, keeping your pet occupied so it will stop following you throughout the house with their demanding meows.

Depending on the variety of pot a stoner smokes and how much of it, they can get into a light dreamy state and still function as a person or be super fried and useless. When they are too stupefied to move, they can become semi-incoherent.

If you've spent any time with stoners, you know what that means. They can't drive more than five miles an hour—anything faster and they say, "WHOA"; give them a simple task and they will do it over and over and over again, stuck in rewind mode; they have no short-term memory; they stare at a wall for hours acting as if it will eventually tell them jokes; they can't get off the couch; they giggle and won't shut up; they write worse than a seven-year-old; and they eat up all your junk food.

Stoners are quite useful when you want to clean out your shelves and test food expiration dates. Cookie dough with freezer burn? Give it to the stoner. A decades old box of crackers? Only a stoner would appreciate that long marinade of formaldehyde fumes from your shelf. If they don't puke, then you know you can eat something way past the *sell by* date.

That said, there are some stoners who will surprise you with their astounding revelations and philosophical theories on the workings of space and time. This subset of stoners is a class above the rest. They can understand the theory of relativity and cite pi to the thousandth digit. They understand how black holes work and are so inspired that they can write long essays on their theories. All you have to do is smoke the same shit they did and stare at the same Lucky Charm's marshmallow carefully in order to understand any of it.

Individuals with serious medical conditions are helped greatly by pot to eliminate nausea, stimulate appetite, manage pain, and reduce tumors. In that case, smoking massive quantities of pot is encouraged.

CAUSE:

Stoners of the highest kind get that way due to the crazy shit circulating these days. There are more stoners than ever, because the potent stuff is so easy to get. No more wimpy "Columbian Gold." Now there's "Hairy Lips" and "I Need to Crawl" and "Where's My Eyebrow"—stuff meant to fry your mind. For an occasional toker, one or two hits of this shit will send you off to the moon.

Even being in the same airspace of Mary Jane secondary smoke has an effect of blissing you out, unless you have an allergy to weed.

With strong weed everywhere and beaucoup stress in this busy world, becoming a spaced out, red-eyed stoner is preferable to dealing with that colony of cockroaches under the kitchen sink.

In the states that have legalized pot, it's hard to get away from the wonder weed; it seems everyone is smokin' some good shit. Even grannies are getting in on it, growing pot in their sewing baskets, baking cookies with it, and hawking it to their friends.

RECOMMENDATIONS:

If you know someone who spends too much of their time lighting up a bong or eating happy treats, steal their stash and give it to the Type A's and Control Freaks you know. Control Freaks and Type A's are the ones who really need to chill out so they can stop pissing off the rest of society.

Replace the stoner's stash with freeze-dried kale so they can be sure to get some healthy greens. Also, hide their smoking paraphernalia. Tell them to stop being wasted and start living.

The Superstitious

aka: the believer, the irrational

variation: the faithful

Every day, promptly at 3 p.m., Misha hears the ice cream man pass down the street pushing his cart. It doesn't make any sense, but she feels somehow comforted by the sound of the bells on his cart. All is right with the world. So it was with great alarm that on a certain Thursday, there was no ice cream man around and no sound of delightful bells in the air. Misha felt a sudden panic, believing the break in routine as a sign of bad things to come. She knew it was a silly thought, but she couldn't help the sense of foreboding.

A superstitious person is one who believes in the cause and effect connection between two different things that may have little or no relationship to one another, basing assumptions on irrational and/or coincidental circumstances, for example, believing a broken mirror in the morning has something to do with being called a douchebag in the afternoon.

Superstitious beliefs and practices are relatively safe and tend to be restricted to the person possessing the belief. In rare cases, however, they can lead a person to make really bad and silly decisions, causing great harm to others such as their own children.

For example, a child with a staph infection, typhoid fever, or tuberculosis would benefit from a visit with a medical doctor. A deeply superstitious or religious person might believe talking to a statue, screaming at the ceiling, throwing salt into the air, or getting yelled at by a trembling guy with a snake to be more effective than medicine.

Most superstitious people are only lightly superstitious and for the most part, don't take it too far beyond rubbing a dead animal's foot for luck or wearing a charm or a talisman. Sometimes, a few words are mumbled under a breath, a plea is made to a particular angel, or a favorite t-shirt is worn before going to a game.

These minor actions can calm a person down and make them believe they have some control over their life. It even makes them think they can prevent a runaway truck from knocking them into an electrical wire that will fry them alive.

CAUSE:

Tripping on drugs should not be done lightly. When a trip is embarked on with purpose and care, psychedelics can help expand a mind. When tripping happens by accident in a mind that is unstable or unprepared, hallucinations can really mess a person up. Bad drug trips may be the origin of superstitious beliefs.

In the old days, before pharmacology or biochemistry was invented, people put whatever looked colorful and appealing into their mouths. Sometimes, those items ended up being psilocybin mushrooms, peyote, salvia divinorum, morning glories, and other pretty plants with psychoactive properties.

Those early poor unsuspecting victims tripped hard and heavy from eating plants out of hunger.

In doing so, they saw fantastical and sometimes horrific things that weren't really there. For example, an accidental tripper who came into contact with a black cat could mistake it for an incubus with flashing eyes. Cracks in a hard dried ground could be seen as veins inside their mother's uterus. Cherry blossoms in a tree could be seen as oozing bloody pimples on a green giant's face.

If the tripper was so scared out of their mind that they made a mad run for it—right into a grizzly bear's arms—bad things were bound to happen.

After the psychoactive ingredient wore off and if the tripper was still alive, they fearfully recounted their experience to the townsfolk. In the case of the poor black cat, the feline was forever maligned as an evil entity. Once a story got planted into simple minds, it became truth and superstitions were created.

Humans seek meaning where none may exist. If shit happens for no reason, why in the world do we bother being good? But if bad things can be linked to something in our control, that makes it easier to wake up in the morning and scramble some eggs.

In an effort to seek control over chaotic circumstances, a person hallucinating under some bad drugs or with a grand imagination may connect dissimilar causes and effects as a way to cope with shitty circumstances. But just to be safe, try not to break mirrors anyway.

RECOMMENDATIONS:

If the superstitious person is interested in being cured, the best way to negate a superstition is by fully immersing themselves into whatever object is feared.

Afraid of black cats? Let a black cat lounge on your face and see how friendly they can be. Afraid of Friday the 13th? Plan a big party for that night.

To rid an unnatural attachment to an object, inflict negative feedback by yanking the person's hair while they hold the charm. That may help reset the superstitious mind back to a neutral position.

For superstitious beliefs involving faith healing, this usually gets remedied by law enforcement, angry relatives, or the public when a child or a spouse is harmed from getting inadequate treatment. It may only take one failure with grave results to cure a superstitious person forever.

The Sycophant

aka: the ass kisser, the bootlicker, the brown noser, the fawner, the flatterer, the teacher's pet

variation: the hanger-on, the parasite

Today, something unusual happened. Alice went out of her way to stop by your office to tell you how nice you looked and how great you smelled. This is the same person who last year—on your first day of work when you said "hello" to her—bared her canines at you. You were terribly hurt by her unfriendly demeanor. Now she is all smiles and syrupy words. Maybe it's the promotion you got recently, which now gives you the power to approve or veto any employee's time off. You don't trust Alice one bit.

A sycophant is a person who fawns over other people to get ahead and gain favors, resulting in an insincere person who can't seemingly be trusted.

Anyone who has been in a situation where they needed to be nice to someone, because their job was on the line, knows how phony they feel being artificially nice to a person they think deserves a big wedgie.

Sometimes bosses, managers, and supervisors have fat egos that can destroy if they aren't sucked up to. In those instances, a fake smile can go a long way, but for a select few, over the top flattery is the way to go.

All those false sugary words are attempts to get something special, making the sycophant appear to be a dishonest turkey with a personal agenda.

Generally speaking, sycophants aren't usually as friendly to those who cannot benefit them and may even seem standoffish to their peers and others of lower status.

This behavior should be exercised with caution as it can inspire co-workers to sneak a squirt of Purell into the brown noser's mocha latte.

People hate a suck-up in their midst, because it puts those who refuse to play the game in an unfavorable light. If Mr. Manager really is a turd in a suit, finding nice words to say is really an odious chore.

CAUSE:

It may seem like sycophants are really self-interested, insincere ass-kissers, but such a quick dismissal ignores the fact that many of them may behave the way they do, because of severe periodontal disease they got from their dogs. This deters people from wanting to talk or get close to them. In order to compensate for this problem, they resort to flattery as a way to hold someone's attention.

When a person loves their dog, they end up exchanging lots of saliva with their little buddy boy. A dog who loves their owner licks their master's face and mouth and anything else they can get their wet, slimy tongue on.

The pet owner who loves their dog welcomes that tongue with a lick of their own. In this loving show of affection the owner gets a good dose of their dog's gum bacteria.

This creates a problem as older dogs tend to have periodontal disease, because they can't grasp a toothbrush with their paws, aren't great at squeezing toothpaste out of a small tube, and have years of accumulated plaque and bacteria in their mouth. As a result, a dog's breath is pretty foul and they spread those germs to their owner whenever they show their love.

For example, when Fido slobbers all over Master Joe's face, Joe may not know Fido is also spreading the microscopic enemies inside their mouth, because Fido smells bad all the time in every way, from his bad farts to the open sores he has from flea bites.

Joe doesn't realize nasty smells on a pet means a visit to the veterinarian is in order. He won't notice the reek from serious gum disease every time Fido smooches him, because he has become desensitized to his dog's god awful stink.

Joe will develop foul breath no one wants to be near and he won't know why. In order to keep someone present, Joe discovers he has to compliment them with copious amounts of flattery. It may not even be a conscious thing but a reflexive response.

Having to keep this up on a daily basis with everyone, however, can get very tiresome and it only seems to happen when someone gets physically close to him. Selectively choosing who to flatter is a matter of self preservation. It can make a big difference in Joe's life. He acts unfriendly to those who don't benefit him in some way because he knows, once he tries to engage in friendly chit chat, the other person will abruptly end the conversation and leave.

This hurts Joe's feelings. As a result of this coping mechanism, he ends up being viewed as a sycophant, because he will only engage in flattery on those individuals he needs something from.

RECOMMENDATIONS:

If you know such a person whose words are sugary sweet while their breath is not, offer them a breath mint. See if you can introduce the subject of canine dental health. Find out whether they have an older dog at home.

Bad breath is a delicate matter. It may not be easy to tell the smelly one their breath could be used as a weapon of mass destruction. Let them know you are concerned for their dog's well-being. Recommend a good veterinarian.

If you find yourself offering profuse compliments in order to hold someone's attention and wonder why people keep their conversations short with you, get your teeth and gums checked out and stop slobbering all over your dog. You're a different species. Knock it off! Your dog has, no doubt, licked up some drunk's barf when it was running loose in the park.

Go take your dog to the vet. Know that you are making enemies with your flowery words, so stop it, and get your gums taken care of.

The Talker

aka: the bloviator, the chatterbox, the gabber, the jabberjaws, the long-winded, the motor mouth, the verbose, the windbag

Words, so many of them flow out of Hector's lips—an endless stream for a half hour. You don't know what the subject is anymore. It started off as a question about your electric shaver, but has somehow morphed into a long lecture on how to grill a bratwurst. Then, suddenly, it's about engine oil followed by a forty minute comparison of car wax brands. The guy will not shut up, and there is no escape from his car. He's on the highway going 55—too fast for you to jump out. The only chance of getting away from the talker is when you fake an oncoming bowel explosion, forcing jabber jaws to stop at the nearest gas station where you can escape for a break.

The talker is a person who aggressively dominates a conversation, able to talk for long periods of time without a break, turning you into a hostage who can only add comments, questions, and opinions after head-butting them in the stomach.

In a discussion between two or more people, there are two roles available, listener(s) and speaker. After the speaker gets what they need off their chest, he or she stops and the listener then becomes the speaker.

In a perfect world, when one is speaking the other listens with rapt attention. Sometimes, two people can vie for airtime, but this causes problems and requires a referee with a bullhorn to fix.

A person who bogarts a conversation is highly problematic; the talker is such a person. The talker has a serious issue of not shutting up.

They will tell you every detail of their brake repair job and will segue way into random topics, like the time they found a dead raccoon pinned underneath their car with guts splattered everywhere and when they grabbed the hose to spray it off, realized the spigot wouldn't turn due to rust so they went to their basement for a wrench, unexpectedly finding not a wrench but a naked gnome with three wives living there. Now they are worried about selling the house before the holidays when the housing market always plummets, because people are busy with Christmas shopping and not house buying and damn it, they need to find a gift for their high maintenance girlfriend who is impossible to satisfy, because she's so damn picky about everything and maybe they should go out with someone more down to earth.

Pleading looks, turning away, clearing your throat, and other polite hints don't work on a talker. They won't stop and will talk you into submission. It takes forceful interruption or tear gas, to stop them.

In rare instances, a talker's non-stop chatter can be useful when background noise is needed as a hypnotic tool for sleep. A talker is also useful in a room full of shy people who are all afraid to say anything, but other than a few special situations the talker is not one you want to engage with if you have a bladder infection.

CAUSE:

Talkative people are driven to talk incessantly by the need to eliminate an excessive buildup of oxygen in their blood due to a large lung capacity.

Humans need oxygen, but too much of a good thing becomes bad, and too much of this vital element can make a person feel really really crappy, enough to cause all sorts of toxicity in their cells, in turn becoming toxic to good manners.

Oxygen gets utilized in our body after it is breathed into our lungs. The oxygen diffuses into cell membranes and gets distributed to various red blood cells. In a talker, however, not all of the oxygen is expended properly, because their lungs can hold a lot more than the rest of their body needs.

With excess oxygen to spare, some of it heads up into the brain where it can cause free radicals to form. This seriously compromises the ability to understand social cues and is probably the reason why a talker is unable to see the irritation on a listener's face as well as failing to hear another person's attempts to speak.

Some of the excess oxygen is retained in the lungs, causing a burst of energy that needs to be dispelled. If a person doesn't get rid of that excess energy, they will feel uncomfortable.

Talking feels good. Talking a lot feels even better for the motor mouth because they are rebalancing how much of the gas is in their system. Talkers are quite literally windbags; they hold a lot of air in there!

When interrupted, the talker sometimes gives a momentary confused stare, but then continues gabbing as if that last detail about their sweaty neck is something you must know right now or your life will be unfulfilled.

Weather may impair a talker's capacity. Extremely cold weather can slow a talker down, as oxygen gets expelled at a faster rate, while warm weather gets that speedy mouth going.

RECOMMENDATIONS:

A talker in need of expelling excess oxygen requires greater measures than verbal interruption; they need a physical workout. Telling them to clam it doesn't work. They need to keep speaking to feel better and if insulted, may scream nonstop at you instead.

To really help a talker, gallop away from them. Tell them a cramp in your foot requires physical intervention. Suggest they follow your lead. Add in jumping jacks and quick sprints while the talker continues. They will have to exert themselves physically to keep up with you as you move away from them.

If the talker has something important to say in the middle of all that rambling, they will want you close by, but the additional workout will rid the excess oxygen in their system quicker, making them feel better faster and they will finally shut the fuck up. Finally, you'll get a chance to say something.

The Tempter

aka: the coaxer, the enchanter, the enticer, the persuader

Nolan's eyes are glued to the rum-infused chocolate buttercream cake at the company picnic. He wants it, but he knows it will hurt his heart. The doctor told him to lose 100 pounds or he'll get diabetes and need a heart transplant—not an attractive proposition. Finally, he breaks away from that plate of sin. He congratulates himself on his iron will. But then Gerald comes over with two plates, each containing a piece of that dangerous sweet. He plops one down in front of Nolan and tells him to enjoy himself. He knows full well Nolan's struggle with dieting, but he tells his weight conscious friend that he should reward himself once in a while. Nolan has to find some way of getting rid of his tempter pal who will help him to an early grave.

When trying to be good, no one needs a tempter or temptress anywhere near them, baiting them with all sorts of goodies that will end up in all sorts of baddies.

Everyone has a weakness. For Superman, it's kryptonite. For a cheesehead, it's a slab of smoked cheddar. For an unhappily married straight dude, it's a sexy woman in a short, tight skirt.

There are things we shouldn't indulge in, because they are bad for us and will get us into a whole mess o' trouble.

But then someone comes along that can throw a person off course. It could be a friend, a cousin, a stranger with something to sell and before you know it, there's five pounds of heart clogging fried butter cubes in your mouth.

Temptation is everywhere. It can take every ounce of willpower not to scarf down that triple decker cheeseburger with extra bacon. When you succeed in saying "no," a noncaloric reward is in order. But when a tempter crosses your path dangling a badly desired object, you may not be able to resist the sinful sight. Then you'll be sorry.

This is especially true when temptation comes in the form of a person who has a big old ring around their wedding finger and their spouse happens to have large biceps, carries a Glock, and wears a dark blue uniform. Don't go there. You could end up unconscious in a gutter clogged with sewage swill, your dick forcibly removed, and placed behind bars with a mentally unhinged maniac who stares at you up close with their crazed eyes while you sleep.

CAUSE:

Tempters and temptresses do not have your best interest at stake and are not truly your friends, but are actually paid minions of big pharma companies who get commissions every time you take one of their drugs.

It may be hard to believe cousin Barry is on the payroll of one of these unscrupulous drug pushers, but it's true. Every time you down a six-pack of cherry cola, you are that much closer to a lifetime of insulin shots, and Barry is that much closer to getting his jet skis.

It can be a very lucrative deal for a commissioned tempter whose purpose is to make sure you are on drugs for life. High cholesterol? Acid reflux? Diabetes? All of these maladies can be remedied with drug treatments that help make the wallets of tempters and pharma CEOs that much fatter.

If you think about it, it makes perfect sense. The people who care about you the most don't tell you to do dumbass things that will screw up your life. When was the last time you heard a mom say, "Go ahead honey, do that line of coke. It'll help you with that algebra assignment." Nope. It's usually someone who has a casual relationship with you or a friend who wants to see you fail.

Tempters who try to get you to cheat on your partner are also out for a commission. Once someone has been caught screwing around (two-timers almost always get caught), an ugly scene usually follows, which ends up in some sort of depressing breakup for the couple involved.

Drugs solve everything and that tempter/temptress in your path just earned a hefty commission if you end up buying mood-enhancing prescription drugs for a few years.

RECOMMENDATIONS:

When you meet someone who tries to persuade you from your noble, disciplined path, know they are not your friend or ally. Know that they are using your demise to fund their trip to Waikiki.

If the temptation is too great for you to bear, use your imagination to help you resist. A chocolate sauce could be reimagined as diarrhea if you try hard enough. A white sausage gravy could pass for vomit. A whiskey sour could be turpentine. A hookup with that hostess could end up with sharp scissors on your balls. Willpower requires that you imagine the tempting item as something nasty and frightening.

You could also try confronting the tempter, demanding to know what company they're on the payroll of.

You can also turn away and let them know you can't be swayed by their sinful attempts—munch a big piece of burdock root right in their face.

If you show yourself to be a hard nosed, disciplined, healthy, faithful person, the tempter will stop tempting you, figuring you to be an unprofitable waste of time.

The Thief

aka: the burglar, the con artist, the hustler, the kleptomaniac, the mugger, the pickpocket, the robber, the scammer, the shoplifter, the swindler

variation: the embezzler

After hanging out with friends for a bit of tasty grub, you go back to your car to find that it is nowhere in sight. After 10 minutes of searching, it dawns on you that it is gone, that someone took your car while you were savoring that almond tart. You have been robbed of your precious wheels by some carjacking prick.

Thieves are people who steal, take, or permanently borrow the most super awesome thing in your possession: a laptop, a Fender Stratocaster, or an Xbox, but never makes off with the stuff you really want to get rid of but can't, namely the ugly reindeer sweater you got from uncle Jim or the overprotective bull terrier your girlfriend brings over whenever she spends the night.

Thievery can start at an early age with kids taking toys and lunch money from other kids, without impunity.

Later, as the young thief grows older, they learn to shoplift from stores. If they get away with it enough times, they will graduate to stealing on a frequent basis from as many places as possible.

In the old days, thieves stole mostly physical items: cash, horses, wagons, food, wives, and husbands. Nowadays, thieves can steal these things and more, such as intellectual property, social security numbers, credit cards, and ideas.

People aren't the only culprits capable of robbing you. There are also banks that steal from you through dishonest practices, offering contracts with hidden terms and conditions in small print buried on page 48 that require you to part with a finger every year. There are also kleptomaniacs, people with a compulsion to steal items big and small, from motorcycles to plastic forks.

There are times when people steal out of necessity, stealing food to feed a family. But sometimes, thievery can happen when someone has an aversion to work.

Many thieves lack an honest moral code and will not hesitate to separate you from your well earned goodies for their own enjoyment.

On rare occasion, there are thieves who steal from the rich, the corrupt, the military, or some other organization for the supposed benefit of society. These thieves get lauded by some but condemnation by others.

When something you cherish is taken from you, it makes you fantasize strange things that are out of character, fantasies that include netting the thievin' bastard, then coating them in a layer of Cheez Whiz and holding them in the basement with hungry city raccoons.

CAUSE:

Thieves have been inspired to do their misdeeds based on the corrupted understanding of the legendary tale of Robin Hood.

Sometime during the 15th century, one man rose as a hero among his peers. His name was Robin Hood and whether he was a real or imaginary figure, he was famous for stealing from the rich to give to the poor.

Today, almost everyone has heard of Robin Hood, but not everyone has gotten his story straight.

Instead of comprehending the noble mission of Robin Hood, burgeoning thieves hear the words "robbin' the hood" or "Robin, the hood." Instead of *stealing from the rich to help the poor*, thieves believe the motto to be *steal from everyone to help myself*.

Somewhere along the way, the story got bastardized in the thief's ear. Perhaps it was wishful thinking, but ethically challenged people have consistently heard or wanted to believe a different story. If anyone does correct them, they argue their own version of the story and use it as a personal justification to unlawfully take from others.

Young punks and spoiled brats are quite prone to mishearing words as they have short attention spans and don't listen anyway.

Institutions that rob you with their shitty practices are run by folks who have also misunderstood the classic tale.

Emboldened by the classic story, thieves tell themselves that robbin' the hood is a good thing, one that they need to keep doing 'cuz some dude got famous for doing that a long time ago.

Right before a thief breaks into a home, they sing a little song about robbin' the hood, making themselves feel righteous in the process.

RECOMMENDATIONS:

Thieves need to understand the real story of Robin Hood so they can quit bastardizing the tale to their offspring and friends. In fact, they may use the Robin Hood story as justification for stealing while poor—a lame excuse as the majority of people in the U.S. and the world is poor.

Once a thief has successfully scored goods with ease, they will not stop. Forced rehabilitation becomes necessary once a thief is captured and imprisoned.

If the thief is not moved by the real legendary story of good, there really is no other choice than to force them into a Robin Hood costume and have them participate in a play about the hero's life.

Repeating the motto *steal from the rich and give to the poor* over and over again will eventually help the thief understand the true story.

Acting out Robin Hood's deeds of giving generously to the misfortunate on a weekly basis may help modify a thief's behavior once they are out of prison; repetition is a good way to form new habits.

If not, then the only other option is glue their fingers together, making it difficult for them to steal but also to do anything else.

The Troublemaker

aka: the agitator, the heckler, the hellion, the hooligan, the instigator, the provoker, the rabble-rouser

Trudy and Noah are in love. They seem to be a perfect fit for one another. He loves walking in lightning storms; so does she. He can't stand the smell of worms; she feels the same way. Both are vegan and have a passion for Tofutti bars. Each appreciates the sound of whirring helicopters on a hot summer's eve and for them, a romantic afternoon means watching the turtles mate at the zoo. They're a match made in heaven and have never had a fight, until Noah's brother Joel came for a visit. He thought they were a little too happy for their own good and decided their relationship could use a little spicing up. He tells Trudy that Noah, as a teenager, had a pet duck he strangled one day for no reason—something Trudy had never heard before. Joel tells Noah Trudy seems to be a little flirty with the guy in the apartment downstairs and is probably bored with her sex life. This brings a frown to Noah's face. By the time Joel leaves, the two have their first big fight ever. Joel has again succeeded in doing what he does best—cause trouble.

Troublemakers are people who instigate problems, dissent, and chaos wherever they go and are quite disgusted when trapped in a room where people hold hands and sing merry tunes.

This bad behavior is rather broad based and not specific to any situation; troublemakers are everywhere. A few examples include the heckler who makes offensive comments to get reactions; the patron who decides a food fight needs to happen right there in a cafeteria; and the instigator who throws the first egg at a cop's face during a protest.

Harmony, peace, and love are three repulsive words to a troublemaker. They can't stand team effort and cooperation. They feel most content when others are crapping their pants.

Troublemakers are easy to identify, because they are repeat offenders.

They should definitely not be invited to your bachelor party. They should also not be allowed to enter libraries and hospitals.

CAUSE:

Sex. People want it. People need it. When that hankering for a hand job comes along, it is best to try and satisfy those primal urges or else you could become a troublemaker.

Being a horny devil puts a person on edge with great urgency to satisfy those needs. This is where problems can arise. If a frisky female or fellow doesn't have a satisfying conclusion to those sexual longings, they can end up being a chaotic, irritable person causing mayhem and trouble wherever they go.

If you haven't been living in a coffin, you have probably heard of Bonobo monkeys and their insanely promiscuous behavior. Females on males, males on males, group sex—it's a free for all! They spend their days humpin' and bumpin'.

Bonobo monkeys don't cause trouble or fight, because they are getting "it" by the hour. This puts a smile on their furry faces. But if the sexual component were removed, they would become as crappy as other primates, easy to anger, full of piss, and ready to brawl over the last blu ray player on sale.

Humans are no different. When an extremely horny human doesn't get any action, they become a little crazy inside. Something needs to get released, to explode, and if it doesn't happen, they become ripe for troublemaking.

For the Joe or Jane with an average libido, masturbation will do the trick, but for the real pent up toad, masturbation doesn't quite satisfy the way another person does, the way food tastes better when it's prepared by someone else.

After all, there is no excitement when you squeeze your own orange juice. You know your own moves while another person's hand offers the novelty factor. Will they start at the top or the bottom? Will they go for the navel or get right down to juicing? There are many ways to squeeze oranges; an extremely horny person needs a little help to do so. Inner dissatisfaction leads to outer dissatisfaction.

When others seem happy, content, and at peace, it bothers the sexually frustrated person. No one has the right to enjoy life when the troublemaker ain't gettin' any.

RECOMMENDATIONS:

If you find a troublemaker in your midst, you've got a randy rascal in front of you.

If they are physically appealing to you, find a room or an available counter for an afternoon grind.

If they disgust you, tell them to go get help. Suggest some hookup apps they can use and if needed, pitch in a few dollars to help them join some of the better ones.

The troublemaker may not realize the connection between sexual frustration and their urge to cause chaos. You may have to spell it out for them. However, it's really not your problem.

Getting laid is not an easy endeavor unless you are female. Females can always get laid if they know how to market their availability.

Men have a trickier time, which may account for why the majority of troublemakers end up being male. This makes it doubly difficult, because men are oftentimes a great deal hornier than women to the point where they end up doing and saying really stupid shit to get laid such as "I see dead people and they tell me we have to make out in the coatroom."

Men can also become overly aggressive and refuse to back down from strong objections, along the lines of "fuck off" and "get off me asshole" and "want your dick diced up into little pieces and served to you on a rusty platter?" If the sexually frustrated can find a local sex club where orgies are available for an entrance fee, it may be a good option.

If you are a troublemaker, understand the source of your frustration. If no partners are present, then it's really up to your own ingenuity to release that bomb inside you.

Perhaps wearing a mask of a hot celebrity while masturbating in front of a mirror will give the illusion of a real partner, or watching porn with decent actors and a good storyline can make you feel like a participant. Otherwise, your troublemaking days are ahead and that can put a damper on gettin' any action.

The Type A

aka: the ambitious, the busy bee, the driven, the "on edge," the stress bunny, the stressed out, the workaholic

You arrive at Mario's desk for a meeting scheduled for 10 o'clock, but he's not ready. As you sit waiting and waiting, you realize you only have an hour before you have to leave for a sperm donor appointment. Mario is having a hissy fit in front of you as he tries to return a call while typing an email and booking travel for a conference. Meanwhile, your pile of to do's is no less than his and you're wasting precious minutes while Mario freaks out. Why he can't stop right now and just meet with you for 15 minutes, you'll never know. Mario is a Type A personality. He has to show you how busy and important he is.

There's no stress bunny quite as frazzled as the Type A personality, a person in a constant state of agitation and busyness as they rush past you en route to giving a very important speech on the proper way to peel a banana.

The Type A always has a mountain to climb and if it turns out to be only a molehill, they will insist on the grand heights of that molehill and the rough terrain of that hill and the expensive gear they had to buy to climb it.

These overscheduled people exhibit impatience, stress, anxiety, rigidity, overachievement, and rudeness. They also sigh heavily, have conniption fits and say on an hourly basis, "I am so busy, you have no idea." They may have a lot to show for their time here on Earth, but they disturb other humans while they live.

Type A's have no time to stop and smell the lilacs, because doing so takes away time they could spend telling you about the important things they are going to do in the next 24 hours.

If you wish to spend time with a Type A, you will need to book a date weeks in advance and when you do get a meeting, made to feel like a cow pie they suddenly notice after a half hour of waiting in a chair—unless you're a VIP that can influence their life in some way. If you are, you can expect a chef plate and a masseuse waiting for you.

When a Type A gets thrown off course or off schedule, they turn red and can be seen shaking, trying very hard to restrain their anxiety.

In conversation the Type A will list their accomplishments as a direct result of their workaholic ethic. This, in turn, gives them an excuse to be rude while they manically check the time in your presence.

You may wonder what the "A" stands for in the term "Type A." It's for "Asshole."

CAUSE:

Type A behavior stems from sleeping with the head in front of or very close to electrical outlets, smart phones, blu ray transmitters, and wifi routers. Doing so releases electromagnetic fields (aka EMF) waves into the sleeper's head on a nightly basis, frying nerves and neurons, causing noticeable physical and behavioral changes that keep the exposed person on edge, eventually turning them into a tool.

EMFs have been studied extensively by numerous scientists who have linked the dangers of long term exposure with brain and blood cancers and a variety of other harmful effects: blood electrification, hair follicle die off, eardrum damage, and nose inversion into the skull.

Having the whole head zapped by EMFs on a nightly basis also dulls the part of the brain that controls anxiety and obsession, causing this person to believe they must accomplish as much as possible, or they will turn into—gasp—an average person.

Anybody, after prolonged bombardment of EMFs over many decades, can't help but become a supercharged dipstick that annoys every colleague they come into contact with.

RECOMMENDATIONS:

Grounding is what these hyped up people need. They need to be at one with Mother Earth and what better way than to be fully immersed in her through hot mud baths.

Type A's would benefit from the comforting feel of warm pasty earth all over their bodies, soaking into their skin, calming their inner crazies. Downing a cup of warm, sanitized liquid clay would also be very useful, offering a way to cleanse the body inside out.

If you recognize your own spazzy tendencies and cannot readily find a good mud bath to soak in, you can lie down naked on a plot of grass in your own backyard. Make yourself do nothing for an hour but enjoy the song birds overhead. Toss your phone into a warm cup of water and forget the worries of the day.

Visit a good hypnotist who can help push your anxieties away and free your mind to believe you are a cow grazing in a grassy meadow.

The User

aka: the false friend, the parasite

Devon broke his foot after snowboarding into a pine tree. He's in a cast and can't move around too well. He calls his buddy Julian, the dude he helped three months ago who was flat broke and needed to move out ASAP. Devon was sick at the time and should have stayed home; he caught pneumonia from being out in the cold. But he's a nice guy, has a big truck, and Julian sounded desperate. Now Devon could really use some help. He rings Julian up asking for a ride to the store sometime during the week. To his surprise, Julian says he's busy surfing and doesn't have any time to spare—ever. The worst thing, though, was how callous Julian was. He didn't ask how Devon was doing or offer to help in any way. WTF? Devon is blown away. Turns out, Julian is no real friend after all. He feels completely used.

A user is a person who falsely befriends another for the purpose of getting something they want or need, misrepresenting their real intentions, allowing the other to believe that a real honest to goodness friendship exists when, in reality, the user is only interested in borrowing that new forklift in the back lot.

The user may sound similar to the psychic vampire (see *The Psychic Vampire*) with the difference being that the latter actually enjoys chowing down a pepperoni pizza with you.

Luckily, users tend to have short-term relationships, unless the other is a dolt, easily swindled over and over again.

People with lots of material things can be targets for users who need what the financially endowed have to offer, more so when the victim possesses the brain of a golf ball. However, people who are broke can be used too.

Users are everywhere and if one is not careful, can end up wasting a great deal of your time and drive you to hit a pillow with an axe.

Users are easy to identify after a few interactions; a pattern emerges where you give everything to them and they give nothing to you.

CAUSE:

A user is a person who hasn't learned the meaning of friendship, doesn't know what a real friendship entails, and is possibly an anti-social person trying to adjust to the human world (see *The Antisocial*).

There are those walking among us who are new to a flesh and blood existence, formerly being display mannequins left in storage rooms, until they were turned human by students of magic.

These previously stiff figures are trying to navigate through social interactions without proper orientation and guidance. They don't know what relationships are. They have a very childish understanding of the give and take exchange between two people in a long-term friendship. No one has offered the user type a manual to read and learn from. The user has a one track mind, that is, to satisfy their immediate needs.

Users sometimes need to borrow an item or get assistance and will ask for help in a friendly manner. If they've been around for awhile, they learn to ask for things in a nice way or others will tell the user to go fuck themselves.

The user has seen how other people speak to one another. Through imitation, they have learned how to mimic polite phrasing. It probably took a few times before they got it right; their early attempts got them nowhere.

However, friendships are much harder for the user to see in action. Feelings between friends are not easily visible to the eye. That is why they are so awful when it comes to reciprocating—these folks do not know any better.

The user may never understand the nuts and bolts of a real relationship and will go from one person to the next in order to get what they need.

RECOMMENDATIONS:

If you have been used by someone, you may feel slighted and hurt. If the user is someone you wish to engage with on a deeper level, you will have to be the one to initiate a real friendship.

Why you would want to is another question, but considering mannequins are created with attractive faces and bodies, their appearance might have won you over. Perhaps they are a babe magnet and you benefit from their company. Perhaps you feel driven to call them out on their shitty behavior?

Whatever the reason, you will have to explain to the former mannequin what "feelings" are and how yours were hurt. You will also have to explain to them how friendships work; show them what they need to do.

Suggest going to a good buddy movie. Try "Butch Cassidy and the Sundance Kid," "Thelma & Louise," or "I Love You, Man" where overt displays of friendship abound.

With practice, time, and a cattle prod, you will get the user trained well enough to understand how to behave in a friendship.

The Victim

aka: the blamer, the finger pointer

Dina peed on your expensive Italian suede shoes. You weren't happy about it. In fact, you were really pissed off you let her borrow them for her big interview. The shoes are ruined and they smell bad. She didn't offer to have them cleaned, she didn't offer to replace them, and she didn't offer to give you money for your loss. What makes you even madder is that she doesn't own up to it. She tells you the reason the shoes are ruined is because she was so happy that her interview went well that she decided to celebrate with a glass of wine at lunch, but the waiter gave her an extra glass by mistake, which made her feel obligated to drink it, which caused her bladder to become too full, and because she was in a rush for her liposuction appointment, she ended up peeing on your shoes when she got out of the car. It's really the waiter's fault your shoes now stink, not hers.

There's no party quite like a pity party for the unlucky one who believes they are the target of the heaviest slings and sharpest arrows in life. The victim is a person who has difficulty owning up to their actions, preferring to blame the dog, the postman, the baby in a stroller, or a childhood trauma for the reason they drove your car into someone else's living room.

The victim always has an excuse for rotten behavior. A conversation with this type might sound like the following:

Dina: You have to understand, my mother would come after me with a spatula when she was in one of her moods. You have no idea what I went through, what it did to me.

Mike: I understand you had a troubled past, but what does that have to do with this cat turd in my coffee?

Dina: You used up all the cream this morning. Putting a cat turd in your coffee is how I've learned to express my anger, because you should have been more considerate. It's your damn fault. You should have known I would do something like this.

Similar to a free *get out of jail* card, the victim pulls up a traumatic incident or blames someone else whenever they need to deflect ownership of a shitty, stupid, mean, reckless, or thoughtless deed.

These people are smart enough to bring up the victim card whenever it's convenient for them, but act too stupid and helpless to do the right thing or take responsibility for their actions.

CAUSE:

What would cause one person with a traumatic past to transform their inner pain into compassion and insight while another, with the same childhood woes, to use their old wounds as an excuse for bad behavior? The reason is quite startling—it's bird shit; the victim is frequently the target of birds taking a big nasty dump from the sky.

Bird shit is everywhere. That is an undisputed fact. Birds will shit while roosting, they will shit while flying. They will shit in place while caged and eating. Out in the world, in a vast open space, there are so many places they could shit on that Earth serves as one giant toilet for them.

A bird's decision to let loose their load, while airborne, is not as random as some would think.

Flying high in the wind, birds seek their food in the sea or the ground below. What catches a bird's attention is a moving target that stands out in some way.

That means a fish that jumps out of the water, a little rodent that darts from hole to hole, or a brightly colored object that moves from one location to another. When a bird of any kind sees a brightly moving colorful object, they zero in on that object, hovering above to get a better view.

But what happens when that colorful moving object is nothing more than a child in a bright red jacket? That means that the bird will concentrate their flight pattern around that child while they are thinking about their next meal.

Birds naturally prepare themselves to dine by emptying their stomach for more intake. In other words, they shit so they can make room for a new meal.

If the birdies happen to be above a person wearing a bright red, orange, blue or purple shirt, that colorfully dressed person is going to get a shower of nasty shit on their head.

It is common knowledge that birds fly in groups and behave in unison. If a whole flock of birds spot a colorfully dressed child or adult, they can release dozens of aerial bombs on top of the poor person's body, dousing them with a palette of white, yellow, brown, and green.

Birds are not the only affliction for a victim type. Bees, wasps, and hornets are also attracted to vivid colors. The brightly clothed child is forever pursued by nature's winged creatures. This can make the child feel victimized, as if the world was full of evil out to get them, that it is an unsafe place to be, compounding the inner pain they have from a bad home situation. They are minding their own business when they get attacked for no reason by these little flying fuckers.

If the person's love of colorful clothes extends to adulthood, they continue to attract these airborne demons wherever they go. No wonder they embrace the role of a victim, because they certainly are when it comes to the birds and the bees.

RECOMMENDATIONS:

Unfortunately, in order to keep birds and stinging insects away, one must forego the happy colors and aim for gloom and doom in fashion attire. Browns, dark greens, dark blue, grey, and black clothing will help the victim blend in better with their surroundings.

However, this makes a person vulnerable to mosquitoes; mosquitoes go for dark colors. But it may be better to deal with a mosquito than it is to deal with the unsanitary mess of bird shit or the painful sting of a hornet or wasp, unless the mosquito carries malaria, dengue fever, West Nile, or Zika virus. It's a hard call.

If you are a victim type and wish not to be, carry an open umbrella to ensure that at least your head won't be messed up if you insist on wearing bright colors. If transitioning to dark gloomy clothes, insect repellent will deter these tiny winged blood suckers, but contains harsh chemicals that can cause your skin to fall off when used long term. Try moving to a geographical location with a lower mosquito count.

If nature is not your friend, it may be wise to stay indoors as much as possible and plaster wall-sized posters of forests around you so you can still enjoy the outdoors without ever going outdoors.

To learn how to take responsibility for your actions, take baby steps by repeating the words, "I screwed up," and "it's my fault," and "I'm to blame" in front of the mirror. You will find that your relationships become much more rewarding. You will also gain a newfound respect from others and will be called "a grown up" in the process.

The Weirdo

aka: the crackpot, the eccentric, the freak, the fruitcake, the kook, the looney, the misfit, the nonconformist, the nutter, the oddball, the offbeat, the peculiar, the unconventional

variation: the individualist

Yoshi delights in being different. He will go out of his way to be as unconventional as possible. Sometimes his antics make people afraid of him, but that's okay. To be authentic sometimes means shocking others. Once in a while, he feels called to listen to Sufi dance music. Hearing fast-moving string chords strummed by the hands of a skilled musician channeling higher powers has the effect of putting his body into an ecstatic state. Instead of repressing those divinely energizing emotions, he lets his body go into a frenzied kinetic dance. It's hard for the people around him on the subway train to understand. He needs more space than rush hour allows, and so what if he accidentally smacks a few passengers in the head while aligning himself to the rhythms of the sacred. People around aren't evolved enough to comprehend his inner process. They think he's a weirdo, but he knows better than them all. He knows he is special.

A weirdo is labeled as such when he or she displays atypical, inappropriate, or eccentric behavior in a setting that requires compliance or consideration for others or surprises or disturbs others. In short, a weirdo can be the little bloke or damsel headed upstream in a downstream run or one who behaves unpredictably.

One person's definition of weirdo might be another's definition of normal. There are varying degrees of weirdness, from harmlessly annoying to really fuckin' scary. For example, a person who eats bizarre food combos—think jello with peanut butter and hamburger sandwiches—might be considered a weirdo around vegans and anyone with good taste, but is generally harmless and doesn't motivate a call to the cops but might motivate others to puke.

One can also be called a weirdo for merely having different preferences. A tween girl who prefers Marilyn Manson over Justin Bieber might be considered cool by older kids but a weirdo amongst her classmates.

Another example would be a guy who wears a lifelike rubber penis on his head. If he went to a bat mitzvah, he would undoubtedly be considered a weirdo and would get thrown out the door with a kick to the groin before he has a chance to load up at the ice cream station. But if that guy went to a frat party, he'd get plenty of fist bumps and an open pathway to the keg. Context is everything.

The weirdo of the scary kind is the one viewed as harmful or confusing to others by their unusual and unpredictable behavior. Having deep conversations with a serving spoon while sunning in your birthday suit in a stranger's yard will cause serious alarm for others who aren't sure what to expect next, maybe a Scottish broadsword from the old backpack?

Weirdoes are sometimes misfits who haven't found their circle of like-minded friends, because when a group of people exhibit strange behavior together, they are somehow more socially acceptable.

The line between *awesome* and *unsettling* can be a fine one. Having the sense to know when that line has been crossed can make you the coolest kid on the block or the craziest one everyone runs from.

CAUSE:

The origin of weirdo behavior can be traced to a singular event in a weirdo's past, an event that brought forth conflicting emotions of shame, pleasure, and self-awareness.

At a young age, the future weirdo was left alone much of the time to entertain themselves. With boredom to kill, any kid eventually becomes interested in tinkering with their own developing body.

If they do so in the privacy of their own room without interruption or judgment, then no harm no foul. But sometimes adults walk in, and that's when things go terribly wrong.

In the case of a burgeoning weirdo, a young kid happily experimenting with their pleasure centers got interrupted by a shocked and disgusted parent, grandparent, or adult guardian sometime during their formative years.

The adult's reaction becomes central to how that child will develop emotionally. If the grandparent makes a big fuss, the bored kid remembers the event as one of gratification (jerking off) mixed with shame (disgusted adult) and a great deal of attention (a long lecture or "the talk").

From then on, the kid recognizes the power of shameful and bizarre acts for grabbing neglectful adults' attention. Thus begins the learned behavior of using shock to get noticed; the more shocking the act, the greater the response.

Adolescents love to rebel anyway, and doing so in the most unusual manner makes them stand out.

Eventually, acting weird gets old as the teen matures, and they develop other talents and skills equally attention grabbing, such as salad arranging and puppeteering.

For the ones who never find anything else to do or don't get recognized for their skills and talents, acting strange becomes a way of life and becomes ingrained into their personality. This sets the stage for a lifetime of weirdo behavior.

In rare cases, there are those who really live by a different tune and in those instances, one hopes that those tunes aren't the off-key kind that can land a jail sentence.

RECOMMENDATIONS:

By the time you meet an adult weirdo, their way of life and habits are usually entrenched. They probably won't change unless forced to. But a younger weirdo is still impressionable.

The best way to discourage a weirdo is to yawn in their presence—the weirdo thrives on strong reactions. Reacting as if they were kind of boring might make them try harder or give up. However, the more aghast you are, the more incentive for a weirdo to continue their shocking behavior.

On the other hand, if you tend to be an uptight schmuck, spending time with a weirdo might give you a new perspective and open you up to a broader world that would normally scare you.

If you want the weirdo to be in your life, accept them as they are and don't act shocked anymore. In time, they will stop trying so hard and may even behave predictably from time to time.

The Worrier

aka: the anxious, the fretter, the nervous, the overly concerned, the troubled, the unsettled

Terrence was nervous as he drove to pick up a woman he met at the gym. He had seen her working out for the past two weeks and wanted very much to meet her. He finally got the chance when he accidentally tripped over some weights and knocked her off the elliptical. He apologized profusely. He struck up a conversation that somehow led to a dinner date. Score! But while showering, he started to worry. What if the date went bad? That would mean he'd have to avoid her and couldn't go to the gym at his usual time anymore. That would screw up his schedule. But if it went well and he ended up sleeping with her, that would be problematic too. Seeing her at the gym might be awkward after that. What if she expected to go out with him after every workout? What if she fell for him? Even worse, what if she got pregnant and named their kid Cucumber or Pickles. And he would have to pay child support for the next 20 years. Shit! She could take his ass to court and tell everyone at the gym he neighs like a horse during sex. What the hell was he thinking?

The Worrier is a person who is overly concerned with disasters, dangers, mishaps, loss, the sky falling, and other potentially terrible things that might happen as a result of a decision, an action, a situation, a job, or a commitment they make. This makes people around a worrier speak louder and use a lot more cuss words than usual.

Sometimes the worrier's worries are warranted, but many times they are not. Worriers tend to be thinkers—generally on the fearful side—with active imaginations leading to worst case scenarios.

These nerve-wracked individuals are very concerned with outcomes in situations they have no control over. They can be consumed by peculiar thoughts. *Will the postal carrier deliver my mail order sex robot to that nice Mormon family next door by mistake? Will an earthquake happen right when the nurse inserts a catheter into my urethra? Will the surgeon fall asleep on my intestines during surgery?*

Worriers tend to be responsible people. If they weren't, they'd be carefree with toilet paper hanging from their butts.

A worrier makes for a great employee, because they are several steps ahead, determining all the possible outcomes for pissing off a boss or missing a deadline.

The people around a worrier type tend to get a little impatient when the worrier indulges in their worst fears. Having to be the voice of reason can be tiring. If you're lucky, the worrier will be so anxious they won't be able to speak.

To be fair, there are some things one should be worried about, such as giving birth to a child that spews green vomit, can rotate their head 360 degrees, and curse you in Latin before they learn to say "mama." That definitely is something to be concerned about.

CAUSE:

If it seems as if worriers are riddled with anxiety and fear, that's because they are. Each night, these poor people are terrorized by visions of brutality, blood, and slaughter.

I must add a warning here. The rest of this section is not advised for vegans, vegetarians, and breatharians. If you don't eat meat, your worries are not nearly as bad as the meat eater's. Your worries are more due to the vibes passed on from making out with a meat eater or having any sort of physical contact with them. You can skip to the last paragraph in this section that starts with "For VVBs." If you are a meat eater, you can proceed.

The worrying soul is a sensitive sort, more so than the average person. For this reason, they are much more reactive to what they put in their bodies. A sensitive person who eats any factory farmed meat becomes haunted by the residual terror lodged in the flesh of an animal at the time of slaughter.

In a factory farm slaughterhouse, the smell of blood permeates the entire facility. Handlers sometimes kick and taunt fearful or sluggish animals to get them moving for slaughter. Anyone who has seen undercover videos of slaughterhouses knows that these animals can be sick from overcrowding, poor food, chemical injections, lack of exercise, and foul air.

At the time an animal is herded for slaughter, they can smell the blood of their brethren and sometimes even see their own kind butchered by sharp painful tools right before their eyes. For them, it's sort of like being trapped in a dungeon with Ramsey Snow (*Game of Thrones*) when he's in one of his knifey moods.

No, I am not a spokesperson for PETA. I am not even a fan of PETA, but I am a great fan of pita with a side of hummus and falafel. However, I will endorse just about anything if you give me a lifetime supply of roasted pistachios. Brazil nuts too.

The factory animals know they are queued for their impending doom. Of course they become frightened and anxious—it's the worst nightmare imaginable to them.

Once these terrified creatures get butchered into edible cuts, packaged, and delivered to your favorite supermarket or restaurant, their flesh remembers the horrors their eyes witnessed.

When a sensitive person reaches for that tasty morsel of horrified flesh, they consume not only the body of the animal but also the emotions. If those emotions are comprised mostly of fear, terror, and anxiety, then the sensitive person becomes saturated with those feelings as well.

These emotions don't dissipate when digested. Instead they express themselves through nightmares. A person haunted by nightmares is sure to be a nervous wreck, making them jittery and anxious, looking around corners, imagining knives from above and dangers at every turn.

For VVBs: Beans, twigs and sticks. No animal tears on your soul. You are happy happy, bliss bliss. Love. Kittens. Purr Purr. Carob coconut shakes. Honey badger kisses. A cow with wings calls your name. A dozen goats follow you to heaven, massaging you gently with their ears.

RECOMMENDATIONS:

It serves the worrier's best interest to stop eating factory farmed flesh. The delicious taste of cooked meat is hardly worth the night terrors inflicted by brutally murdered animals.

Instead, sweet tasting fruit grown on a bright sunny farm might be the best antidote (with the exception of pomegranates and blood oranges).

It will take a while before the worrier can rid themselves of the lingering feelings of terror, anxiety, and pain of a creature headed for sharp blades.

Spending quality time among the animals they consume would be helpful. For example, if a New York cut steak precipitates a night of terrors, then spending time in a field with content free-ranging cows and nudging your forehead against theirs in a friendly way may actually help combat the terrors of the eaten flesh.

Likewise, nuzzling a happy porker in a large pigpen may be the best remedy for a morning of Italian sausage made from screaming pigs. This allows the worrier to replace all those horrified feelings in their body with happy animal experiences.

Becoming a vegan would eliminate many of the night terrors plaguing a person. It would also be wise to surround yourself with pictures of Yoda, baby pandas, little ducklings, and smiling dogs for the rest of your life.

About the Author

It takes one to know one and no knows more annoying personality types than Abraham (Abe) Surde. Gifted with a compassionate ear, Surde has served as a professional listener for more than two decades.

He has listened to all types of people and all kinds of complaints during his numerous years of public service as a bartender in upscale establishments.

Hailing from a small conservative town in Wyoming, Surde knew from an early age he was destined for something great. He packed his bags and headed for the big city lights of Cheyenne where he studied traditional bartending, learning to make such classics as the Whiskey Sour, the Sea Breeze, the Gin and Tonic, the Mai Tai, the Margarita. Once he accomplished the basics, he set his sights for more exotic libations.

He headed to New York City where he was mentored by the best and brightest bartenders in the nation. After earning his bachelors degree in bartending, he went on to do his scholarly work on drinks from the Hellenistic age, comparing the practices of each continent during that time period. He wrote his thesis on the fermentation practices of ancient times and recreated several beverages using old methods.

During his tenure as a bartender, Surde discovered his gift for therapeutic consultation. It was in the atmosphere of a darkly lit room where patrons, with a whiskey or vodka to help soften inhibitions, openly discussed their divorces, exploits, complaints, dreams, and desires.

After many hours of interactions with his troubled customers, he realized he had a knack for giving helpful advice. In time, his reputation as a therapist grew. Even nondrinkers began to seek him out. However, these extra customers upset his regular clientele. Many of the new folks also failed to follow the one-drink minimum rule, causing friction between Surde and his employers.

Some of these advice seekers were also extremely obnoxious, caustic, mean, and demanding. They came in droves, making Surde not only the most popular bartender in the area but also the most burned out. This demanding period led to serious soul searching, a time Surde calls "the turning point" in his life.

For the next three years, Surde read psychological texts, took classes, read reports, met with therapists and psychiatrists, went on vision quests, partook of ayahuasca and peyote ceremonies, and smoked excessive quantities of super strong cannabis to understand how difficult personalities came into being.

He wanted to understand what could turn a good person into an annoying ass. Why divas are such douchebags and how bullies got made. He documented the many stories he heard and in doing so, discovered patterns to rotten behaviors that could be identified and categorized into at least a hundred different types. But what remained unanswered was: *What caused these shitty behaviors in the first place?*

He felt the literature available in the field failed to truly answer his questions in a meaningful way, leaving him less than satisfied but driven by a profound need to understand *why* people behaved badly.

Through an unexpected journey into the unconscious, Surde received divine guidance when he accidentally fell one day, hitting his head on a statue of Athena. The Greek goddess of wisdom seemed to answer his queries. From that point on, Surde was able to divine the origin for many difficult, annoying, and rotten behaviors. He became a psychological intuitive.

Seemingly ludicrous at times, Surde has nonetheless added to the extensive body of work currently available in the psychoanalytic field. By doing so, Surde has offered an alternative to the time consuming and expensive mainstream therapist/client dynamic. His down-to-earth remedies offer quick and satisfying results that are simple and sensible.

Surde currently resides in upstate New York. He no longer bartends and spends much of his time in his garden, reading and writing next to several Athena statues he now has on his property. Yes, even in winter. Currently, he is commissioning an additional statue for his garden—a curvaceous Aphrodite. He hopes to gain insight from the goddess of love as he penetrates the depths of the female psyche.

Made in the USA
Lexington, KY
01 November 2016